Growing Up in America

Children playing "Cut the Pie" and "Fox and Geese" during noon recess at a rural school in Morton County, North Dakota, 1940. Photograph by John Vachon. (courtesy of the Library of Congress, LC-USF34-64805-D)

Growing Up in America

Children in Historical Perspective

Edited by
N. Ray Hiner *and* Joseph M. Hawes

University of Illinois Press
Urbana and Chicago

Illini Books edition, 1985

© 1985 by the Board of Trustees of the University of Illinois

Manufactured in the United States of America

P   8   7   6   5   4

This book is printed on acid-free paper.

Library of Congress Cataloging-in-Publication Data

Main entry under title:

Growing Up in America.

Includes bibliographies.
1. Children—United States—History—Addresses,
essays, lectures. 2. Children—United States—Social
conditions—Addresses, essays, lectures. I. Hiner,
N. Ray. II. Hawes, Joseph M.
HQ792.U5G75   1985   305.2'3'0973   84-16323
ISBN 0-252-01218-6 (alk. paper)

To All Our Children

Contents

Preface

The basic purpose of this anthology is to provide an introduction to the rapidly growing body of scholarship on the history of childhood in America. Because this field of history is relatively new and because space limitations made it impossible to include more than a few of the best articles available, our intent has been more to raise questions than to answer them, to whet the intellectual appetite rather than satisfy it. Thus, for those who want to read more about this subject, we have provided carefully selected bibliographies at the end of each unit. Just a glance at these bibliographies will reveal the vitality and scope of this emerging field.

We want to take this opportunity to thank those who assisted us with this project. We are very grateful to Richard Wentworth and Elizabeth Dulany of the University of Illinois Press for their consistent support and their judicious and helpful suggestions. We are also pleased to acknowledge the assistance we received from the Bureau of General Research at Kansas State University, the History Department and the Department of Educational Policy and Administration at the University of Kansas, and the History Department at Kansas State University. Finally, we wish to express our special appreciation to Paul Pruyser, Director of the Program for Interdisciplinary Studies and Henry March Pfeiffer Professor at the Menninger Foundation. It was during our tenure as fellows in the Interdisciplinary Studies Program that this project was conceived. Professor Pruyser's erudition, his irrepressible curiosity, and his genuine openness to new ideas provided an excellent example of interdisciplinary scholarship at its best.

Acknowledgments

Part I: The Child in Colonial America

"In Search of the Historical Child: Miniature Adulthood and Youth in Colonial New England," by Ross W. Beales, Jr. Reprinted by permission of the author and publisher from *American Quarterly*, Oct. 1975, pp. 379-98. Copyright, 1975, Trustees of the University of Pennsylvania.

" 'From the *Cradle* to the *Coffin*': Parental Bereavement and the Shadow of Infant Damnation in Puritan Society," by Peter G. Slater. Reprinted by permission of the author and publisher from *Psychohistory Review*, Fall-Winter, 1977-78, pp. 4-24.

"Autonomy and Affection: Parents and Children in Eighteenth-Century Chesapeake Families," by Daniel Blake Smith. Reprinted by permission of the author and publisher from *Psychohistory Review*, Fall-Winter, 1977-78, pp. 32-51.

"Family History and Demographic Transition," by Robert V. Wells. Reprinted by permission of the author and editor from *Journal of Social History*, Fall 1975, pp. 1-20.

Part II: Perfectible Children in an Imperfect World: Perspectives from Nineteenth-Century America

"Evangelical Child Rearing in the Age of Jackson: Francis Wayland's Views on When and How to Subdue the Willfulness of Children," by William G. McLoughlin. Reprinted by permission of the author and editor from *Journal of Social History*, Fall 1975, pp. 20-43.

"Infant Abandonment in Early Nineteenth-Century New York: Three Cases," by Paul A. Gilje. Reprinted from *Signs*, 8 (Spring 1983): 580-90 by permission of the author and publisher, the University of Chicago Press. Copyright 1983 by the University of Chicago. All rights reserved.

"Socializing Middle-Class Children: Institutions, Fables, and Work Values in Nineteenth-Century America," by Daniel T. Rodgers. Reprinted by permission of the author and editor from *Journal of Social History*, Spring 1980, pp. 354-67.

"Families and Foster Care: Philadelphia in the Late Nineteenth Century," by Priscilla Ferguson Clement. Reprinted from *Social Service Review*, 53 (Mar. 1979): 406-20 by permission of the author and publisher, the University of Chicago Press. Copyright 1979 by the University of Chicago. All rights reserved.

Part III: Growing Up Red and Black in White America

Part IV: Children in the Twentieth Century: Trends and Issues

Introduction

The history of childhood is coming of age. Once viewed as a trivial subject of interest only to antiquarians, it is now part of the cutting edge of American historical scholarship.[1] Much of the growing volume of historical work on American children is a direct reflection of the strong new interest among historians in the many powerless and inarticulate members of society whose experiences and perspectives have generally been ignored by traditional history. Convinced that history should be more than the story of elites, the new social historians are committed to constructing a history that includes the historical experiences of all groups of people regardless of their class, race, gender, religion, ethnicity, *or* age.[2] From this perspective, the fact that children as a group were relatively weak and inarticulate does not justify their exclusion from written history. Given that they were present in large numbers from the beginning of American society, living side by side with adults, experiencing hardship and suffering as well as happiness and joy, children deserve to have their experiences studied and their stories told.

Beyond the concepts of social justice and equal access to the past implied by the new social history, there is a growing awareness that all human relationships are to some degree reciprocal and dynamic, and that no one, even the most powerless person, is without influence on others. Social historians have demonstrated that even in the most uneven relationships, such as those between master and slave, influence is exchanged, not just passed from the "powerful" to the "powerless." Slaves normally obeyed their masters' commands, but they sometimes "obeyed" in ways that undermined their master's authority and required him to modify his own behavior to maintain "control" over them. Influence was also exchanged more subtly, in language, food ways, music, work patterns, and other social customs where the sheer numbers of slaves made them influential if not "powerful." We know now that slavery cannot be understood without consideration of the dynamic reciprocity between master and slave, between the "powerful" and the "powerless."[3]

Children were certainly no less powerful and influential than slaves. If slaves were numerous, children were ubiquitous. Their numbers alone made them an important force in American history. Those under the age of twenty have never constituted less than 30 percent of our population,[4] and social demographers are only now beginning to understand the profound political, economic, social, and cultural implications of shifts in the age structure of populations. A society with many children is significantly different from one whose population is older. For this reason alone, the presence of children and their influence should not be ignored.

Children in the past were also influential as individuals. From the time they made their first eye contact with their parents or elicited friendly responses to their first social smiles, American children have never been without the capacity to influence the adults around them, in part because American adults, especially parents and other caregivers, were deeply interested in and concerned with their development. American parents have had enormous legal and economic authority over their children, but children, like slaves, have never been only the passive recipients of this authority. The individual and collective responses of American children to the demands of adults have shaped adult behavior and experience to the extent that it is impossible to construct an adequate history of American adults without a knowledge of the history of childhood.

The new history of childhood reflects another major trend in American historiography — the growing interest in the psychological dimension of human experience. Psychohistorians believe that the rationalistic, utilitarian, and materialistic models of human behavior often used implicitly or explicitly by historians are one-sided and simplistic, and fail to reflect the full range and complex character of life in the past.[5] For psychohistorians, learning what a person felt, what a person experienced, and what experiences meant to a person in the past is as important, if not more important, than discovering what a person did. Without knowledge of the inner life of persons in the past, without some insight into their private, subjective, sometimes irrational worlds, psychohistorians doubt that it is possible to understand their behavior or write valid history.

This psychohistorical perspective has had a direct influence on the history of childhood because historians of childhood generally hold the view that being a child is to some extent a unique experience, never entirely synonymous with being an adult. To be sure, American children have often been expected to act as adults, they have been treated as adults, but they could never be adults because they were children, because their physical, cognitive, and emotional conditions required them to experience the world in special, unique ways that were eventually closed off or changed by their normal growth and development. It cannot be automatically assumed that events or experiences in the past had the same meaning for children as they did for adults. Thus, for example, historians of childhood have usually not been content with simply describing the strikingly high rates of infant and adult mortality during the colonial period, but have sought as well to understand the implications of these rates for children's emotional development and the character of child-parent relations. Similarly, historians of childhood have been interested not only in outlining theories of child rearing, but also in determining the emotional consequences of these theories when and if they were put into practice. The best, perhaps the only, avenue to understanding the unique qualities of children's experience in the past is through an empathetic study of their inner lives.

Even though the history of childhood has been heavily influenced by psychohistory and the new social history, it has fortunately not been dominated by one methodology or a single ideological orientation. Because the relatively powerless and inarticulate condition of children makes them difficult subjects for historical study, historians of childhood have been reluctant to reject any approach or method that promises to help them in their complex task. Moreover, interest in this new field is too widely dispersed to be the expression of a single ideology. Scholars in several fields outside of history — psychology and human development, sociology, social work, education, medicine, and law — have begun to publish research on the history of children. The history of childhood has been and will no doubt continue to be a cooperative, interdisciplinary process.

How can the dramatic surge of interest in the history of childhood be explained? Although many factors have contributed to this phenomenon, one of the most obvious and probably the most important was the extraordinarily powerful impact of the so-called baby-boom generation.[6] As this unprecedented demographic bulge began to work its way through the American social and cultural system, it left its imprint on nearly every major institution. Families, schools, colleges, churches, the media, the entertainment industry, the military, and the government were profoundly affected by this phenomenon. From the time the first children of this generation entered kindergarten in the 1950s until they arrived on college campuses in the 1960s, their influence grew. Few people, including historians, could fail to be impressed by the importance of children and young people as a force in American life. By the late 1960s, papers on the history of childhood and youth began to appear on the programs of the annual meetings of the major historical associations; historian John Demos reported that "in March 1970, the first conference devoted entirely to the investigation of 'childhood and youth in history' was held at Clark University in Worcester, Massachusetts."[7] Childhood had clearly become a subject for serious historical inquiry.

One of the most influential early works in the history of childhood was written by Philippe Ariès, a French demographer and social historian. His *L'Enfant et la vie familiale sous l'ancien régime*, published in 1960, appeared two years later in English translation as *Centuries of Childhood: A Social History of Family Life*.[8] Concerned with the origins of the modern family, Ariès expressed succinctly what many American historians had come to understand, that "our experience of the modern demographic revolution has revealed to us the importance of the child's role in this silent history."[9] Furthermore, Ariès challenged traditional assumptions about the changelessness of childhood and argued instead that the idea of childhood had not even existed before the fifteenth or sixteenth centuries. Before this period, during the Middle Ages, Ariès says "children were mixed with adults as soon as they were considered capable of doing without their nannies," and were in some respects better off than children in later periods when, under the influence of the modern idea of childhood, adults began to deprive children of their freedom, confine them to prison-like schools, and subject them to the severe discipline of schoolmasters.[10]

Although not everyone shared Ariès's nostalgia for the medieval period, his basic thesis that childhood was in part a social category and therefore subject to the historical process proved to be an immensely popular idea among American social historians and helped justify research into its historical development. Although *Centuries of Childhood* has recently been labeled "a superb piece of rhetoric,"[11] and Ariès has been justly criticized for his selective and sometimes uncritical use of evidence, no one has successfully challenged his essential point that childhood is *not* an immutable stage of life, free from the influence of historical change.

Another European scholar who had considerable influence on the development of the history of childhood during the 1960s and 1970s was Erik Erikson, the well-known child analyst and psychohistorian who emigrated to the United States in the 1930s. His first book, *Childhood and Society*, written in the 1940s and published in the 1950s, was not widely discussed by American historians until the 1960s when his interdisciplinary approach, integrating psychological, social, and cultural perspectives, took on a special relevance for many Americans who were puzzling over the complex issues raised by the post–World War II generation. Scholars were now more willing to consider the implications of Erikson's critical observation in *Childhood and Society* that "one may scan work after work on history, society, and morality and find little reference to the fact that all people start as children and that all peoples begin in their nurseries."[12]

Erikson's developmental or epigenetic model of psychosocial stages which he described in *Childhood and Society* attracted a favorable response from several historians, including John Demos, who used it to assess the experience of children in his important and well-received study of seventeenth-century Plymouth published in 1970.[13] Demos argued that unlike the approach followed by scholars such as Ariès, "who study the child as a kind of mirror which focuses and reflects back cultural themes of central importance," Erikson's model encouraged historians to treat the child as "not just a mirror, not only the creature, but also the creator of culture, and in this sense, a dynamic force in his own right."[14]

Whereas Erikson and Demos sought to establish the historical importance of children and childhood, Lloyd deMause went even further and asserted that children and parent-child relations constitute "the central force for change in history," independent to some extent from social and technological trends. According to deMause, a scholar with training in psychoanalysis, political science, and history, the primary source of this change lies in "the ability of successive generations of parents to regress to the psychic age of their children and work through the anxieties of that age in a better manner the second time they encounter them than they did during their own childhood." DeMause therefore concluded that each generation of parents grew in their capacity to love and care for children, became better parents than those of previous generations, and thereby provided an essential foundation for general social progress: less narcissistic, better integrated, more autonomous adults who were able to develop deep and lasting bonds with others. For deMause, then, "the history of childhood is a nightmare from which we have only recently begun to awaken. The further back in history one goes, the lower the level of child care, and the more likely children are to be killed, abandoned, beaten, terrorized, and sexually abused."[15] DeMause thus completely reversed the portrayal of childhood provided by Ariès. Whereas Ariès believed that the creation of modern childhood often made life worse for children, deMause claimed that their lot has become progressively better. However, Ariès and deMause agreed on one point — that childhood as an experience and a social category is part of the historical process and subject to change over time.

Like Ariès, deMause has seen his work sharply challenged by other scholars.[16] Few American historians have accepted his strikingly optimistic psychogenic theory or agreed with his thesis that parent-child relations constitute an independent source of historical change; nevertheless, deMause has played a vital role in stimulating and encouraging research on the history of childhood which should not be overlooked. He not only generated interest in the field through his own sometimes controversial writing, but as founder and editor of the *History of Childhood Quarterly* (now the *Journal of Psychohistory*), and the Psychohistory Press, he has supported the publication of important articles and monographs on the history of childhood.[17]

In addition to Ariès, Erikson, and deMause, one other scholar who has played an essential role in the development of the history of childhood should be mentioned. In 1966, Robert Bremner, a respected social historian at Ohio State University, was named director of a major research project on the history of children sponsored by the American Public Health Association and funded by the U.S. Children's Bureau. Designed to update Grace Abbott's classic *The Child and the State* (1938), this project culminated in the publication of *Children and Youth in America* (1970-74), a massive, three-volume documentary history of public policy toward children and youth that goes far beyond Abbott's earlier study in the scope and variety of its contents.[18] Even though Bremner, who edited the work, says that it does not comprise a history of childhood in America, and although the collection is by definition heavily institutional in focus, even a cursory glance at its contents reveals that it offers great insight into the historical experience of children in America. Bremner and his associate editors, John Barnard, Tamara Hareven, and Robert Mennel, have created an indispensable resource for anyone who wishes to do research in the history of childhood. They have also demonstrated the great relevance of the history of childhood to the discussion and formulation of public policy affecting children.

The rapid development and expansion of the history of childhood, stimulated in part by the work of Ariès, Erikson, deMause, and Bremner, was in many respects parallel to and at times heavily influenced by the development of women's history, history of the family, and the appearance of new trends in the history of education. Long dominated by a pronounced institutional bias, historians of education until the 1960s concentrated almost entirely on schools, their organization, administration, and curriculum, and gave little direct attention to children as children. Lately, a more comprehensive view of education as a psychological, social, and cultural process has emerged, and historians of education are now more inclined to include the perspective of the child in their research. Two important works that reflect this new awareness of children are Sol Cohen's comprehensive, five-volume

Education in the United States: A Documentary History (1974), and *Regulated Children/Liberated Children: Education in Psychohistorical Perspective* (1979), a collection of original essays edited by Barbara Finkelstein.[19] As more historians of education have come to share Cohen's and Finkelstein's sensitivity to the historical importance of children, the history of education has become an increasingly valuable source of insight for the historian of childhood.

Another field with important implications for the history of childhood is the rapidly expanding history of the family, which since the early 1970s has produced an enormous volume of studies either directly or indirectly concerned with children.[20] As family historians have extended the scope of their inquiry beyond the narrow emphasis on household structure that dominated the early work in this field and have begun to investigate the character of emotional relationships within the family, they have produced knowledge which is vital to the reconstruction of children's daily lives. Several important collections of articles and essays in this field are now available. Among the most valuable for the historian of childhood are Michael Gordon's *The American Family in Social-Historical Perspective* (1978); Vivian Fox and Martin H. Quitt's *Loving, Parenting and Dying: The Family Cycle in England and America, Past and Present* (1980); and *Family Life in America, 1620-2000* (1981), edited by Mel Albin and Dominick Cavallo.[21] Many of the documents reprinted in Donald Scott and Bernard Wishy's *America's Families: A Documentary History* (1982) will also be useful to the historian of childhood.[22]

One might expect that research in the dynamic, new field of women's history would be at least as valuable to the historian of childhood as that in the history of education or the family, especially since the lives of women and children have been tied so closely together throughout American history. Unfortunately, historians of women have devoted surprisingly little attention in their studies to children, even female children. Recently, however, there has been evidence of a greater interest among historians of women in the relationships between women and children in the past. If this new interest in children among historians of women continues, which seems very likely, our understanding of the history of childhood will be greatly enhanced.[23]

Even though family history, women's history, and the history of education are closely related to the history of childhood, it is important to note that they are not synonymous with it. Indeed, these fields are guided by purposes and assumptions that make it impossible for them, separately or together, to develop a comprehensive understanding of children in the past. By definition, the historian of education is ultimately concerned with the educational process, and knowledge of children is therefore important to the extent that it enhances historians' understanding of that process, even if this knowledge incorporates the child's perspective. Furthermore, the historian of education is not always concerned with children because not all persons who experience education are children, but are adults with their own special perspectives and interests. Similarly, the family historian's primary object of study is an institution, not children. To be sure, children are a very important part of that institution, yet knowledge of children is not an end in itself for the family historian, but a means to understanding the family. Also, American children as a group have never spent all of their time at home, interacting with other members of the family. Family historians, therefore, are limited in what they can tell us about what children have experienced in other institutions or environments such as schools, churches, playgrounds, streets, and gangs where they have interacted with children and adults who were not necessarily members of their own families. Finally, it is clear that until recently the history of women has produced little direct knowledge of the historical experience of children, although this will undoubtedly change as the field continues to develop. Historians of women, the family, and education have much to offer the history of childhood, but historians of childhood should be careful not to be unduly restricted by the methods or purposes of these fields if they hope to produce a comprehensive, integrated understanding of children on a level of complexity consistent with that of the subject itself. If the history of childhood is to reach its full potential, it must be interdisciplinary in scope and method, and historians of childhood must remain flexible and accommodative in spirit, always bearing in mind their commitment to keep children at the center of inquiry.

One way to clarify these issues is to identify the basic questions that scholars in the history of childhood have sought or should seek to answer. These questions will serve to differentiate the history of childhood from other, related fields and provide a guide for future research.[24]

1. *What have been the attitudes of adults toward children and childhood?* In some respects this is one of the easiest questions for historians of childhood to answer. Although most adults who left records about what they thought of children and childhood were usually middle or upper class, there is still an enormous amount of historical material which has yet to be fully examined. Care must be taken, however, not to assume that parental attitudes are synonymous with behavior or experience, or that there is any simple and direct relationship among them. Even with these difficulties, a thorough knowledge of adult

attitudes concerning children is basic to the construction of a comprehensive history of childhood.

2. *What are the conditions which helped to shape the development of children?* It is here that the new social historians have a great deal to offer. Whether they are studying the broad social indicators that influence the duration, scope, and intensity of childhood as a stage of life; examining the institutions in which children have spent much of their time; or analyzing the intricate patterns of relationships within a particular household, their insights will be indispensable to an understanding of childhood. A caveat: this question must not be studied in isolation from the other questions or there will be a tendency to treat the child only as a cipher for social processes rather than as an important variable in his or her own right.

3. *What has been the subjective experience of being a child in the past?* This is one of the most hazardous questions faced by historians of childhood, in part because they may be tempted to rely too heavily on reductionist psychological theories in their efforts to fill in the gaps left by the sources. It is, nonetheless, a crucial question because the essence of childhood is the child's special mode of experiencing life, his or her unique way of being in the world. No history of childhood will be worthy of its name if it ignores this critical dimension. Unless historians are willing to confront this question, they will only be probing the periphery of childhood, not penetrating the heart of the subject itself.

4. *How have children and childhood influenced adults?* This question concerns not only the influence children have on the adults around them but also the impact of childhood experiences on the character of the adults the children become. Almost without exception historians have assumed that most of the influence in adult-child relations flows in one direction, from the adult to the child, while blithely ignoring what modern research has confirmed: that all human relationships are inevitably reciprocal and dynamic. For example, what informed person today would deny that infants manipulate their caretakers or that the proportion of children in a population has profound implications for almost all aspects of society? We have only begun to apply these insights to our study of history. With respect to the second dimension of this question, historians have not usually questioned the proposition that childhood experiences shape adult character to some degree, but they have despaired of actually demonstrating this influence in concrete historical terms. If it is ever to be demonstrated, it will have to be accomplished through some sort of longitudinal (i.e., historical) study, a task which the historian above all should be willing to undertake.

5. *What have been the social, cultural, and psychological functions of children?* Children have inevitably been assigned both explicit and implicit roles in American society and culture. For example, throughout most of American history child labor made a significant contribution to the economy, although today children are more important as consumers than as producers; religious groups have always tended to view children as a basic means of perpetuating their beliefs; and parents have often used children directly or indirectly to realize their own personal aspirations. In this sense, children are no different from any other social group: they are part of a larger system that places demands on them and structures their behavior in very precise ways. Historians of childhood must be sensitive to this reality.

Taken together, these five basic questions and their many permutations constitute a means of generating, organizing, and assessing knowledge about children in the past which is not restricted to any specific methodology or ideology but is precise enough to establish the history of childhood as a separate area of inquiry.

This volume provides a concrete demonstration of the breadth and depth of the interest among scholars in the history of childhood, and the high quality of the work that has already appeared in this field. The articles reprinted here were selected after a systematic review of hundreds of articles in scores of journals. Many excellent essays could not be included, so the ones selected should be viewed as *samples* of the best work that is available. The reader is urged to consult the lists of selected readings placed at the end of each unit for additional examples of solid scholarship in this field.

Several general principles were used in selecting the articles for this volume. First, no article was included unless it provided a substantial response to one or more of the five questions listed above. Second, all major chronological periods are represented in the collection. Third, an effort was made to provide some discussion of each "stage" of childhood, which for the purposes of this volume includes infancy (birth to age seven), latency (seven to fourteen), and adolescence (fourteen to twenty-one). Fourth, a special section was devoted to black and Native American children to illustrate the extent to which the historical experience of minority children has been different from that of the children of the majority. Finally, each article was screened for its literary and scholarly quality.

As the editors, we wish to conclude this introduction with a personal observation. After several years of teaching and research in the history of childhood, we continue to be impressed by the accommodating and cooperative spirit that exists among scholars we have encountered in this field. This is in sharp contrast to the petty competitiveness that too often mars contemporary scholarship. To some extent this spirit of cooperation exists because historians of childhood recognize that their task is so difficult and complex that cooperation and sharing are absolutely necessary. We also believe that it may have something to do with the special character of children as historical subjects. To study children in the past or present is to be confronted with fundamental issues, with human origins, with the human capacity for nurture, growth, and creativity. We do not mean to sentimentalize children or glamorize their history. Indeed, the history of childhood is often most unpleasant. Many American children were and are very badly mistreated, and very few, even the most fortunate ones, have ever reached their full potential as human beings. In spite of this, each successive generation of American children has exhibited a capacity for spontaneity, freshness, and playfulness that is testimony to the resilience of the human spirit. Somehow narrowness or pettiness seems inappropriate in the study of children. They invite openness and sharing. It is in this spirit that we invite you to join us in the fascinating and rewarding study of children in the past.

Notes

1. For a comprehensive review of research in this field, see Joseph M. Hawes and N. Ray Hiner, eds., *American Childhood: A Research Guide and Historical Handbook* (Westport, Conn.: Greenwood Press, 1985). Also see Patricia Rooke, "The Child 'Institutionalized' in Canada, Britain and the United States: A Trans-Atlantic Perspective," *The Journal of Educational Thought* 2 (Aug. 1977): 156-71; Ruby Takanishi, "Childhood as a Social Issue: Historical Roots of Contemporary Child Advocacy Movements," *Journal of Social Issues* 35 (1978): 8-28; and Hiner, "The Child in American Historiography: Accomplishments and Prospects," *The Psychohistory Review* 7 (Summer 1978): 13-23. John Sommerville provides a useful overview of the history of childhood in Western culture in his *The Rise and Fall of Childhood* (Beverly Hills, Calif.: Sage Publications, 1982).
2. Peter N. Stearns, "Toward a Wider Vision: Trends in Social History," in *The Past Before Us: Contemporary Historical Writing in the United States*, ed. Michael Kammen (Ithaca, N.Y.: Cornell University Press, 1980), pp. 205-30.
3. John W. Blassingame, *The Slave Community: Plantation Life in the Antebellum South* (Rev. ed.; New York: Oxford University Press, 1979); Thomas J. Webber, *Deep Like the Rivers: Education in the Slave Quarter Community, 1831-1865* (New York: W. W. Norton, 1978).

4. U.S. Bureau of the Census, *Historical Statistics of the United States, Colonial Times to 1957* (Washington, D.C.: U.S. Government Printing Office, 1960), pp. 10-11; U.S. Bureau of the Census, *Statistical Abstract of the United States, 1982-83* (Washington, D.C.: U.S. Government Printing Office, 1982), p. 27; Robert V. Wells, *Revolution in American's Lives: A Demographic Perspective on the History of Americans, Their Families, and Their Society* (Westport, Conn.: Greenwood Press, 1982).

5. Peter Lowenberg, "Psychohistory," in *The Past Before Us*, ed. Kammen, pp. 408-32.

6. Stearns, "Trends in Social History," p. 221. For a comprehensive discussion of the baby boom, see Landon Y. Jones, *Great Expectations: America and the Baby Boom Generation* (New York: Coward, McCann, Geohegan, 1980).

7. John Demos, "Developmental Perspectives on the History of Childhood," *Journal of Interdisciplinary History* 2 (Autumn 1971): 315.

8. Philippe Ariès. *Centuries of Childhood: A Social History of Family Life*, trans. Robert Baldick (New York: Random House, 1962).

9. Ibid., p. 10.

10. Ibid., pp. 33, 128, 411-13.

11. Paul G. Spagnoli, "Philippe Ariès, Historian of the Family," *Journal of Family History* 6 (Winter 1981): 439. See also Linda Pollock, *Forgotten Children: Parent-Child Relations from 1500 to 1900* (Cambridge: Cambridge University Press, 1983).

12. Erik H. Erikson, *Childhood and Society* (second ed.; New York: W. W. Norton, 1963), p. 16; John J. Fitzpatrick, "Some Problematic Features of Erik H. Erikson's Psychohistory," *The Psychohistory Review* 5 (Dec. 1976): 16-27.

13. John Demos, *A Little Commonwealth: Family Life in Plymouth Colony* (New York: Oxford University Press, 1970); Lowenberg, "Psychohistory," in *The Past Before Us*, ed. Kammen, pp. 417-20.

14. Demos, "Developmental Perspective on the History of Childhood," p. 327.

15. Lloyd deMause, ed., *The History of Childhood* (New York: The Psychohistory Press, 1974), pp. 1-4, 6-7, 51-54.

16. Clifford S. Griffin, "Oedipus Hex," *Reviews in American History* 6 (Sept. 1976): 305-17; Miles F. Shore, "The Child and Historiography," *Journal of Interdisciplinary History* 6 (Winter 1976), 495-505; Henry Ebel, "The Evolution of Childhood Reconsidered," *Journal of Psychohistory* 5 (Summer 1977): 67-80.

17. See, for example, Barbara Finkelstein, ed. *Regulated Children/Liberated Children: Education in Psychohistorical Perspective* (New York: The Psychohistory Press, 1979): Vivian C. Fox and Martin H. Quitt, eds., *Loving, Parenting, and Dying: The Family Cycle in England and America, Past and Present* (New York: The Psychohistory Press, 1980).

18. Robert H. Bremner, et al., *Children and Youth in America: A Documentary History*, 3 vols. (Cambridge, Mass.: Harvard University Press, 1970-74); Grace Abbott, ed., *The Child and the State*, 2 vols. (Chicago: University of Chicago Press, 1938).

19. Sol Cohen, ed., *Education in the United States: A Documentary History*, 5 vols. (New York: Random House, 1974); Finkelstein, ed., *Regulated Children, Liberated Children*. See also Finkelstein, "Literature Review: Incorporating Children into the History of Education," *Journal of Educational Thought* 19 (Apr. 1984): 21-41.

20. Lawrence Stone, "Family History in the 1980's: Past Achievement and Future Trends," *Journal of Interdisciplinary History* 12 (Summer 1981): 51-87; Daniel Blake Smith, "The Study of the Family in Early America: Trends, Problems, and Prospects," *William and Mary Quarterly* 39 (Jan. 1982): 3-28.

21. Michael Gordon, ed., *The American Family in Social-Historical Perspective* (second ed.; New York: St. Martin's Press, 1978); Fox and Quitt, eds., *Loving, Parenting, and Dying*; Mel Albin and Dominick Cavallo, eds., *Family Life in America, 1620-2000* (St. James, New York: Revisionary Press, 1981). John Demos and Sarane Spence Boocock, eds., *Turning Points: Historical and Sociological Essays on the Family* (Chicago: University of Chicago Press, 1978), and Tamara K. Hareven, ed., *Transition: The Family and the Life Course in Historical Perspective* (New York: Academic Press, 1978) are also useful, but include less material dealing directly with children.

22. Donald M. Scott and Bernard Wishy, eds., *America's Families: A Documentary History* (New York: Harper and Row, 1982).

23. Carl N. Degler, "Women and the Family," in *The Past Before Us*, ed. Kammen, pp. 308-26. For examples of recent scholarship that include more direct concern for children, see Nancy Cott, "Notes Toward an Interpretation of Antebellum Childrearing," *The Psychohistory Review* 6 (Spring 1978): 4-20; Ruth Block, "American Feminine Ideals in Transition: The Rise of the Moral Mother, 1785-1815," *Feminist Studies* 3 (Fall 1975): 159-72.

24. The discussion of questions one through four is reprinted in edited form from Hiner, "The Child in American Historiography," pp. 15-16.

PART I

The Child in Colonial America

Introduction

Colonial children have been elusive creatures, difficult to study, more difficult to understand. The problems normally associated with studying children in the past have been compounded because of the relative lack of sources concerning colonial children as compared with those for later periods. For this reason and others, historians often do not agree about the basic character and shape of childhood in colonial America. For example, one group argues that colonial children were expected to think and act like adults and did not experience a childhood as we know it today. Other scholars maintain that there is a great deal of continuity between colonial and modern childhood, and that colonial children and modern children have much in common, including parents and other adult caregivers who loved them deeply. In what has become a classic article in the field, Ross Beales challenges the traditional belief that colonial Americans viewed their children as "miniature adults" and did not recognize the years following childhood as a distinct stage of life resembling modern adolescence. By studying colonial essays on children and carefully analyzing age patterns in catechism, conversion, military service, courtship, marriage, and voting, Beales builds strong support for the argument that, at least in colonial New England, children were not seen as small adults, and that colonial "youth" was in fact similar in many ways to modern adolescence.

Historians do agree on one thing about colonial children: they died at an astonishingly high rate when compared with children today. In his essay on parental bereavement in Puritan New England, Peter Slater explores the emotional responses of Puritan parents to the high mortality rates among their children. Most Puritan parents lost at least one child and some lost several. Slater finds that this experience did not, as some have argued, lead Puritan parents to reduce their emotional involvement with their young children, although there is evidence that some anticipatory mourning occurred in specific cases. Puritan parents loved their children deeply, and when children died their parents went through the basic stages of mourning experienced by persons today; however, this mourning process was experienced within the framework of traditional Puritan theology which raised the possibility of infant damnation.

Much of the research on colonial children has concentrated on New England, and we are only now beginning to see work on other areas. Daniel Blake Smith's article on parent-child relations in eighteenth-century Chesapeake families illustrates this welcome trend and provides an excellent comparison piece to the essay by Slater. According to Smith, the infant mortality rate in colonial Virginia and Maryland was even higher than that of New England, perhaps as high as 40 percent during the seventeenth century when malaria was prevalent. Smith suggests that this high rate of infant mortality may have led some seventeenth-century parents to restrict their emotional involvement with their children, but he says that by the eighteenth century there is abundant evidence of affectionate and tender relationships between parent and child, which he believes promoted a sense of security in the children.

The changing attitudes of colonial parents toward their children may have played a significant role in producing the simultaneous decline of birth and death rates that occurred in the nineteenth century. Robert Wells argues that a critical factor in this demographic transition was the growing feeling among colonial parents, especially in the eighteenth century, that disease could be controlled and that the loss of large numbers of children did not have to be accepted passively. Also, Wells thinks that increased population density in the eighteenth century may have changed the economic *meaning* of children and contributed to the decision of many parents to limit their childbearing. Wells's essay demonstrates the importance of adult attitudes toward children in explaining one of the most important shifts in American social history.

The Mason Children, David, Joanna, and Abigail, Massachusetts, 1670. Artist unknown. (courtesy of the M. H. de Young Memorial Museum of the Fine Arts Museums of San Francisco)

In Search of the Historical Child: Miniature Adulthood and Youth in Colonial New England

Ross W. Beales, Jr.

"I shall miss the little grown-ups — were there no children in those days?" This question about an eighteenth-century portrait of four American children essentially states the widespread scholarly and antiquarian view of children in colonial America. Not only is it assumed that colonial Americans treated their children differently than we do today, but it is also believed that they regarded their children as "miniature adults" and recognized no stage of development like twentieth-century adolescence. While this essay does not suggest that colonial Americans treated their children as we treat ours, it does conclude that notions of "miniature adulthood" and the absence of adolescence in colonial New England are, at best, exaggerations.

Much of the myth of miniature adulthood stems from the belief that children in colonial portraits appeared old and dressed like their parents. Until the Revolution, writes Alice Morse Earle, "As soon as a boy put on breeches he dressed precisely like his father — in miniature." According to Arthur M. Schlesinger, "The older generation as late as Independence still displayed its basic assumption that children were miniature adults by continuing to dress the young like little grownups. . . . The vital distinction between youth and age as yet remained unrecognized." Monica Kiefer finds that eighteenth-century children occupied "a submerged position in an adult setting"; only through the child's "gradual emergence" from that status would he come to occupy "a place of honor as a cherished social entity." Like other observers, she concludes that "as children of Colonial times were expected to behave like adults, they quite logically wore clothes appropriate for the role." Michael Zuckerman also states that there was "no clear distinction between child and adult" in eighteenth-century

Massachusetts. Children in Puritan portraits are "only scaled-down adults," who wear both wigs and the same clothes as their parents. "If clothes do not make the man," he asserts, "they do mark social differentiations; a distinctive mode of dress for children never developed before the Revolution." New Englanders did not believe that children had "distinctive needs and desires," and children were therefore given "no distinctive places or roles." Eighteenth-century Massachusetts children "did not live separated from the society in a protected preserve of carefree innocence; they were part of a single undifferentiated community."

Accounts of childhood in early America are marked by condescension, sentimentality, and even blank incomprehension. In describing Cotton Mather's admonitions to his daughter, Earle confesses, "I hardly understand why Cotton Mather, who was really very gentle to his children, should have taken upon himself to trouble this tender little blossom with dread of his death." None of Earle's concern for Mather's "tender little blossom" appears in her discussion of Nathaniel Mather, whose diary contains the admission, "Of the manifold sins which then I was guilty of, none so sticks upon me as that, being very young, I was *whitling* on the Sabbath-day; and for fear of being seen I did it behind the *door.* A great *reproach* of God! a specimen of that *atheism* I brought into the world with me!" For Earle, "It is satisfactory to add that this young prig of a Mather died when nineteen years of age."

Certain that modern parents know best how to rear children, authors like Earle believe that their knowledge is an appropriate standard by which to judge other cultures and eras. They insist that colonial child-rearing practices were not only incorrect but also harmful. Arthur W. Calhoun thus emphasizes the ill effect of "precocity" on children. The seventeenth century was "an age of precocity," which was encouraged in America by Puritan theology and a scarcity of labor. Parents' "zeal for education," for example, "overstimulated and forced baby minds"; the churches encouraged "infantile conversion"; and, in economic life, children were overworked and exploited. In Calhoun's judgment, the Puritans failed "to make the child appear valuable or noteworthy to himself or others." Such a "curtailment of infancy" was both a "distortion" of and "a crime against childhood."

Sandford Fleming argues that in Puritan society "children were regarded simply as miniature adults, and the same means and experiences were considered as suitable for them as for those older." This view of children resulted partly from the general attitudes of a society which lacked the benefits of modern psychology. Furthermore, Puritan theology "had banished the child, and classed everyone indiscriminately, infants and those of maturity, as sinners who were in urgent need of being saved from hell." The necessity of encouraging early conversions was particularly unfortunate in the century after the Great Awakening, when an "overdependence" on revival methods caused the "child mind" to develop "wrong" and "perverted" ideas of God. Indeed, the emotional excesses of revivalism "could hardly fail to do permanent physical, mental and spiritual injury to many of the children wrought upon."

John Demos finds that childhood in Plymouth Colony lasted a short, but crucial, six to eight years. Although a child's first year was "relatively comfortable and tranquil," his second year was likely to be traumatic. Not only would he be weaned and later be confronted by the birth of a rival sibling, but his parents, heeding the repressive advice of minister John Robinson, would seek to crush his "assertive and aggressive drives." As Robinson warned, "Surely there is in all children . . . a stubborness, and stoutness of mind arising from natural pride, which must, in the first place, be broken and beaten down." Demos suggests that this early childhood experience, in which the desire for "autonomy" was beaten down, instilled a lasting sense of "shame and doubt" in the Puritan character. As a result, adult life in Plymouth Colony was characterized by numerous personal conflicts and court cases, especially incidents involving slander, defamation, and fear of public exposure.

At about six to eight years of age, a child in Plymouth Colony became, in effect, a "miniature adult." Clothing symbolized this new status: previously dressed "in a kind of long robe which opened down the front," boys and girls now dressed very much like their parents. This implies "a whole attitude of mind," in which "there was no idea that each generation required separate spheres of work or recreation. Children learned the behavior appropriate to their sex and station by sharing in the activities of their parents." Six- or seven-year-olds began "technological" training, the boys perhaps working with their fathers at planting or fencemending, the girls helping their mothers with the cooking, spinning, or candlemaking. There may also have been some academic training, including more intensive religious instruction. The pattern of age at apprenticeship and service in other families also leads Demos to stress the years from six to eight, "the most common age for such arrangements."

Children's religious experiences also suggest miniature adulthood, for whole families attended the same church services, and "the young no less than the old were expected to digest the learned words that flowed from the pulpit." While nineteenth-century conversions typically occurred among young people in their teens, "no similar pattern" was found at Plymouth. In fact, many conversions apparently took place well before puberty. "Perhaps, indeed, a religious 'crisis' can more reasonably be connected with the whole matrix of changes customary for children at the age of about six to eight." Thus, with the evidence converging on this early age, it is likely that "the culture attached a very special importance to this particular time of life. Further 'proof' is lacking, but perhaps it was now that children began to assume the role of little adults."

After these crucial early years, the development of the child was relatively smooth. "The way to maturity appeared not as a cliff to be mounted in a series of sudden and precarious leaps, but as a gradual ascent the stages of which were quite literally embodied in the many siblings variously situated along the way." Adolescence was not the turning point that it is today, for "at Plymouth the 'teens' formed a period of relatively calm and steady progress toward full maturity." Courtships began during this stage of development, and following marriage, "the later years of life in Plymouth Colony brought, in most cases, no new departures of a major kind."

Joseph F. Kett agrees with Demos's findings with respect to adolescence. "Verbal distinctions between childhood and youth" were "practically nonexistent in the seventeenth century and still rare in the eighteenth." While there were numerous references to "youth" as early as the seventeenth century, the Puritans used "youth" as a noun rather than as a concept. Thus, their sermons commonly "mixed up children, youth, young people, and young men." Indeed, even if they experienced adolescence in a social sense, seventeenth-century "Puritans would have had difficulty coming to terms with it," for they viewed life as a highway rather than as a series of stages.

Substantial agreement thus exists among authors who discuss attitudes toward children and adolescents in colonial New England. That New Englanders regarded and treated their children as miniature adults is, in C. John Sommerville's words, "one of the hoariest shibboleths." Similary widespread is the belief that there was no stage in human development comparable to today's adolescence.

Recently, however, David E. Stannard has suggested that "there is no real evidence to support the contention that in 17th-century New England, as in 15th- and 16th-century France, there was little or no distinction between children and adults." He notes, for example, that Puritan journals, autobiographies, histories, and family manuals make "clear distinctions between adults and children well into their teens" and that the law definitely discriminated "between acceptable behavior and appropriate punishment for children, post-adolescent youths and adults." Stannard's observations are confirmed by an examination of the language New Englanders used to describe the "ages of man," by legal distinctions among age groups, and particularly by religious thought and practice.

Colonial New Englanders included both children and youth in the "ages of man," with youth extending from the early teens well into the twenties. When Gilbert Tennent preached in Boston in 1741, he used four familiar chronological divisions in addressing his audience: "old" and *"aged Persons"; "middle-ag'd People,* of thirty Years old and upwards"; *"my younger Brethren,* of fourteen Years and upwards"; and *"little Children,* of six Years old and upwards."

Tennent's age-groups approximated the concept of the "ages of man" held by New Englanders. These ages included old age, middle age, youth, childhood, and sometimes infancy. Anne Bradstreet, for example, wrote "Of the Four Ages of Man," while Ellis Gray spoke of the "Old, and the middle Aged, the Young and little Children." Samuel Moody included "infancy" when he warned that "Judgment shall be Universal with respect to Persons, *viz.* Youth as well as Children and Infants below them, and Middle, with Old Age above them. . . ." Jonathan Edwards advised "every one that is yet out of Christ, and hanging over the Pit of Hell, whether they be old Men and Women, or middle Aged, or young People, or little Children, now [to] hearken to the loud Calls of God's Word and Providence." William Cooper also addressed "MANY of you *Children,* you *Young People,* you that are *middle aged,* and you that are *old. . . ."*

Edwards placed the upper limits of childhood at fourteen when he described the revival of 1735 at Northampton. It had been unusual for children to be converted, but now, he reported, "near thirty were to appearance so wrought upon between ten and fourteen years of age, and two between nine and ten, and one of about four years of age. . . ." Thomas Shepard also saw the early teens as a dividing point. When his fourteen-year-old son was admitted to Harvard College in 1672, Shepard urged him to "remember . . . that tho' you have spent your time in the vanity of Childhood; sports and mirth, little minding better things, yet that now, when come to this ripeness of Admission to the College, that now God and man expects you should putt away Childish things: now is the time come, wherein you are to be serious, and to learn sobriety, and wisdom in all your ways which concern God and man." While young Shepard ended his childhood at fourteen, Cotton Mather dared call himself a "youth" at thirty-one. "I am willing now," he told an audience of young people, "at an Age thus far Extending, to conclude my own *Youth,* with one Affectionate Endeavour more" to encourage youthful piety.

The early teens were recognized as special years in other aspects of Puritan culture. The laws of Massachusetts, for example, established fourteen as the age of discretion in cases of slander. (Neighboring Plymouth Colony set the "age of descretion" at sixteen for slander and lying.) Fourteen was also the age for "chusing of Guardions." Sodomists were to be executed, but if one party was forced to commit sodomy or was under fourteen, he was only "seveerly punished."

The "ages of man" and the different ages of legal responsibility might be dismissed, however, as mere conventions that had no real social meaning. Such an argument might be especially persuasive with respect to the law because of Puritan attempts to institute Mosaic law in New England. But another area of New England culture — religious thought and practice — provides abundant evidence to confirm the patterns of language and law described above.

Historians like Calhoun, Fleming, and Demos argue that Puritans treated the young and old equally and encouraged early conversion experiences. "The young no less than the old," writes Demos, "were expected to digest the learned words that flowed from the pulpit." John Cotton would have disagreed. "Bring them to Church," he urged, "and help them to remember something, and tell them the meaning of it, and take a little in good part, and encourage them, and that will make them delight in it." This suggests that because children's capacities were limited, loving parents should take care that children understood at least something. William Williams later warned that "because of the weakness of their Understandings, and narrowness of their Capacities, in their younger Years, Pains must be us'd to convey Truth in such a manner as they may be able to *conceive* of it, and not meerly learn Things by rote."

Puritan descriptions of the age-groups from which God was most likely to call His elect show that infants and children were not miniature adults. God would not, of course, restrict His call to any one age-group. "Should God call only children, middle aged men, or old men onely," explained Thomas Hooker, "then men would conceive that there were something in the persons that moved him to this, either the weakenesse of the child, or else the innocencie thereof did move God to shew mercy thereunto, or else that God did delight in the strength or in the gifts and parts of a young man, or if he should call men in their old age onely, then men might thinke that their experience and gravitie did move God to call them onely." God called "some in all ages and at all times, some young ones chosen, and some refused, some old men called, and others cast aside." The selection of some for salvation and others for damnation resulted not from particular men's natural qualities but "from the freenesse of Gods mercy."

Despite its freeness, God's mercy was extended to some groups more often than to others. "Some are called in their youth, some in their middle age, some in their old age, some in their tender yeares, some in their riper age, some old, some young, but this is most true that those whom God doth call it is most commonly in their middle age before they come to their old age." According to Hooker, the middle age "hath better Materials . . . wherein, or whereupon the frame of Conversion may be erected, or imprinted by the stamp of the Spirit."

The special fitness of middle age for conversion followed naturally from the attitude summarized by John Norton: "Though knowledg may be without grace, yet there can be no grace without knowledg." Infants were incapable of the knowledge that preceded grace. "In Infancy," explained Hooker, "a man lives little other than the life of a Plant, or Beast, feeding and sleeping, growing and encreasing; or else he takes up himself with delights of outward objects most agreeable to his Sences." This did not mean that God would not save infants, but rather that His manner of converting them was special. "Calling," said Norton, "is either extraordinary, as in Elect Infants, dying in their Infancy: or ordinary." Thus, in John Cotton's view, children were "capable of the habits and gifts of grace from their first Conception . . . and the reason is, as soon as capable of sin, capable of grace." Hooker noted that there was "a number of children" whom it was God's purpose to save "according to election." They were to be saved, however, not because they were children but while they were children, for "all the men in the world are either vessels of mercy, or vessels of wrath, according to the good will of God." The operation of God's grace on infants was "extraordinary in mans account," but Hooker cautioned against curiosity, "for secret things belong to God," and man should be content to know "that some children are elected, and God will sanctifie them, and glorifie them; but the number, and manner, I leave that."

A child who lived through infancy could exercise his understanding little more than an infant. In Hooker's opinion, a child of ten or twelve lived "the life of a beast," and it was "almost impossible" for him "to consider of the mysteries of life & salvation." In his "tender yeares" a man had "such a weake understanding" that he could "hold nothing." If a child were told of the wonders of salvation, it was "impossible unlesse God workes wonderfully that hee should receive them." However, when a man arrived at "the ripenesse of his yeares, from 20. years untill he come to be 40. or thereabouts," Hooker believed, "the Understanding begins to shew itself in her operations: Invention is then most quick to apprehend, the Judgment to discern, Memory to retain, and the Affections tenderest and nimblest to imbrace any thing offered, and most pliable to be wrought upon." At this age "a man is able to conceive and partake of the things of grace, and fadom [sic] them, and the power of his understanding comes on whereby he is able to embrace them." The middle years were therefore "the fittest time that God should bestow his graces upon a man."

Puritan ideas about the age-groups from which God called His elect were borne out in practice. At Dorchester, Massachusetts, for example, in the period 1640-1730, only 34 (8.9 percent) of the 382 new communicants whose ages are known were under the age of twenty; only 3, all girls, were under seventeen (one each at age thirteen, fifteen, and sixteen). In the same years, 202 (52.9 percent) of the new communicants were in their twenties, and 94 (24.6 percent) were in their thirties. At New Haven, in the years 1685-1739, only 54 (7.9 percent) of the 681 new communicants whose ages are known were younger than twenty. Data from eighteenth-century Andover and Norton, Massachusetts, and Norwich and Woodbury, Connecticut, reveal the same pattern. One must conclude, therefore, that the most famous conversion of the eighteenth century, that of four-year-old Phebe Bartlet of Northampton, was a remarkable exception.

Provisions for catechizing children in the churches at Dorchester and Norwich also indicate that the Puritans treated children and youth differently. At Dorchester in 1672, the minister compiled a list of "all children & servants that weer under any famely government in order to catechising or some other way of instruction." The names for 1672 did not survive, but the church records do contain a list of catechumens for 1676. Males aged thirteen to twenty-eight are separated from the younger males designated "children from 12 et infra" and as young as seven. The list of "young Maids," aged seven to thirty-one, is not so explicitly divided, although there are spaces between ages twelve and thirteen and between ages eight and nine. The church at Norwich decided that "all the Males who are eight or nine years of age, shall be presented before the Lord in his Congregation every Lords Day to be Cate[c]hised, until they be about thirteen years in age." At thirteen the boys and girls attended "the Meeting appointed in private for their instruction," and they continued to meet as long as they lived "under Family government of Parents or others" or until they became full communicants.

Communion presupposed a degree of knowledge that children could not achieve. "Children are not capable sabjects [sic] of the Lords Supper," wrote John Cotton. "For receiving whereof, the Apostle requireth wee should examine and judge our selves." Among "men of years, the Spirit . . . worketh faith by the hearing of the Word, and by revealing and tendering Christ as the al-sufficient and onely way of life." Aware that individuals matured at different rates, Puritan thinkers did not set an arbitrary age when individuals might be said to arrive at the "years of understanding." As early as 1643, Richard Mather recognized the problem of "how long Children should be counted under age." He noted that the New England churches had no occasion to look into the question. "Onely this we thinke, that one certaine rule cannot be given for all, whereby to determine how long they are under age, but according as God gives experience and maturity of naturall understanding, and Spirituall; which he gives sooner to some then unto others." Mather was somewhat more specific a number of years later when he asked, *"Till what age shall they* [children] *enter into Covenant with their Parents, whether sixteen, twenty one, or sixty?"* He answered that "as long as in respect of age or capacity they cannot according to ordinary account, be supposed able to act in a matter of this nature for themselves, so long they shall enter in by means of their Parents covenant, because whilst they are children and in their minority, they are not otherwise capable of covenanting: When adult, they are to covenant in their own persons." Thirteen years of age was not too old for a child to be included in his parents' covenant, for Ishmael (Genesis 17:25) had been "admitted to the Seal by his Fathers covenant at thirteen years of age." Nevertheless, Mather cautioned, in "the bounding of adult and in-adult age, depending upon the judgment of prudence, much is to be left unto the discretion of Officers and Churches in this case."

Charles Chauncy agreed with Mather on this point. "It cannot be concluded," he wrote, "that all persons are to be looked upon as adult at the very same age, some persons coming to years of discretion before others; and some ... having weaker parts and less means of instruction then others have, therefore we see not how there can be any *particular time* fixed when all *persons* shall be accounted adult, (or of age) to answer for themselves at this or that age, but a latitude must be allowed in this case."

At Northampton, the congregation of Richard Mather's son, Eleazer, sought to "come to som[e] de[ter]mination respecting the continuing [or] expiring of the state of minority," but did not find it "limited in Scripture to any perticular yere or tyme." They therefore followed Richard Mather's advice and voted that "the fixing of Adult, and not Adult age bee left to the wisdome, discretion and judgment of the Elders of the Church from tyme to tyme, and as they upon tryall and Examination of the Ability and capacity of each person respectively shall determine them to bee in that state either of Adult or inadult, accordingly shall Such persons bee accounted and walked towards by this Church."

Solomon Stoddard, Eleazer Mather's successor, departed significantly from the Mathers' point of view. Stoddard came to believe that the sacrament of the Lord's Supper was a "converting ordinance" that should not be restricted to God's visible saints; it should rather be offered to the regenerate and to the unregenerate alike with the expectation that it would help bring the latter to Christ. But Stoddard did not follow his doctrine to its logical conclusion, for it was said that he permitted only those who were "Civilized & Cathechised above 14 years old" to come to the Lord's Table. He thus demanded good behavior, knowledge of doctrine, and a minimal age. In discarding an older conception about the purposes of the Lord's Supper, he also discarded a flexibility in assessing the age when individuals arrived at years of understanding. It was certainly easier to classify a person as "adult" or as "inadult" merely by his age than to examine the ability and capacity of each person under fourteen, but one wonders whether this decision did not reflect a certain loss of spiritual energy, perhaps a waning of piety, that led to a less personal treatment of each soul. Put in slightly different terms, Stoddard's open communion and the arbitrary restriction of communion to persons over fourteen can be viewed as movement away from Puritanism's sect-like qualities toward an increasingly church-like form of religion.

Not all churches made such arbitrary distinctions among persons of different ages. At Barnstable, for example, the church baptized a sixteen-year-old boy "by vertue of his fathers Covenant bec[ause] upon examination, before the Elders & divers brethren of the Church thereto appointed, hee was Judged An Inadult person though 16 years old when his father Covenanted." Another case was that of Jane Bump, who, "being about fourteen or 15 years old, was examined, & being one of the family & looked upon in her minority, was Baptised." The minister declared seventeen-year-old John Howland "to be adult" and "that he could not baptize him on his mothers faith but finding In him Such pious dispositions declared that he Could baptize him on his own faith and Covenant." The members of the church agreed that John was "a Subject of baptism," but since "this was a new Case" and the members could not agree on the reasons why he should be baptized, they concluded that "this Instance [was] not to be made a precedant In time to Come." Jedidiah Lumburt's eighteen-year-old son was baptized at the West Parish of Barnstable "by vertue of his fath[er's] Covenant, for upon examination of him before the elders of the Church, he appeared not of maturity to act for himself," and "therefore he was Judged an In[adult?] & received baptism as one In minority."

At Chelmsford, the church decided in 1657 that children might be baptized if they were under the age of fourteen or fifteen when their parents became communicants. Six years later, it was agreed that the minister and at least one other church member were to examine the knowledge and spiritual experience of children who had grown to years of discretion. As a result of this examination, some children were taken into communion, but others were found to have a better memory than a real understanding of doctrine. In this case, the age of discretion was probably regarded as sixteen years, for in 1666 the church agreed on a course of catechism for all persons under sixteen. Unmarried men over sixteen were given special treatment: they had the choice either of publicly demonstrating their knowledge of religion or of attending the catechism classes.

These kinds of records confirm the practice of what men like Richard Mather and Charles Chauncy held in theory: that there was no set age at which a person might claim, merely by virtue of accumulated years, a new standing in the church. Recognition that an individual had arrived at years of understanding or at years of discretion depended on an examination of that understanding or discretion. Even Stoddard's church required an examination, for a person who sought communion had to be both fourteen and "Civilized & Cathechised." Persons under fourteen, regardless of their precocity, were automatically excluded from communion; persons over fourteen were only conditionally eligible for communion.

Language, law, and religious thought and practice thus suggest that New Englanders, far from regarding children as "miniature adults," recognized their immaturity. But what about individuals who were no longer children? Did "youth" in colonial New England in any sense resemble twentieth-century adolescence? "The adolescent as a distinct species," writes F. Musgrove, "is the creation of modern social attitudes and institutions. A creature neither child nor adult, he is a comparatively recent sociopsychological invention, scarcely two centuries old." In contrast to this viewpoint, S. N. Eisenstadt observes that "however great the differences among various societies, there is one focal point within the life span of an individual which in most known societies is to some extent emphasized: the period of youth, of transition from childhood to full adult status, or full membership in the society. In this period the individual is no longer a child (especially from the physical and sexual point of view) but is ready to undertake many attributes of an adult and to fulfill adult roles. But he is not yet fully acknowledged as an adult, a full member of the society. Rather, he is being 'prepared,' or is preparing himself for such adulthood." Eisenstadt's generalization is applicable to colonial New England, where the stage of development, commonly called "youth," resembled today's "adolescence."

In physiological terms, adolescence is the biological and sexual maturation of a child, extending from puberty to the achievement of full reproductive capacity. In a broader sense, adolescence includes both sexual maturation and the social and psychological development of the individual. Sociologically, adolescence has been described as "the transition period from dependent childhood to self-sufficient adulthood." It ends with the attainment of full adult status within the limits prescribed by one's culture, class, and sex. Adolescents and children are thus distinguished from adults by the adult activities from which they are excluded: for example, marriage and the rearing of families; economic self-sufficiency; participation in the political life of the community to the extent that their sex and station permit. Psychologically, adolescence "is a 'marginal situation' in which new adjustments have to be made, namely those that distinguish child behavior from adult behavior in a given society." Chronologically, adolescence continues "from approximately twelve or thirteen to the early twenties, with wide individual and cultural variations."

The transition from the dependence of childhood to the self-sufficiency of adulthood was not made suddenly in early New England. This can be seen, for example, in the individual's gradual assumption of the legal rights and obligations of adulthood. Massachusetts children over sixteen, "and of sufficient understanding," were to be executed if they cursed or struck their parents. Likewise, "a stubborn or RE-BELLIOUS SON, of sufficient years & understanding (viz) sixteen years of age," risked capital punishment for incorrigible disobedience. Another law provided that "the minoritie of women in case of marriage shall be till sixteen years." Although Plymouth youths were eligible for militia service at sixteen, "noe single persons under twenty yeares of age either children or servants" could vote in "milletary concernments." In Massachusetts, twenty-one was the age both for "passing away of lands, or such kinde of hereditaments, or for giving of votes, verdicts or sentences in any civil courts or causes," and for making "Wills & Testaments & other lawfull Alienations of their lands and estates." A statute of limitations affecting inheritances in Plymouth Colony permitted minors to bring suit within five years of reaching twenty-one. Finally, in the town of Barnstable in Plymouth Colony, a person had to be either twenty-four years old or married in order to share in a division of the town lands.

"Where land was abundant and labor at a premium," writes Bernard Bailyn, "it took little more to create a household than to maintain one. Material independence was sooner or later available to every energetic adult white male, and few failed to break away when they could." Oscar and Mary F. Handlin assert that "the passage of the child to adulthood ceased to be a gradual progression through well-defined stages and became a single great leap away from home."

Recent studies show that Bailyn and the Handlins overestimate the ease with which the economic self-sufficiency of a separate household might be attained. "A man ready to marry," observes Kenneth A. Lockridge, "did not just go out and get a job; he prepared a farm of his own to support his family or else he made sure that he could expect to inherit the family home and acres." The creation of a household, contrary to Bailyn's premise, often must have required considerable labor, parental assistance, and capital outlay. Land had to be acquired, cleared, and fenced; buildings, however rough in the first years, had to withstand New England winters; animals and tools, as well as household utensils and furnishings, were also needed.

Philip J. Greven, Jr.'s, study of the first four generations in Andover, Massachusetts, documents the slowness with which sons achieved economic independence. The key to independence was land, and fathers often retained until death legal title to the lands on which their sons were settled. Those sons who purchased their shares of the paternal estate were more often than not "mature men rather than youths just out of adolescence or in their early twenties." Some sons, particularly in the third and fourth generations, did choose to leave Andover, and their fathers often helped them to achieve autonomy relatively early.

Patterns of apprenticeship in New England also suggest that a "youth" of thirteen or fourteen would not assume autonomous economic status for several years. In the seventeenth century, according to Edmund S. Morgan, a boy typically chose his calling between the ages of ten and fourteen. Most apprenticeships required seven years of service to a master and lasted until the age of twenty-one. Thus, while an individual made an early choice of his life-long occupation, his actual economic independence was delayed seven years while he learned the skills of his calling. And even if he were fully trained at the age of twenty-one, it is unlikely that a young man would have had the capital or connections necessary to establish his economic independence.

Political rights also came slowly. In Plymouth Colony, the revised laws of 1671 established twenty-one years as the earliest age at which a man might become a freeman. John Demos finds no "set age" at which men became freemen, for his sample of sixty adult males achieved that status between twenty-five and forty. "This privilege and responsibility... was perhaps the last in the series of steps leading to full adult citizenship in the community." Delayed political adulthood followed naturally from the economic qualifications for freemanship and late economic adulthood.

Marriage was closely connected to economic independence, for marriage presupposed the ability to provide for a family. Parents played an important role in their child's choice of a spouse, for successful courtship, at least in the seventeenth century, depended on the parents' directing influence, goodwill, and skill in negotiating a marriage settlement. Like the ability to earn a living, marriage was often delayed until the middle twenties and later.

"The most sensitive register of maturity," writes Greven, "is the age at marriage, since the responsibilities and duties involved in the establishment of a new family suggest the recognition that the married couple were ready to function as adults." This insight is confirmed by other evidence. The provisions for catechizing at Norwich and Dorchester took special notice of unmarried non-communicants, who were apparently required to receive religious instruction either until they became communicants or until they married and set up independent households. The laws of Plymouth Colony also accorded special recognition to the married vis-à-vis the unmarried. A married man under the age of twenty could presumably vote in "milletary concernments," while his single counterpart could not. Finally, at Barnstable a single male had to wait until the age of twenty-four in order to share in a division of the town lands, while a married male under twenty-four was eligible for a share.

From these varied data emerges a picture of a prolonged "adolescence" or "youth" experienced by young people in colonial New England. Youth, in Benjamin Colman's words, was a "chusing time." "*NOW* O Young People is *your chusing time,* and commonly your *fixing time;* and as you fix it is like to last. Now you commonly chuse your *Trade;* betake your selves to your business for life, show what you incline to, and how you intend to be imploy'd all your days. Now you chuse your *Master* and your Education or Occupation. And now you dispose of your self in *Marriage* ordinarily, place your *Affections,* give away your hearts, look out for some *Companion* of life, whose to be as long as you live. And is this indeed the work of your Youth?" For today's adolescent, at least in his idealized type, this "chusing time" presumably provides the opportunity to try out a number of life styles or roles, for the choices are abundant and the pressures for early decision are often not great. In this respect, adolescence has been called a "moratorium," during which the adolescent is dependent on parents and society, yet free from significant responsibilities. As a result, the adolescent in an age-stratified society is likely to be part of a peer group based on age and having its own distinctive "culture."

In colonial New England, the range of choices open to youth was narrow, particularly outside Benjamin Colman's Boston, and decisions tended to be irrevocable: "As you fix it is like to last." As Demos points out, "The profesional and 'artisan' classes were relatively small" in seventeenth-century Plymouth, "and the vast majority of the populace was engaged simply in farming. In the typical case, therefore, the choice of a calling was scarcely a choice at all; instead it was something assumed, something everywhere implicit in the child's surroundings and in the whole process of growth." Kenneth Lockridge suggests that "most men showed the typical peasant's satisfaction with the *status quo*. It worked for his father and for his father before him, why tinker with success? Why, especially when it could be dangerous?" In addition to having limited choices, sons — to say nothing of daughters — were heavily dependent upon their parents both in timing and in making their choice of education or occupation, economic independence, and marriage. Under such circumstances, a son's bold assertion of independence from his parents or adoption of an alien life style was surely difficult if not unthinkable. Neither the desire nor the ability existed.

This is not to say, however, that elements of a distinctive youth "culture" did not exist in colonial New England. Ministers' descriptions of youthful behavior before and after the revivals of the eighteenth century reveal a deep strain of anxiety about the apparent collapse of family government and a rejoicing that the revival had prompted a measure of youthful self-control and reformation. Jonathan Edwards, for example, reported that there was "a time of extraordinary dullness in religion" just after the death of his grandfather, Solomon Stoddard. "Licentiousness for some years greatly prevailed among the youth of the town," many of whom were "very much addicted to night-walking, and frequenting the tavern, and lewd practices, wherein some, by their example exceedingly corrupted others." The youth "very frequently" gathered "in conventions of both sexes, for mirth and jollity, which they called frolics," and in which they often spent "the greater part of the night . . . without regard to any order in the families they belonged to: and indeed family government did too much fail in the town." The Northampton revival of late 1734 and 1735 radically changed the behavior of the town's young people. The conversion of a young woman, "one of the greatest company-keepers in the whole town," was "almost like a flash of lightning, upon the hearts of young people all over the town, and upon many others." As Edwards looked back on the revival, he expressed the hope that those young people who were "on other accounts most likely and considerable" had become "truly pious and leading persons in the ways of religion." Similarly "those that were formerly looser young persons are generally, to all appearance, become true lovers of God and Christ, and spiritual in their dispositions."

This pattern of youthful reformation was repeated frequently during the Great Awakening. At Somers, Connecticut, "those *Youths* that delighted themselves in Frolicking and Mischief" were reported to "have wholly left it off" and reputedly found "more Pleasure and Satisfaction in serving GOD, than ever they did in the Ways of *Sin* and *Satan.*" The young people of Halifax, Massachusetts, abandoned "all Frolicking and Carousing, and merry Meetings" and now "took more delight in going to a Meeting than ever they did to a Frolick." The minister of Wrentham rejoiced that the *"young People"* had "generally and voluntarily *done* with their *Frolicking* and *merry Meetings"* and bitterly lamented the time they had wasted in such pursuits. Even "some of the *late Ring-leaders* of their Merriment" shared these sentiments. The Awakening at Bridgewater convinced many of the young "of the Sin of spending away Days & Nights in Singing and Dancing, and other youthful Sins, which they were much addicted to before, and greatly delighted in." As a result they stopped "their youthful Practices, of Singing, Dancing, Company-keeping, which before they esteemed lawful Recreations, and took abundance of Pleasure in."

These and other accounts of pre-revival patterns of youthful behavior — night-walking, frolicking, company-keeping, carousing, merry-meeting, dancing, and singing — suggest that there were elements of a separate youth "culture" at least in eighteenth-century New England. If this culture were not so sharply separated from the adult world as today's adolescent "cultures," the explanation may be that Puritan youth did not live in as highly an age-stratified society as today's adolescents. This is probably the source of Arthur W. Calhoun's alarm at Puritan "precocity." Puritan hagiography includes accounts of children who learned their letters and catechism at remarkably early ages. Moreover, it was not unusual at Harvard and Yale for brothers of different ages to be in the same class, or for a class to contain members whose ages ranged from the early teens to the twenties.

It thus appears that in colonial New England, childhood was not succeeded by "miniature adulthood" but by "youth," a lengthy transitional period preceding adult status. During this "chusing time," when the young were expected (in Thomas Shepard's words) to "putt away Childish things," the youth remained dependent on his elders for his education, for his choice of and training in a calling, and for the material means, usually land, which would support a family. While this dependence carried with it a measure of parental control, it also provided a moratorium, a freedom from adult responsibilities, during which the elements of a youthful "culture" might emerge.

What do these findings suggest about the history of family life in America? On the one hand, as Stannard argues, the Ariès paradigm of French parent-children relationships is not applicable to the American experience. In part, this may arise from America's relatively short history, and therefore the Ariès model can be tested only in the context of the longer Anglo-American experience. On the other hand, recent investigations suggest that the Ariès paradigm may not apply to England and may not even be wholly correct in terms of the French experience. In any event, historians must re-examine parent-child and intergenerational relationships from the earliest American settlements through the nineteenth century. Recent studies offer some outlines of a new, possibly American paradigm. Greven's study of Andover shows that first-generation fathers exercised remarkably strong and enduring control over their sons' lives. If this relationship existed elsewhere, perhaps we can attribute it not only to an abundance of land but also to a high degree of religiosity among the first-generation settlers. The weakening of patriarchalism in successive generations would fit not only into the narrowing economic base of farming communities but also into the weakening or dilution of religious zeal, the "declension" which Perry Miller has so masterfully analyzed. The slackening of parental discipline, one symptom of the declension, gave the younger generation more latitude to develop their own "culture," which at times might seem very much at odds with parental authority. Both Marion L. Starkey and John Demos, for example, identify a structural conflict between generations in Salem Village in 1692. Although their interpretations of the sources of this conflict are markedly different, does not the conflict itself partly reflect the development of a youthful "culture" not subject to parental supervision and control?

The most startling manifestation of weakened parental control can be seen in the dramatically increasing rates of premarital pregnancies which occurred from the late seventeenth to the mid-eighteenth century. Equally dramatic, however, were the decreasing rates of premarital pregnancies that took place a century later. When the New Lights of the 1740s observed an apparent reformation of manners and morals among the youthful converts of the Great Awakening, their rejoicing was perhaps premature, for, at best, the reformation may have affected only the new converts. Nineteenth-century revivalists were more successful than their predecessors, for early conversions were expected and widespread and may have contributed to an alteration in premarital sexual behavior — at least among middle-class Protestants. The submergence or temporary denial of adolescent sexuality may have prepared the way for the "discovery" of adolescence in the late nineteenth and early twentieth centuries, as well as the mistaken belief that earlier generations treated their children as miniature adults. As a result, the idea of "miniature adulthood" must be seen, not as a description of social reality, but as a minor chapter in the history of social thought.

Child's high chair used during the seventeenth and eighteenth centuries by the Mathers, a New England clerical family. (courtesy of the American Antiquarian Society, Worcester, Mass.)

2

"From the *Cradle* to the *Coffin*": Parental Bereavement and the Shadow of Infant Damnation in Puritan Society

Peter G. Slater

In contemporary America children seldom die in infancy, though parents are a bit apprehensive about the possibility anyway. A child psychologist notes: "A new mother may be so unsure of herself that every little thing tends to worry her. She has not had enough experience with young babies to know how to interpret different things that may happen. If the baby is sound asleep, he may not seem to be breathing. She rushes over to see if he's still alive!" And, of course he is, as she knew he would be. Parents worry about many things — kidnappings, accidents, animal attacks — without truly expecting them to happen to their children.

In the Puritan era (defined as New England's first century, the 1620s to the 1720s), parental apprehensiveness about death had a different quality. Mothers and fathers genuinely expected to lose some of their infants, because they saw these fragile, death-prone beings passing away at a disheartening rate. Describing her late grandchild, Anne Bradstreet used *similes* evoking transciency: "Like as a bubble, or the brittle glass, or like a shadow turning as it was." After losing several youngsters, Samuel Sewall was so disturbed by his awareness of a child's tenuous hold on life that he dreamt that all his surviving offspring but one had died. Cotton Mather, who suffered in waking hours the torments the less anxiety-ridden confined to nightmares, lived "in a continual Apprehension" that his son Samuel "(tho' a lusty and hearty Infant) will dy in its Infancy," which alas, was what eventually happened.

Recent historical research has demonstrated that the actual rate of infant mortality was not as high as the Puritans thought and as scholars had long believed to be the case. The objective figures are high enough, however, to indicate that the death of a young child was a frequent occurrence. In the healthiest communities, such as Andover and Ipswich in the mid-seventeenth century, one of every ten infants died, as contrasted with one of every sixty in present-day America. In less-favored places during the seventeenth century, like the towns of Salem and Boston, as many as three infants of every ten expired. The probability that parents would lose at least one child was increased by the high birth rate. With seven or more children per family, even repeated bereavements were not unusual, especially during epidemics. In the first marriage of the poet Edward Taylor, five out of the eight offspring died in infancy. Of his fourteen children, Samuel Sewall buried seven who were under two years old. Cotton Mather saw eight of his fifteen children die before reaching that age, and one soon thereafter. Three of these Mather children perished from the measles in a period of five days. Death seemed to sit on the doorsteps of unfortunate families, waiting to devour their young.

Having expected one or more of his children, as well as those of his close kinsmen, to die in their earliest years, even a Puritan who was fortunate enough to escape this misfortune was likely to be concerned about what happened to infants in the afterlife. Those most knowledgeable about the future state, the clergy, let it be known that some infants would go to heaven. They were less certain about the fate of the rest, but generally upheld the doctrine of infant damnation: children dying during the first years of life who were not recipients of saving grace would spend eternity in the fires of hell. Ministers tended to be brief when discussing this doctrine, but as long as they made people aware of what it meant, anyone pondering the fate of deceased infants would have to reckon with it. The doctrine especially had to be taken into account by grieving parents and those seeking to comfort them. Like an insane relative pacing the attic in a nineteenth-century novel, hardly mentioned by the characters yet throwing a pall over their lives, infant damnation cast its shadow over Puritan households in mourning for deceased babies.

Love for Infants

When someone dies, people's feelings about the loss are to a large extent determined by the relationships they had with him while he was alive. Those in the immediate family are expected to mourn, a process that is not confined to bereavement, but represents a general way of responding to loss. Mourning reactions to the loss of a loved one include shock, grief, and pain, which develop as the survivor's ego struggles to cope with the experience. If an individual does not mourn the death of a family member, either he is suffering from an abnormal emotional condition or he has not been involved in an affective relationship with the deceased. The application of this pattern to the Puritan past raises important questions. Were parents emotionally attached to their children, or were they indifferent to them? Did they grieve when infants died, or were they uncaring?

Evidence shows that Puritan parents often had sufficient affective investment in their offspring to make a death deeply felt. At the demise of Samuel Sewall's daughter, the family gave way to "general Sorrow and Tears." "I lost my hope," wrote Wait Winthrop after the expiration of his child, "and the greatest part of my comfort." Thomas Shepard described his young son who had sickened and died shortly after a stymied departure from England as "very precious to my soule & dearly beloved of me."

The children so warmly spoken of in these citations were all less than four years old when they died. This point is important because some scholars have made a sharp distinction between parental feelings for little children and for older ones, claiming that in the past the very young were seen as somewhat less than human, "unconsciously regarded like the embryos of marsupials." This assertion is hard to sustain for New England. Even still-borns or babies dying after a few days of life could be described as "my poor litell infant," or "a child of a most *comely* and *hearty* Look." Samuel Sewall, away from home during his wife's labor, "was grievously stung" upon his return soon after to "find a sweet desirable Son dead, who had none of my help to succour him and save his Life. . . . These Tears I weep over my abortive Son." Such statements were not expressions of love, which took time to develop, but did represent recognitions of the fundamental humanity of the newborn. On that basis, a genuine love for infants who survived could be established during the first months of their existence.

This love relationship was complicated by the Calvinist doctrines of original sin and native depravity. According to the "Augustino-federal" version of original sin, which held sway in New England until the reformulations of Jonathan Edwards, infants entered the world carrying the crushing burden of a multiple sinfulness. Ministers told parents: "Your *Children* are born with deadly *wounds* of sin upon their souls"; "there is a *Corrupt Nature* in Every Child, in its Infancy: Yea from the *very Birth*, they Go *Astray Speaking Lyes*." In the nineteenth century, opponents of Calvinism argued that parents who believed such doctrines could not genuinely love their children. By contrast, our post-Freudian understanding of the psychodynamics of the family allows for the compatibility of these doctrines with love relationships.

Most likely, Puritan mothers and fathers did not see vessels of sin and depravity every time they glanced at one of their infants. The images parents maintained of their children during the bustle of daily family life were not hard and constant, but varied among positive and negative shadings. Puritan infants could, on occasion, be as attractive as those of any other era, capable of charming all but the most austere of Calvinists with their "pretty features, pretty speeches, pretty actions." During such moments of affection the fundamental iniquity of the child would not be uppermost in a parent's mind. "We have seen *Lovely Qualities* in our *Children*, by which they have been mightily Endeared unto us," noted Cotton Mather. Yet, if the sleeping baby, the smiling little one, or the prattling tot did not evoke unfavorable theological depictions, the inevitable fits of crying and of pique readily brought to mind condemnatory doctrines. Such thoughts could even occur without specific provocation. Cotton Mather's daughter Katherine appeared in the recesses of his diary as the very symbol of innocence, "a *Lamb* that was indeed unto me as a *Daughter*," but he dutifully made occasion to speak to the girl of her depravity and of how she must pray for grace.

Despite the ambivalences that it fostered, the doctrine of infantile depravity may have played a stabilizing role in parent-child relationships. If the Puritan nuclear family had but a small part of the charged emotional atmosphere of contemporary nuclear families, feelings of intense jealousy and of acute annoyance must have at times arced between parent and child, even an infant in a cradle, as well as between siblings and between husband and wife. Such feelings might not have been explicitly verbalized by parents, as the society disapproved of their expression. But by talking about a child as iniquitous in the eyes of God, the parent's own sporadic dislike of his offspring could be vented in a socially approved way. The doctrine of original sin thus served as a lightning rod for what Dr. Benjamin Spock calls "the inevitability of parental impatience and resentment," forestalling that anxiety which many twentieth-century parents experience because "when they detect such emotions stirring in themselves, they either feel unbearably guilty or try strenuously to deny them."

Although images of child loveliness and of child sinfulness could not simultaneously occupy center place in parental consciousness, ultimately there was no contradiction between them. The Puritans viewed the child as a paradox — an innocent facade behind which lurked all sorts of wicked desires — a perspective not unlike the one Freud later employed to shatter the nineteenth-century idealization of the very young. The child in an Anne Bradstreet poem is characterized by "A perverse will, a love to what's forbid,/ A serpent's sting in pleasing face lay hid." Samuel Willard made the same point in describing infants as *"innocent vipers."* In the nineteenth century the paradox would be dissolved by those who accepted the Romantic notion that the physical qualities of a person were symbols of his inner state. William Ellery Channing would exclaim, "What! in the beauty of childhood and youth, in that open brow, that cheerful smile, do you see the brand of total corruption?" That is just what the Puritans had visualized, without relinquishing their love for their children.

The Theological Quandary

In the routine of everyday family life, a precise determination of the spiritual worth of children was not a paramount problem even for so intellectual a group as the Puritans. A parent could wash, dress, feed, and supervise a little one without consciously thinking of him or her in moral terms, imagining neither depraved serpent nor sinless lamb. The situation reversed itself in the event of the child's death. The body had ceased to be, but the soul endured, its spiritual qualities now central in any consideration of that child. In this context, the fact of juvenile depravity and the possibility of its removal by divine grace were matters of intense concern. Parents and close relatives longed to know what became of deceased infants on the other side of the grave.

If a Puritan mourner turned to theology for the answers, he would soon discover that they were not readily forthcoming. What made the matter so troublesome was that infants while on earth gave little evidence of the state of their souls, lacking the actions, and presumably the thoughts, which in older children and adults offered clues. "They doe not put forth acts of Reason," explained Increase Mather. Faced with an enigmatic issue which could cause deep anxiety, but which had little value for homiletic purposes, the clergy were not inclined to dwell upon it. There were numerous Puritan sermons and treatises which explored such subjects as the Last Judgement, heaven, and hell in great detail, but provided no treatment of the problem of infants. Even when willing to say something about the issue, Puritan ministers often pleaded ignorance of many of its aspects.

The one member of the clergy willing to abandon the cautious approach to the doctrine was Michael Wigglesworth, a man unusually morbid, even by Puritan standards. His well known poem of 1662, *The Day of Doom,* presented infant damnation in detail. Its verses depicted Christ at the Last Judgement condemning reprobate infants to hell because Adam's original sin, "both his and yours it was." Christ charitably acknowledged that:

> ". . .to compare your sin with their,
>   who liv'd a longer time,
>
> I do confess yours is much less,
>   though every sin's a crime."

> "A crime it is, therefore in bliss
>   you may not hope to dwell;
>
> But unto you I shall allow
>   the easiest room in Hell."

This lame attempt by Wigglesworth to be lenient with the condemned infants only made the horror of their fate all the more patent. Anxious relatives could gain little solace from imagining the little ones in the devil's mildest chamber for they soon read that in hell,

> The least degree of miserie
>   there felt is incomparable
>
> The lightest pain. . .
>   more than intolerable.

In its insistent detailing of the process of infant damnation, *The Day of Doom,* on the whole the most representative of Puritan poems, was unrepresentative.

But everyone read it. Hawked about the region in broadsides, recited by adults who as children had memorized sections of it with their catechisms, *The Day of Doom* had a dissemination second only to that of the Bible itself. The poem became so familiar to the Puritans that it must have contributed to their mental pictures of situations for which they had no experience to draw upon — Judgment Day, heaven, hell — as in the twentieth century, mass media like the movies shape widely shared images of strange monsters, remote planets, and so on. One such Puritan was Mrs. Elizabeth Fitch Taylor: "The Doomsday Verses much perfun'de her Breath,/Much in her thoughts." This poem alone guaranteed that the Puritans understood what infant damnation was all about, but it failed to provide them with ways to determine which particular children were doomed.

Puritan Mourning: The General Pattern

Since theology offered, at best, only partial answers to pressing questions about the fate of deceased infants, further answers arose out of the complex emotions of the bereaved. To discover these responses, the mourning process of early New England must be reconstructed, which is a difficult task. The lack of substantial psychohistorical materials from the Puritans, as well as the incompleteness of our present knowledge of the mourning process, necessitates that much of the discussion be hypothetical.

"We have our CHILDREN taken from us; the *Desire of our Eyes taken away with a stroke*." This outcry of Cotton Mather suggests both the emotional investment of the Puritans in their children, and their well warranted fear of sudden death for these loved ones. The seemingly healthy infant could expire in but a few days' time. Without the opposition of antibiotics and similar devices of modern medicine, viruses and other infections, once they had overcome the body's natural defenses, could be quickly lethal. There were also many deaths that in a physiological sense were not sudden at all, but nevertheless appeared that way to Puritan parents who had not the questionable advantage of a physician's previous diagnosis of a disease or congenital condition as fatal. Continually on the lookout for the swift killing stroke, the Puritans multiplied the situations in which death seemed to be looming, keeping many last watches that turned out to be, happily enough, unnecessary. Diaries are filled with stories of vigils over groaning, feverish, fading children who, despite all expectations, managed to survive: "Our son Edwd has been so bad with a cough that we thought several times he had been quite dead. . . . Our son Benja was very sick of a fever, and near unto death"; "My Little Dauter Molly was extremely ill. So that we thought between 9 and 10, She would have expir'd."

Because Puritan parents were involved in many more scenes that suggested death as the outcome than is indicated by actual mortality statistics, they must have often been in a state of anticipatory mourning. There is something of a paradox in this reaction, for the sudden deaths that were common in early New England by their very nature usually precluded anticipatory mourning. However, the conviction that death often came quickly made the Puritans anxious not to be caught unready. Part of this orientation would have been established even if dying was always prolonged — the relatively high mortality rate was obviously itself a major causal factor entirely apart from the tempo of death — but the large number of rapid expirations spurred the vigils at a moment's notice. When the death watches where the youngster actually did succumb are added to those which proved unfounded, the likelihood is that a Puritan family during its child-rearing years experienced successive expectations of the demise of various offspring.

In these vigils, whatever their eventual outcome, parents prepared themselves emotionally to cope with the anticipated loss.

As a result, the responses to juvenile deaths were often subdued in comparison with modern reactions which, moreover, tend to be most extreme when triggered by the type of sudden demise the Puritans so often witnessed. This fact has fostered the suggestion that the Puritans did not have deep attachments to their children. The truth is that where some of the mourning process is worked through before the actual death, there is that much less left to do afterwards. Thus, the ready weeping of modern mothers when informed of the terminal illnesses of their children changed during vigils of several months into "calm acceptance of the fatal outcome. There was almost no tendency to weep." In a similar fashion, one can imagine a Puritan mother crying copiously at the first death-threatening illness of her first child. By the time of the third such illness of her fifth child, she was likely to be more restrained, the periodic intervals of anticipated mourning having the same cumulative effect as the one prolonged vigil of the modern mother.

Although anticipatory mourning moderated the Puritan reaction to death, grief (which is "the response of emotional pain ... to the deprivation") was still present when there had been an affective investment in the child. The rules on mourning approved its expression. Intuitively recognizing the abnormal nature of lack of grief when a loved one died, Puritan ministers advised the bereaved not to suppress their emotions. Instead, healthy relief should be obtained by venting pain and sorrow in the ritualized gestures and actions of the mourning process. As with the other areas of life, a good Puritan was required to keep such behavior well under control. The ministers were more alarmed by what today would be termed acute grief than by signs of the absence of grief: "We must not be Stocks and Stones: But yet, we may *do much Amiss* in our *Lamentations.*"

A proper moderation in mourning required an attitude of resignation. Clergymen worked hard at impressing their congregations with the importance of accepting the divine decision that had brought about the loss of the loved one. Fatalistic acceptance of the inevitable was merely the minimum expected. The grief stricken were advised to make a virtue out of a necessity by cheerfully approving what God had willed, demonstrating that they valued Him above their dearest relations: "We are to Bless God even when He takes away."

An attitude of resignation was supposed to prevail before the loved one expired as well as afterward, but that was a more difficult requirement to fulfill. Even when in a state of anticipatory mourning, a parent could retain considerable hope for a child's life. Unlike modern parents, Puritan fathers and mothers did not receive a physician's report showing their child's illness to be terminal. If the lack of reliable prognoses meant on the one hand that the Puritans expected death in many situations where they need not have, it meant on the other hand that they would not go as far in anticipatory mourning as modern parents who may come to regard the still living child as in essence dead. Furthermore, in periods of crisis psychological states tend to be shifting and not fully integrated. A parent can be resigned one moment and hopeful the next, or even contradictorily hold both attitudes at once.

Cotton Mather represents an elaborate example of the Puritan whose outlook during vigils fluctuated between resignation to whatever God had chosen and schemes to influence His choice. This counterpoint paralleled the larger cultural interplay, brilliantly depicted in the writings of Perry Miller, between a Puritan fatalism expressed in the doctrine of predestination and a Puritan activism expressed in the notion of preparation for grace. The form this activism took when death threatened could not be that of the modern parent's frenzied search for the best treatment, hospital facilities, and physicians, but would be a last ditch attempt to convince God, that omnipotent doctor, to spare the child. Time after time, Cotton Mather looked heavenward and "begg'd for the Life of the Child in the World," ignoring his own public and private counsels about the necessity of contented resignation. He supplemented these pleas with fasts and abundant tears. When in desperate straits, Mather even "wrestled with the *God of Jacob* for my threatened family." While life remained in a child, the attitudes that death was likely and that it should be readily accepted warred with various paternal or maternal affections, hopes, and expectations, including economic and dynastic calculations. After death, when these were irrevocably dashed, full resignation was easier to attain.

Puritan Mourning: Visions of Heaven and of Hell

Unfortunately for Puritan mourners, the maintenance of an attitude of resignation did not eliminate all of the difficulties of bereavement. This attitude contained fundamental ambiguities that gave very different shadings to prospects in the afterlife depending upon the parent's mood. Was he resigning his infant to joy in heaven or to agony in hell? Since even the experts on religious matters could not provide definitive information, the answers would have to arise out of the complex, fluctuating attitudes of the parent before and after his child's death.

The truest resignation was ready acquiescence in whatever God had decreed for one's child in the afterlife, be it heavenly glory or hellish torment. A completely open resignation was not, however, the predominant attitude of Puritan parents. Just as they asked God to extend the life of a dying child, so they bombarded the deity with requests that in the event of death the little one be taken into heaven. Such pleas were the last things that a parent could do for a child, the final gestures of Puritan activism. One parent noted, "My little Judith languishes and moans, ready to die. . . . Told Mr. Walter of her condition, . . . desiring him to give her a lift toward heaven." No theme was more common in private writings about departed children, indicating that bereaved Puritans had to assume that their perished offspring were going to glory in order to make resignation a viable attitude. Only a definite determination of the final outcome could give satisfying meaning to the course of events; to have left the outcome unknown and the ultimate meaning of the death inscrutable would have meant intensification of the pain of loss. Parental love required that the outcome not only be definite (damnation is definite), but positive in meaning — salvation.

The psychological processes of *idealization* and *rationalization,* which are commonly found in mourning, furthered the assumption of infant salvation and the emotional relief it provided. In idealization the dead child becomes endowed in the memory with superior characteristics, often in invidious contrast to still living siblings. For Puritan mourners, the images of departed offspring would no longer be scored with reminders of depravity, but would evoke rare goodness: "a most lovly and pleasant child," "sweet Flowers," "innocent children," heightening the credibility of the assumption that the deceased were heaven bound. In rationalization, the loss of the child is justified on the basis that his death is advantageous for all concerned. As Cotton Mather put it, " 'Tis better for our Children to be safely Lodg'd among the Angels of God in *Heaven,* than for them to be sinning against Him like *Devils* on *Earth.*"

Those parents and close relatives who believed themselves to be regenerated could look forward to one day being reunited with their young in heaven. The bereaved had become aware, consciously or subconsciously, of their own mortality, for in the death of the infant a part of their own being had died. Beloved children were both extensions of the self, now severed — "the dying of a child is like the tearing of a limb from us" — and internalized elements in the self, now ripped out. The massive wounds in the ego raised in the mind doubts about the continuation of its own existence. Both the threat to the survival of the mourner's self and the pain of its raw incompleteness could be partially overcome by positing an eternal future amidst the restored love objects. The vision of a heavenly reunion made for a powerful rationalization theme: "I say, take, Lord, they're thine./ I piecemeal pass to Glory bright in them"; "The death of our children is not the loss of our children. They are not lost, but given back; they are not lost, but sent before."

Reinforcement of the assumption that individual infants were bound for salvation came from friends, relatives, ministers, and the community in general. When the Winthrops' little son died, Samuel Sewall penned a reassuring poem which concluded, "JESUS will call John from the Grave,/ From Sin eternally to save." John Cotton sent a similar message to a grieving grandmother. Although Puritan clergymen like Cotton allowed in their theology for the possibility, even the likelihood, that some infants were damned, when they discussed specific children the presumption was almost always made that heaven was the destination.

Explicit suggestions that a particular child might be bound for hell were put forth only in exceptional circumstances. In one case, a young mother had murdered her illegitimate infant. If any baby was likely to arrive in hell, this was the one. The product of an illicit union, it had passed from the world without benefit of even initial subjection to the means of grace. In a harangue directed at the nineteen-year-old mother, condemned as both a fornicator and a killer, Increase Mather intoned, "Methinks you should sometimes hear the blood of your woful Infant, Crying *Vengeance! Vengeance! Lord,* upon my unnatural Mother, who murdered me as soon as I came into the World. And what if you murdered its Soul as well as Body." A similar accusation was made against a mother who had slain two illegitimate children.

A more terrible charge could not be levied against a parent in Puritan society. Only cases of extreme iniquity allowed it to be presented openly, and only the worst enemy of an ordinary mother or father would whisper it. Yet, if sympathy for the bereaved, hardened into a convention, dictated that friends and acquaintances speak of the afterlife of the dead child solely in terms of heaven, this ritual did not prevent the parents themselves from entertaining, perhaps only fleetingly or subconsciously, the possibility of hell. What others would not charge against a parent — the responsibility for the eternal damnation of an infant — he would charge against himself in some inner portion of the psyche.

For one thing, Puritan mourning occurred in a milieu in which hell fire was real. The bereaved had heard about it all their lives and had been highly aware of the threat it posed to their children, not to mention their own souls. The menace of hell acquired a special immediacy when a death occurred. A bereaved parent had almost certainly read in *The Day of Doom* about infants condemned to its torments. If these sections of the poem disturbed him, he may have repressed them, but a time of grief is a time when repressions can become unsealed. Fragments of the Wigglesworthian vision of babes in hell could readily flit across a mind subjected to the upheavals of bereavement.

They were all the more likely to do so because in the Puritan outlook the act of dying itself suggested depravity. The curse of death had originally come upon the human race as a punishment for the transgressions of Adam. Death meant sin, and sin meant hell, an unavoidable association. Idealization of the deceased child with related assumptions about the availability of purifying grace somewhat obscured the death-sin-hell triad, but it remained a palpable part of the mental environment in which the mourning process was encompassed and could cast an occasional pall over the bereaved's spirits.

During the mourner's mood of optimistic resignation, when he was imagining his infant approaching heaven with an angel escort, the grimmer pictures of the afterlife did not intrude, just as in moments of familial affection the notion of juvenile depravity was shut out. Comforters did their best to sustain the bouyant mood and the pleasing image. Nevertheless, during mourning mental states tend to fluctuate and the bereaved often has periods of depression. A depressed individual is inclined to think in ways that heighten grief and increase pain, obsessively torturing himself with frightening images and unpleasing interpretations. Samuel Willard told of many mourners "who seem to take a kind of sullen contentment in nourishing and giving way to sinking reflections on their spirits, whereby they may aggravate instead of mitigating their Grief." How better to heighten grief than by entertaining, even for a moment, the prospect of one's infant suffering in hell? The Reverend Jonathan Mitchel was in this frame of mind when he anguished over the death of his infant without baptism, although he did not believe that this sacrament was necessary for salvation: "*Yet, as it is appointed to be a Confirming Sign, and as it is an Ordinance of Grace, so to be deprived of it, is a great Frown, and a sad Intimation of the Lord's Anger: And though it may be well with the child notwithstanding (that it becomes me to leave unto the Lord!) yet it is to us a Token of Displeasure.*"

In the case of infants who lived long enough for feelings of love to develop, the bereaved's periods of depression were deepened by the feeling that in losing the child he had lost a part of himself. If in optimistic moods he obtained some relief by rationalizing an eventual reunion in heaven, in pessimistic periods he confronted the possibility of permanent loss. Wigglesworth played upon this form of separation anxiety in *The Day of Doom,* providing a very different type of rationalization:

> The pious Father had now much rather
> his graceless Son should ly
> In Hell with Devils, for all his evils
> burning eternally,
> Than God most high should injury,
> by sparing him sustain;
> And doth rejoyce to hear Christ's voice,
> adjudging him to pain.

If the mourning parents who pondered such images were engaging in a form of self-torture, they were also expressing a degree of gratification. Insofar as the bereaved were depressed, they intensified their suffering, and thus fell under the masochist's paradox: pain is satisfaction. When not depressed, bereaved parents might be gratified by the image of the infant damned, which served as the consummation of their long-standing hostility toward the child, who was all the more resented because his death had caused further pain. This expression of strong dislike, even hatred, for one's own offspring existed to a degree in every parent. Even the best of young children had often been an annoyance and a burden, especially for the mother who had risked her life in labor and pained her nipples in nursing. Those women who had murdered their infants were exceptional, yet probably other mothers had at times felt similarly inclined. The death wish the parent harbored for a child was in normal cases consistent with love and affection for him. Freud wrote in regard to a mourner's convoluted feelings: "There was something in her, a wish of which she herself was unaware, which was not displeased with the fact that death came, and which would have brought it about sooner had it been strong enough.... Such hostility, hidden in the unconscious behind tender love, exists in almost all cases of intensive emotional allegiance to a particular person, indeed it represents the classic case, the prototype of the ambivalence of human emotions." The part of the parent that was gratified by the death of the child could also be gratified by the image of damnation, particularly if, as some have conjectured, the image of the devil was a projection fantasy.

To a great extent, the "opposition between the conscious grief and the unconscious satisfaction at death" unfolded in unconscious levels of the mind, only occasionally sending fleeting images and thoughts into the mourner's everyday awareness. However, other types of bereavement reactions entered more directly into conscious experience, being somewhat easier to face openly. Many of them involved guilt. The Puritan parent's web of guilt embodied so many complex twists that it could lead to both expectations of infant damnation, some of which have been seen, and to expectations of infant salvation, furthering those engendered by optimistic resignation, by idealization, and by rationalization.

One line of guilt arose from the belief of the bereaved that he had caused, or contributed to, his child's demise by failing to provide proper care. This form of self-reproach has been commonly found among present-day parents of fatally ill children, although there is usually no medical evidence indicating that negligence brought on the sickness. Such self-reproaches must have been all the stronger among the Puritans with their hazy ideas about disease. A related consideration was whether the parent had paid sufficient attention to the spiritual welfare of the child: "It will be a great damp to our minds, to have such a reflection upon them as this, I do not so much as pray earnestly to God for the soul of this Child, and now it is gone past all prayers." The fires of hell loomed out of the bereaved's guilt over negligence, as forbidding when the negligence was merely a projection as when it had been real.

A further source of self-blame was the parent's own religious and moral qualities. God took children to punish adults for hearts set too much on worldly affairs and too little on spiritual ones, for lack of sufficient gratitude when He bestowed mercies, and for overt sins of thought or deed. These ideas were so common a refrain among the Puritans that they can be considered a standard element in the mourning process. Their function was to turn the anger at God, which might arise if He were held culpable for the child's death, back upon the parent himself.

A search for someone or something on which to lay the responsibility for the death of a loved one is a part of the bereaved's effort to imbue the event with significant meaning. Blame can be directed both against the self and against others. Modern parents who believe that they have somehow caused disease in their offspring often also bear accusatory attitudes toward the attending physicians for not achieving a cure. In the Puritan case the equivalent figure would be God, except that He was supposed to be beyond criticism and blame. Even so, the need to find fault was so strong that some muted resentment came His way, expressed through a covert language that depicted God as the abductor of children: "It pleased God to send ye Messenger of Death to sease and Carry away my little Babe." The same perception of God as a voracious agent of death revealed itself in a dream of Samuel Sewall's in which his little daughter vanished from a closet while in prayer. Some mourners made explicit what remained latent in most and openly muttered against God for the harshness of his providences.

Since good Puritans could not give way to outbreaks against God, they had to turn the anger back onto themselves, adding that much more to the burden of guilt. "I desire to acknowledge ye hand of God in all," wrote Joseph Green, "& quietly to submit unto him, and I think yt I never did once murmur agt God for ys stroke: but have cause to say yt God has punished me far less yn I deserve." An individual who craved still more severe chastisement, perhaps out of guilt over his ambivalence toward God, could find it in imagining a child not only dead, but damned because of parental transgressions. Cotton Mather's emotional reaction to a household accident in which a daughter was seriously burned, vividly symbolizing the threat of hell, suggests this pattern of response: "Alas, for *my Sin* the just God throwes *my Child* into the *Fire!*"

Entwined with the negative side of the bereaved's ambivalence toward God, the web of guilt led toward damnation; entwined with the positive side it led toward salvation, forming the last element in the intricate cycle of mourning. In wrath against parents, God had seized their beloved babies, but this aggressive act could be balanced by the awareness that the little ones had been His bestowals to begin with, and that out of mercy He had many times intervened when children had lain at death's door. Whereas God's punitive actions were less than parents had due, His kindnesses were more than they merited. During bereavement, such divine goodness could be most convincingly demonstrated by viewing God as gathering to His side departed infants, undeserving though the parents might be of such a glorious outcome. Cotton Mather declared, "This is, by far the best of all to have children this day in heaven. Truly this is an honour which neither you nor I are worthy of. But so it is; The King of kings has sent for our children to confer a kingdom on them." While emphasizing the guiltiness of man before God, this feeling alleviated some of the guilt stemming from the bereaved's belief that as a parent he had contributed to the death of his child by faulty care. If the little one attained heaven, things had turned out for the best after all.

The End of Mourning

The normal mourning process requires the bereaved to turn over and over in his mind memories and images of the lost loved one in ways that we have seen. By doing so, he gradually comes to terms with the full significance of the loss and begins to accept it. This process does not take place in isolation, but is influenced by the death-related roles, rituals, and beliefs of a particular society. Such "death systems" can serve to lower the stresses of mourning or to raise them. In the case of the Puritans the death system did both. With heaven and hell as facts, deeply embedded in Puritan culture, the pressing questions were who would go where, rather than as later became the issue, whether these realms actually existed. By providing no sure answers about the fate of specific children, the Puritans left the way open for the fluctuating emotions of the bereaved to flow successively, or even simultaneously, into channels that diminished stress and channels that heightened it.

In normal situations the mental crisis which constitutes bereavement eventually subsides, the rapid oscillations of thought, feeling, and behavior giving way to a state of equilibrium. Often the transference of emotional investment from the lost object to a substitute eases this change. According to the official Puritan death system, God was to be the recipient of the love detached from the deceased. After the loss of his three young children in a span of two years, John Hull exclaimed, "The good Lord, by all these various changes, make me more his own, and wean me more from myself and all fading comforts, that he alone may be my portion." Hull soon had two other children who undoubtedly competed with God as sites for emotional transference. The high birth rate of Puritan society provided a steady succession of infants who in capturing the attentions and affections of parents and grandparents helped to alleviate their grief for the perished siblings, if somewhat at God's expense. Naming a new baby for a dead one, as was common, emphasized its role as a substitute.

A successful termination of mourning requires a resolution of the conflicting thoughts, images, and feelings that pour through the mind of the bereaved. The Puritan death system made this achievement a difficult one by raising anxieties about the afterlife that it could not completely allay. Samuel Willard observed, "*We are apt to say, oh! if we were but sure of their well-being, we could then be quiet and contented; but, this is to fight against God: it is his pleasure to keep these things secret for the present.*" The mourner was cast upon the twisting stream of bereavement emotions in which guilt could raise expectations of heaven or of hell for perished infants, rationalization could make a case for their comfort or torment, and God could appear as an agency of salvation or of damnation. The Puritan death system, which is sometimes touted as exemplary in contrast to the much-criticized present American way of death, did not function that smoothly at all.

In the long run, most Puritans seem to have achieved an equilibrium which allowed them to be convinced that their infant children had indeed reached salvation, although perhaps exposing them to tinges of the old bereavement doubts whenever they reread *The Day of Doom* or heard it recited, or saw a tombstone adorned with bats of hell. This resolution was the easiest to achieve because throughout the mourning process the possibility of heaven had appeared large, detailed, and persistently in the foreground of the conscious mind. The alternative possibility of hell had been a smaller, less definite presence flickering on the periphery of awareness. When the mental conditions of the bereaved reached the final stage of equilibrium, the shadow of infant damnation faded away, leaving in the historical record almost as little trace as the shadows cast by material objects.

The Peale Family, 1773. Painted by Charles Willson Peale, a Philadelphia artist. (courtesy of the New York Historical Society, New York City)

3

Autonomy and Affection: Parents and Children in Eighteenth-Century Chesapeake Families

Daniel Blake Smith

Most parents in eighteenth-century Virginia and Maryland were deeply attached to their children and they structured family life around them. Such an assertion could not be confidently made about parental conduct in much of the pre-industrial West. For as historians of childhood have pointed out, until the very recent past children played a distinctly secondary role in the family; they were valued chiefly for the labor they would eventually provide the household economy. In well-to-do families of Chesapeake society, however, the presence of infants and small children was an important source of pleasure and diversion, providing a central emotional focus in the life of the family. Indeed, the child-centered family which became commonplace in the nineteenth century first emerged in these planter households of the eighteenth century. The following discussion of childhood in the eighteenth-century Chesapeake suggests that child rearing in this plantation culture bore a closer resemblance to that in modern society than in the "world we have lost."

The world of family and kin that surrounded a new-born child in Chesapeake society usually offered a warm, affectionate environment for his development. Indeed, an "increase in the family" brought considerable pride and elation to parents and kin. The paternal self-pride engendered at childbirth is suggested in the praise Thomas Davis gave St. George Tucker at the birth of Tucker's daughter in 1779. Davis was excited "at learning my much-esteemed, Thy amiable Fanny had escaped the Danger of Child-Birth and had presented to my Friend such a lovely Image of himself." James Parker was away from home when his daughter Susan was born in the winter of 1777, but he wrote affectionately of his new baby girl, "The Summer Duck": "God bless the Dear little [one] how I long to hold it to my heart."

Parents arranged christenings and baptisms — usually within a few weeks after birth — to bring kin and friends together in celebration of parenthood. These ceremonies, held in private homes in most cases, were often quite festive affairs with dinner and dancing. Relatively small crowds of perhaps a dozen or so kin and close friends usually attended. William Byrd went to the christening of the Reverend Charles Anderson's son in 1709 where, according to Byrd, everyone dined and danced well into the evening. Anderson, Byrd noted, "was beyond measure pleased with the blessing God had sent him." Phillip Fithian, plantation tutor for Robert Carter of Nomini Hall, reported in 1773 that christenings were "one of the chief times for Diversion here." Godparents were announced on these occasions; parents frequently chose a brother or sister or close family friend as symbolic guardian of the child. For some men, such as Presbyterian James Gordon of Orange County, a child's baptism carried a significant religious meaning. Gordon named his son Nathaniel at the baptismal ceremony in September of 1762 and later recorded in his diary a solemn wish for his son's spiritual fate: "O, may the Lord grant that he be a Nathaniel, indeed: the gift of God, and his name written in the Book of Life."

A child's first important experience in the world comes in his relationship with his mother or nurse, especially in the feeding process. In this earliest stage of development, until about age two, a child is mainly concerned with the simple but essential tasks of "getting" and "taking," as Erik Erikson has suggested. His success in this incorporative mode of behavior depends in part on parental willingness and ability to provide the nourishment a child needs and demands. And most important, the nursing bond significantly influences a child's earliest perceptions about the trustworthiness of the people around him.

Studies of childhood suggest that children in the pre-industrial West often failed in their crucial efforts at "getting" and "taking." Many remained underfed and left in the hands of mothers and nurses who distrusted their "primitive" demands for survival. Seventeenth-century European parents were ambivalent about children whom they felt obligated to protect, but who were also, they believed, "demanding and dangerous little animals." As a result of these tensions, the relationship between nurses or mother and child in early modern Europe resembled more a struggle than a cooperative effort. Mothers, especially after a difficult delivery, viewed breastfeeding as a debilitating experience, one in which an infant drained a mother of her vital substances for his own survival. Some mothers feared that breastfed children might transmit to them some dreaded disease. Consequently, most women who could afford it put their children out to nurse, despite the advice of physicians that an infant would thrive best when nourished by his mother. Moreover, poorly prepared solid food was often fed to children before they were fully able to digest it. High infant mortality rates of between 20 and 30 percent for seventeenth-century Europe reflect in part this low level of maternal care of children. It was not until the mid-eighteenth century that critics of child care in England and France became effective in encouraging maternal nursing.

In the colonial Chesapeake maternal nursing was probably the most common form of infant feeding. Little is known about parent-child relations in Virginia and Maryland during the seventeenth century because of the scarcity of personal documents such as family papers and diaries. The fragmentary evidence that does exist, however, indicates that mothers probably breastfed their children. Nonetheless, infant and childhood mortality rates remained extremely high, perhaps as high as 40 percent, because of an endemic malarial environment which prevailed in the early Chesapeake. Infants frequently received from diseased mothers a short-term immunity to malaria which allowed many of them to survive infancy, only later to succumb to the disease as small children when their immunity had worn off.

In the eighteenth century, even though a larger number of families could afford to hire wet nurses, most women, barring illness, seem to have continued to nurse their own children. One woman in 1780, for example, was reported to be "too weakly to Suckel her little Girl — and is Obliged to Put it out to nurse." In sharp contrast to parents in early modern Europe who feared that infants communicated diseases to those who nursed them, parents in the eighteenth-century Chesapeake worried more about children becoming ill from their contact with sick mothers. For instance, Margaret Parker of Norfolk, Virginia, in 1771 wrote to her husband that their infant boy had "sucked the fever from me I believe." "I was obliged to get a woman to suckle him a while till I get my milk again which the fever dryed up." Other women nursed their infants despite the pain and inconvenience. Breastfeeding, many women believed, ruined the shape of the breasts and doubtless some women hesitated to nurse their children for this reason. The experience of Mary Dulaney of Maryland, however, suggests that a mother's affection for a child could outweigh such concerns. A friend noted that Mary breastfed her infant boy despite her fear that "her good looks may be injured by nursing her fine son. . . ."

Maternal love, though, was not always the central motivation for mothers who decided to nurse their own children. Given the discomfort of frequent pregnancies and the danger and violent pain associated with childbirth — especially in the eighteenth century — some mothers chose to nurse their offspring because the lactation period tended to delay conception. Landon Carter certainly felt that this was the strategy of his daughter-in-law in 1770 when, according to him, she continued to breastfeed her baby girl despite being sick herself. Carter complained that: "The poor little baby Fanny is every time to share her Mamma's disorder by sucking her, and this because she should not breed too fast. Poor children! Are you to be sacrificed for a parent's plesure? I have been a Parent and I thought it murder and therefore hired nurses or put them out." Despite Carter's protest, his grand-daughter "little Fanny" continued "to suck the poizon" from her mother's "morbid breast."

In exceptionally wealthy and large families (of perhaps ten or more children) mothers sometimes relied on nurses — both black and white — to breastfeed some of their children. Philip Fithian noted this practice in 1773. "I find it is common here for people of Fortune to have their young Children suckled by the Negroes!" Mrs. Carter, who had given birth to thirteen children, told Fithian that "wenches have suckled several" of her infants.

Fithian, however, was speaking of a very small minority of women — only those with great wealth and burdened by huge families, like Mrs. Carter. Most mothers, except when seriously weakened by childbirth or sickness, nursed their own infants — often out of strong maternal sentiment. As a result of this natural maternal nursing bond, deep emotional attachments were established between mothers and children. And as a child gained confidence in the accessibility of his mother as an attachment figure, his anxiety and fear about the world around him declined. It was from such an early atmosphere of maternal warmth that planters' children developed a strong measure of self-confidence and independence.

The weaning process, however, threatened to disrupt the close ties between a child and his nurse or mother. Some time in their second year children were removed from their secure source of nourishment. Weaning was critical in the child's first efforts toward autonomy which normally characterize the second year of life. It proved to be a difficult time for parents, too, for they worried incessantly about children becoming ill during this uncertain stage of development.

Parents separated children from the breast at different times in early modern Europe and America. In the seventeenth and eighteenth centuries, children in England and France were weaned at around twenty-four months, and often abruptly among wealthy families. Parents in colonial America appear to have allowed for a more gradual weaning, but began the process earlier, which suggests that they encouraged an earlier sense of autonomy in the child than their European counterparts. In seventeenth-century Plymouth and the colonial Chesapeake, the scattered evidence indicates that weaning began between twelve and eighteen months. A starchy mixture of flour and milk such as gruel or pap was introduced into the child's diet sometime in the first year to begin to accustom him to eating solid food. Mothers often dabbed mustard, pepper, or some bitter substance on their breasts to discourage the child from nursing.

Weaning was particularly trying on parents since many probably felt ambivalent about separating the child from his mother's breast. Parents were clearly relieved when weaning was accomplished without pain or illness. In September of 1728 Dolly Jones was reported to have "weaned herself," at age one. As her nurse explained to Dolly's mother, she "won't touch the breast when offered her, which I think you'll have no reason to be sorry for, but it was first occasioned by her being kept from it when she took the bark, but she never seemed to desire it." Mothers or nurses clearly controlled the weaning process. Frances Tucker, her husband noted, had gone to Port Royal, Virginia, in the spring of 1784 where she was "weaning our last little Brat."

Parents also found teething a difficult period in the child's early development. It was an event that usually signaled the beginning of weaning, for mothers stopped breastfeeding near the time that children began cutting teeth — at the end of the first year. Teething brought on a period of pain and sickness which left parents and kin fearful and anxious. William Prentis, for example, worried that his one-year-old son John had the same "disease" that all of his children had developed the year they were weaned: "a disorder in the bowels, and cutting of Teeth." In 1725 Elizabeth Pratt empathized with her suffering two-year-old son: "Poor Billy has been pulled down by his hard breeding of teeth." And Martha Jefferson Carr was anxious to hear whether her fourteen-month-old granddaughter Martha Terrell had "got safely through the worst of her teething."

Teething concerned parents and kin mainly because of the physical discomfort children experienced during this period. The biting stage also represented an important test of the child's basic trust in the nurturant and protective attitudes of his parents, for teething compelled the child to bite to ease the pain just as the mother was beginning to withdraw the breast. But as we have seen, parental sensitivity to the difficulties children faced during weaning and teething probably helped to create a trusting relationship between a mother and her child.

Anyone who reads through the family letters and diaries from the eighteenth-century Chesapeake will discover a welter of evidence of parental tenderness and affection toward young children. These sources clearly suggest that children were not treated as depraved beings whose willfulness and sense of autonomy had to be quashed by age two or three — as children were apparently seen in early Plymouth. Rather, parents in Virginia and Maryland during the eighteenth century seemed to delight in the distinctively innocent, playful childhood years of their offspring. Parents and an assortment of kin — grandparents, uncles, aunts, and cousins — who frequently helped in childrearing were usually quite fond of children and considered them pleasant diversions. Indeed, as we shall see, family and kin often indulged young children and granted them considerable freedom.

It is not likely that during the seventeenth century children enjoyed such a prominent place in Chesapeake households. Because of oppressive infant and child mortality rates and a short life expectancy in early Virginia and Maryland, parents probably invested less of their emotional life in their children than did eighteenth-century parents. When infants or children died, parents — especially fathers — showed little emotion or deep concern. Moreover, Protestant religious thought, which stressed the inherently sinful and inferior condition of children, shaped the character of family life in the seventeenth century. Fathers remained emotionally detached from infants and small children, insisting on the child's acceptance of self-control and obedience to paternal authority.

In the increasingly secular culture of eighteenth-century Virginia and Maryland, which was committed to an expanding tobacco economy based largely on slave labor, religious values rarely intruded into family life and childrearing, especially in Anglican planter households. As a result, Chesapeake parents felt free to stress more of the positive, pleasurable capacities of children. Indeed, the personal documents of eighteenth-century Chesapeake families, especially after mid-century, reveal a familial and social environment in which children were often the centerpiece of family affection. Mothers and fathers and kin, at least in well-to-do families, lavished attention on their children. One father from Queen Anne's County, Maryland, for example, was reported to be "excessively fond of his Daughter a fine sprightly girl." Richard Tilghman confided to a friend in 1763 that his three-year-old daughter Anna Maria was "the plaything of the family." James and Margaret Parker struggled to avoid spoiling their young son. "I endeavour as much as possible to [guard] against it," Margaret wrote her husband in 1765, "but find it requires more resolution than I am mistress of to help doting on him." When away from their families, fathers almost always asked to be remembered to their children. While staying in Williamsburg in the fall of 1755, George Braxton told his wife to "give little Molly a thousand kisses for me." St. George Tucker was particularly fond of his children and stepchildren. His letters to his wife Frances during his service in the Revolution suggest the pleasure he derived as a parent. "Remember me with a Tenderness Truly Parental to my Boys," he wrote Frances, "and let Patty and Maria be assured I am neither unmindful nor indifferent in regard to them." Tucker, like many parents, used affectionate nicknames for his children. "My poor little Monkies are insensible to all that a parent can feel for them."

Parents were diverted by, rather than impatient with, the nonsense language and "childish" behavior of their offspring. Jane Swann wrote to her uncle of the satisfying moments she and her husband spent with their four-year-old girl. Their daughter, she said, was "very lively and full of Inocent Prattle with which She often pleasantly amuses her Father and my Self. May the almighty preserve her long with us." Surrounded by the familiar and attentive faces of parents and kin, children provided their caretakers with uninhibited and seemingly irrational behavior which was unacceptable in the adult world. The experience of Eliza Custis as a child growing up in Virginia in the 1770s demonstrates vividly that children were welcome diversions to their parents.

I can now remember standing on the table when not more than 3 or 4 years old, singing songs which I did not understand — while my father and other gentlemen were often rolling in their chairs with laughter — and I was animated to exert myself to give him delight — The servants in the passage would join their mirth, and I holding my head erect, would strut about the table to receive the praises of the company, my mother remonstrated in vain — and her husband always said his little Bet could not be injured by what she did not understand that he had no Boy and she must make fun for him, until he had — he would then kiss her to make his Peace, and giving me a Nod my voice which was uncommonly powerful for my age resounded through the rooms, and my Mother who could not help laughing, used to retire and leave me to the gentlemen, where my fathers caresses made me think well of myself.

Custis's treatment of Eliza, at least in her retrospective view, suggests that he was asking Eliza what most parents expected of their children: to give pleasure and comfort in return for parental tenderness and nurture.

For Thomas Gilpin of Maryland in the 1790s proper child rearing involved a close friendship between parents and children. Parental participation in a child's world of play, he believed, encouraged sound character and virtuous conduct in the child as he matured. Gilpin's wife observed that her husband took great pleasure in cultivating "a freedom and sociability with his Tender offspring in order to Unite Fillial Obedience with [paternal?] affection in the Closest tyes of

Friendship which he often used to say was the surest way for Parents to Secure the affection of their Children." According to his wife, Gilpin spent a lot of time with the children, often giving them "little Inocent amusements to keep them in from the street and out of others [pernicious?] Company and would often be one of their party himselfe thereby discovering the great pleasure that their little Inocent Company and Diverting Actions Afforded him." This kind of intimate, parent-child relationship, Gilpin assumed, helped a child to choose proper "Friends and Confidents and none was so proper as their Parents." By this affectionate form of paternal childrearing, planters like Thomas Gilpin nurtured a sense of deference and duty in their children without resorting to authoritarianism or coerced obedience. Respect and filial devotion came much easier to sons secure in the knowledge that their parents, especially their fathers, derived pleasure from their presence.

Childhood had clearly become a distinctive period in the minds of Chesapeake parents and kin during the eighteenth century. The presence of grandparents was extremely influential in shaping these child-centered families. The short expectation of life in the seventeenth century — to about the mid-forties among adult men and women — precluded the development of an elderly generation and a large body of supporting kin. Indeed, family life in the early Chesapeake was often limited to contact between two generations, and with such high death rates these relationships usually proved to be rather short-lived as the profusion of stepparents and orphans in this period suggest. If relationships between parents and stepchildren in modern families are any guide to the past, then many of these seventeenth-century Chesapeake households, filled with half- and stepbrothers and sisters, may have been unable to develop strong emotional ties within the family. With the improvement in life expectancy during the eighteenth century — to about the mid-fifties for adult men — family relationships among three generations became commonplace. As a result, by mid-century planters frequently sent their children to stay with grandparents and other relatives where they were often indulged and fondly cared for.

Family letters from this period allow us to glimpse the quality of kin attachments to children. Six-year-old Betty Pratt spent much of the fall of 1728 with her aunt who admitted to Betty's mother that she was receiving too much attention. "She is exceedingly fondled at [the] other House, more than I think, is necessary tho she manages herself with it better than one cou'd expect from a Child of her age." Charles Carroll of Annapolis was particularly attached to his granddaughter, Molly Carroll, the daughter of Charles Carroll of Carrollton.

He ended almost every letter to his son or daughter-in-law with affectionate expressions for Molly, such as: "I long to kiss my little Gran-daughter." Carroll sent her gifts — once a pocket book, purse, and money — and when she received them, Carroll instructed his son to "tell her I sent it." Children and their grandparents sometimes exchanged pictures — or "miniatures," which were usually placed in a locket — or other personal items as permanent expressions of their affection and kinship. In 1784, Henry Tucker, Sr., sent his granddaughter Nancy Tucker a lock of his hair which, as he told his son, he hoped would please her — "the device is paternal affection."

Despite the pleasure parents and kin clearly derived from young children, they approached child rearing with serious purposefulness. They expected to develop in their offspring powers of self-discipline which, parents believed, would produce self-reliant, independent adults. And it was the warm, nurturant attitudes of Chesapeake parents which we have described above that allowed them to shape children into dutiful sons and daughters.

Parents were especially mindful of developing powers of self-sufficiency and strength in their children. They applauded but rarely demanded precocity in their children, unlike seventeenth-century Anglo-American parents who sought to hurry children out of their childhood dependency. Still, initial signs of mobility and autonomy, suggested in early efforts at walking and talking, attracted close attention from observant parents. Lucy Terrell, according to her grandmother, Martha Jefferson Carr, "prattles Everything she hears," and was "very spritly." Years later, Mrs. Carr expressed the same interest in another granddaughter, one-year-old Martha Terrell. She was anxious to see "little Martha's attempts to prattle and to see her shuffling across the room." Frances Randolph was equally proud of her daughter "Mopsey," who "talks *prodigiously.* She will walk in a fortnight."

Parents took a special interest in the early muscle control and coordination of their sons, who were especially encouraged to move about on their own. The observations of Thomas Jones are revealing in this connection. In July of 1728 Jones reported at length to his wife Elizabeth, then visiting relatives in England, on the growth and character of their three children. Lusty, exuberant children clearly appealed to Jones. His youngest son, two-year-old Tom, particularly pleased him, for, as Jones noted, "he runs about the house, hollows and makes a noise all day long and as often as he can, gets out of Doors." Tom's father was keenly aware of the boy's progress in walking. After returning from a trip, Jones noticed the "great alteration in the use of his Feet in so short a time, and I believe [he] is as forward in that as most children of two years old." Taking his first tentative steps became a lesson in self-sufficiency for young Tom: "When he falls I order him not to be taken up by which means he takes it patiently, unless he hurts himself pretty much." Young Tom was a less remarkable talker, however, which seemed to bother his father somewhat: "He is very backward with his tongue, I use him to pa-pa; and Ma-ma, and in a morning he say (not Tea) but Tee, and sometimes mo' which is all the improvement he has made that way; he grows Tall and is a fine Boy."

To encourage a hardy constitution in children, parents followed the advice of John Locke by dressing them in loose-fitting clothes and allowing them plenty of time in the open air. Locke's prescriptions for early child care seem to have been in the mind of one father who, while away from home on business, inquired about his son's upbringing: "How goes the dear little thing. Do you permitt Charles to run half-naked as he should do, feed him on Mush Milk &c, do you sufficiently correct his little [fancy?] faults, keep him in due Subjection toward his little [servant?]. . . ?" During early childhood boys and girls were dressed alike in distinctively children's clothing — a kind of long robe which opened down the front to provide unrestricted movement. A pair of ribbons hanging from the back of the gown, which was used in the seventeenth century to support children in their early ambulatory efforts, became simply an ornament of child's dress by the eighteenth century. Girls wore more confining clothes, especially the stays placed on the neck to promote straight posture. By age six or seven boys were put into breeches and shirts, perhaps symbolic of their first step toward manhood.

The goal of most eighteenth-century Anglo-American parents was to develop honest, republican virtues of self-discipline and self-reliance in their children. Child-rearing literature since the late seventeenth century advised parents to inculcate these values as early as possible in their offspring, preferably in infancy or early childhood when a child's character and temperament were most pliable and susceptible to parental guidance. Parental authority should be moderate in nature, Locke argued, a strategic combination of indulgence — to gain a child's lasting affection and gratitude — and firm discipline — to ensure obedience and a continuing sense of duty to his parents. Punishment was most effective when administered through shame, rather than through whippings — which, at best, produced only a temporary remedy. Only by inducing an apprehension of parental displeasure and shame early in a child's life could parents instill habits of obedience and self-control.

While Chesapeake parents in general seem to have adopted many features of this child-rearing style — especially its emphasis on developing hardy, self-reliant children — parent-child relationships in this eighteenth-century agrarian society took on a form different from what Locke and other critics would have advised. The wide open nature of the plantation environment, uncrowded with an abundant supply of land and free of many of the vices of the cities, allowed planters to raise their children under more optimistic and permissive assumptions about childhood and parental conduct. Obedience and respect for parental authority remained important for the development of strong character and stable family life, but Chesapeake parents placed considerably more emphasis on developing a child's, especially a son's, freedom of movement and sense of personal autonomy.

Chesapeake households were often complex units with servants and kin living on the plantation, making constant parental supervision of children unnecessary. Indeed, one senses from the letters and diaries of the period that children were allowed — perhaps encouraged — to explore their immediate environment with little parental supervision. While visitng his friend Colonel Eppes in February 1711, William Byrd was asked to help locate a small child who had just learned to walk but had wandered off from his little friends. "All the people on the plantation were looking for it," Byrd explained, "and I went likewise to look [for] it and at last found it, for which the women gave me abundance of blessings." Parents clearly admired rambunctious, energetic children to whom they seemed to have given the run of the plantation. Margaret Parker reported to her husband that their young son was doing well, as he had been "imployed all day making bonfires." One woman who went to see her cousin noted that her cousin's two children, a two- and a three-year-old, "were fighting on the carpet, during the whole visit."

Children thrived on companionship and vigorous play with other children, parents believed; confining them at home weakened their important instinct for sociability. White and black children often mingled freely on the plantation, relatively unsupervised by parents. Parents and kin did become concerned when children missed opportunities for companionship in their early years. One man, fretting over the limited social contacts his eight-year-old nephew had with other boys, complained that it "is not no proper for a boy to be under so much Confinement; and to live so remote without any Company."

Not only did young children experience considerable frreedom of movement on the plantation, but they also lived under few parental restraints on their conduct. Parents and kin, at least in middle- and upper-class families, apparently made little effort to stifle childhood willfulness and self-assertion. To be sure, overt disobedience was not countenanced, but parents did not attempt as a matter of principle to root out autonomous behavior in young children, in sharp contrast to Anglo-American parents in the seventeenth century. Paternal indulgence, anathema to Locke and other child-care advisors, appears far more frequently in the records than does concern for strong discipline in the family. William Byrd, for example, stood up for his three-year-old daughter, Evie, when his wife forced the child "to eat against her will." Thomas Jones seemed almost pleased that his young nephew Frederick "Strutts around the House and is as Noisy as a Bully." Jones's sister-in-law commented on his excessive fondness for his two-year-old son, Tom. Tom's boisterous behavior, she noted, "is enough to distract all about him except his papa and to him I believe all his noys is musick if he can't have and do everything he has a mine to he is ready to tare the house down, but if Nanny has opertunitys, she will bring him to better order before you return."

The presence of uncles and aunts, grandparents, and other kin, who sometimes stayed with a family for weeks or months at a time, probably lent an even more permissive tone to Chesapeake family life. Disciplining a child was largely a father's responsibility, so relatives who helped care for children tried to avoid this aspect of child rearing. Instilling a sense of shame or guilt in disobedient children came hard for Rachel Cocke, an aunt of the Jones children. Mrs. Cocke had grown so close to one of her nieces who often visited her that she could not bring herself to chastise the girl for telling lies. "For all I can do I cant make her think there is any harm in a ly if she is not found out in it, nor can I be angry with her if she does it so innocently." Despite her fondness for her niece, Mrs. Cocke eventually succeeded in shaming her into compliance: "if she thinks I'm angry in good earnest she's sadly frightened and falls to beging my pardon and promises never to do so again and I do assure her that she is one of the most orderly, best children that ever was borne."

Committed to the principle of self-sufficiency, Chesapeake parents tried to avoid crushing the assertive instincts of children. Rather like modern parents, planters employed reason and parental affection to control unruly behavior in their offspring. As a result, parental discipline was often accomplished by negotiation and bargaining rather than by a show of authority. Thus, one finds a father like Thomas Jones explaining to his wife how he had managed to win an argument with his ten-year-old son. "Saturday after you went, Tom and I had some difference, but I got the better. Since which he has been a very orderly good Boy and is very good Company." Other parents offered rewards as incentives for orderly conduct. Lewis Joynes asked that his daughter Susanna "be a good girl and I will bring her a Book and a Thimble." Susanna's younger brother Jack, age five, was likewise instructed "to be a good Boy and not go near the Steers and I will not forget his great coat."

The relatively permissive and nurturant environment that parents and kin seem to have provided infants and small children in the eighteenth-century Chesapeake shaped children's perceptions about parental authority and the larger society. The evidence from the personal documents of planter families, fragmentary as it is, suggests that fathers, far from remaining indifferent to young children, entered their affective world very early on, perhaps earlier than fathers do in modern families. Thus children, especially sons, may have absorbed paternal values and feelings of affection long before reaching the age, usually after age six or so, when paternal guidance became more explicit. Recent psychological studies of parent-child relationships demonstrate that children are more likely to adopt the behavior of nurturant models than those who are indifferent to them. The strong ties of affection and filial duty which bound many children to their parents in the eighteenth-century Chesapeake — often until the parents' deaths — were in part rooted in the close emotional regard that fathers, as well as mother, displayed toward them during childhood. In short, many planters appeared to have gained the life-long gratitude and respect of their children more out of paternal fondness during childhood than out of early assertions of authority and coerced obedience.

That fathers took such an early, affectionate interest in their offspring probably encouraged a strong sense of emotional security in their children. Parents seem to have offered themselves more as a collective unit for nurturance and discipline than as a sharply differentiated one in which mothers provided the affection while fathers distanced themselves as stern disciplinarians. In the absence of clashing child-rearing styles, children could form a clearer, more secure self-identity. It does not strain the evidence to suggest that the independence training Chesapeake parents gave their children provided the psychological roots for the generations of strong-willed planter gentry who rose to such political prominence in Revolutionary America.

The nature of childrearing in planter families also encouraged children very early in life to sense the meaning of the world beyond the immediate family. From infancy on, children were introduced to a network of grandparents, uncles and aunts, and in-laws who helped in the child-rearing process. Young children were not confined at home with their parents, but lent out freely to relatives whom they sometimes visited for weeks or months at a time. Because of this early experience with other planter families, children could perceive their parents, especially fathers, as immediate representatives of a "known community of adults" with whom they could easily identify. A supporting web of kin helped ease the transition from childhood to adulthood in this plantation society.

The McGoldrick Family, c. 1835. Attributed to Ethan Greenwood. (courtesy of the Nelson-Atkins Museum of Art, Kansas City, Mo.)

4

Family History and Demographic Transition

Robert V. Wells

In recent years, the family has emerged as a major subject of historical inquiry. Numerous books and articles have appeared describing, among other things, the composition, kinship, and other interpersonal relationships, economic functions, and political importance of families. In addition, other works have dealt with values and attitudes toward the family and its members. Venturous scholars have even tried to relate family matters to such subjects as the Salem witchcraft trials, the development of a revolutionary milieu in eighteenth-century New England, and the nature of British politics in the seventeenth and eighteenth centuries, or in the case of the *Annales* school, to the total environment of a locality.

Characterized by a wide range of approaches, these efforts have produced an extraordinary number of interesting findings. However, on the surface at least, historical research on the family has lacked unity and a common sense of direction. Not only have individual scholars often pursued answers to their own idiosyncratic questions, using their own definitions, but the appearance of disunity also has been fostered by the wide temporal and geographic distribution of work on the family. Thus, while our knowledge about families in the past has been increasing rapidly, it has generally been difficult to relate the results of one investigation to conclusions reached in other studies.

Certainly this broad attack on the history of the family is to be encouraged. To study only one aspect of the family or families of only one time or place would be unnecessarily limiting. Furthermore, it is important to recognize that current methodologies available to historians of the family tend to focus on the details of the lives of relatively few persons. In such a situation generalization becomes possible only after a reasonably large number of similar studies have been done. Nonetheless, it seems desirable that historians of the family, of whatever persuasion, try to approach their work with at least some reference to a broader picture.

It is easy to call for some organizing theme to give unity and direction to work on families of the past; it is more difficult to suggest what such a theme should be. At the risk of being presumptuous, however, my purpose here is to do exactly that.

Perhaps the most popular theory among demographers today is the theory of Demographic Transition, which describes (and often attempts to explain) the historic decline of both death and birth rates in the industrialized nations of the world. However, in the light of recent work on the history of the family, this theory needs to be recast if it is to make any sense. When I attempted to do this, it became apparent that not only could history help to reshape the theory of Demographic Transition, but that the altered version of the theory also gave coherence to many of the hitherto remotely connected studies in the history of the family.

Thus, the purpose of this essay is fourfold. First, I want to offer a critique of the theory of Demographic Transition as it currently stands. Second, I want to suggest in abstract how the theory might be reformulated to account for the historical evidence which challenges the current model. Third, by surveying families in American history, I will try to relate the revised theory to the facts of the past. I will conclude by indicating some areas of research in family history which appear to be worth further study. In so doing, I hope to show how closely integrated much of the research in family history has been in the past, and how unified it can be in the future.

Because my own special area of competence happens to be American history, I shall rely heavily on evidence from this country, especially in testing the revised hypothesis. However, I shall attempt to indicate how data from other countries also seem to fit the new model. If the evidence appears scattered sometimes, that is in part the result of my own knowledge (or lack thereof), but is more the result of the sizeable gaps in our knowledge of the relevant areas of history. In any case, it should be emphasized that I am putting forth this model of the Demographic Transition with the awareness that future research will probably revise it. My main concerns, then, involve both the accuracy of the theory as revised here and a hope that this essay will serve to give a greater sense of common purpose to students of family history.

The theory of Demographic Transition can be usefully divided into two parts for purposes of analysis and criticism. The first area which we will consider *describes* the general decline in birth and death rates in industrialized countries. The second part deals with *attempts to explain* why the change occurred.

In the past, according to Transition theory, all populations were characterized by birth and death rates which were much higher than those found in industrialized countries today. Although these rates might vary over the short term, over a long period of time they tended to be rather closely balanced, with the result that natural increase was small and population growth was slow. Starting in France, and possibly Scandinavia, in the late eighteenth and early nineteenth centuries, the death rate began to decline noticeably. Since the birth rate did not fall until later, there was a transitional period (hence the name of the theory) of rapid population growth as births exceeded deaths by a considerable margin. However, in the long run the birth and death rates once again came into rather close balance, though at much lower levels than before, and rapid growth ceased. While France was the first nation to experience this transition, other nations (all industrialized) have followed much the same path, although the timing of the change, the rate of decline of fertility and mortality, and the extent to which the transition has been completed vary considerably from one nation to another. Much of the current interest in this theory stems from the fact that in many of the nonindustrialized countries of the world, death rates have fallen remarkably since World War II, leading to rather rapid transitional growth at present. Obviously, demographers are interested if and when fertility will fall in these parts of the world, slowing the growth rate and bringing the birth and death rates into balance at a relatively low level.

In the light of recent historical investigations, about the only parts of this theory which are clearly beyond question are that rapid growth occurred during the demographic transition, and that birth and death rates are now lower in some parts of the world than they ever have been for any extended period in the past. The assumption that relatively slow growth was universal before the transition began needs to be qualified in light of recent findings suggesting rather remarkable oscillations of population in Egypt between about 700 B.C. and the present, the depopulation of Europe during the plague of the fourteenth century and its ultimate recovery, and the rather remarkable short-term variations found in the populations of some British colonies in America around 1700.

Interestingly, when most demographers and historians deal with the demographic transition, they make remarkably few clearcut statements about the cause of the change. Almost all demographers note carefully that the decline in mortality and fertility always is well under way wherever literacy is high, over half the labor force is employed in nonagricultural pursuits, and the majority of the people live in urban areas. Although few specify the exact relationships, it seems to be a common assumption that these trends (whether called development, industrialization, or modernization) have caused both mortality and fertility to decline.

The explanation for why death rates might have fallen in such a situation is quite plausible. It seems safe to say that the changes noted above were generally accompanied by better and more available medical aid. In addition, standards of living tended to improve as well, producing better diets and more healthful environments.

The reasons why the birth rate should have declined as well are less obvious. Perhaps the best summary of the possible causes behind falling fertility have been given by David Heer in his article, "Economic Development and the Fertility Transition." Heer notes first that the decline in infant mortality accompanying rising living standards may reduce the need for parents to have large numbers of children in order to have a few reach maturity. The change from agriculture to industry, and from rural to urban, also may have led to reduced childbearing according to Heer, simply because children were no longer economically valuable in a new environment. Closely related to these factors was the emergence of governmental care for the aged, which meant that parents no longer needed children to care for them when they grew old. Finally, social attitudes stressing education and achievement in an industrial society and recognizing birth control as acceptable may also have fostered decreased fertility. Put simply, Heer and others stress the fact that in an urban, industrial environment children are no longer benefits, but may actually be detrimental to parental aspirations, and hence fertility declines.

In spite of the plausibility of the theory, historical evidence suggests that these causal relationships may not have existed. One assumption which seems common to most advocates of Transition theory is that urbanization and industrialization occurred *before* fertility began to decline. Yet, we have evidence of family limitation being practiced by English and Genevans in the seventeenth century, and by some French, American, and Japanese people in the eighteenth and early nineteenth centuries. In every case, these fertility declines predated any significant industrial development. Ironically, in England and possibly elsewhere as well, the move to industry and the cities was associated with an *increase* in the birth rate, quite in contrast to what Transition theory would lead us to expect. Finally, the baby boom which followed World War II is an extraordinarily puzzling phenomena from the perspective of the theory of Demographic Transition. The explanations cited by Heer implicitly assume that once the birth rate declined it would probably stay low. Certainly it should not increase during times of rising prosperity and movement into cities. In fact, so inconsistent was behavior with theory that the prosperous United States had a much greater surge in fertility than did Europe, where war devastation might presumably have led to a reversion to early patterns of reproduction.

Two questions thus arise. The first is, why did fertility rates fall in the historical change known as the Demographic Transition? The second is, does any connection remain between this decline and the processes known as industrialization or modernization?

In order to answer these two questions we should look at four possible models which might explain a widespread decline in fertility. First of all, it is possible for birth rates to drop for unintended reasons. Changes in health, sexual customs, or marriage patterns all can depress fertility, even though reduced childbearing may not have been the purpose of the initial change. It is clear, however, that the demographic transition involved a deliberate reduction in fertility, and so we must concentrate on conscious efforts to reduce the birth rate. The second model (and first one positing a conscious effort to control reproduction) assumes that when the birth rate was high, there was neither the knowledge of how to limit families nor any desire to do so. Within this framework, the demographic transition is seen as the result of new environments which lead to pressures to control childbearing for the first time, as well as make available the knowledge which allows these desires to be put into effect. Once again, however, the historical evidence makes it difficult to accept this possibility. We noted above that several populations in various parts of the world seem to have practiced family limitation well before industrialization and urbanization introduced new life styles which might have altered the desires of parents to have children. In addition, this evidence and the extraordinary study by Norman Himes on the *Medical History of Contraception* make it clear that knowledge that births could be limited was reasonably widespread before industrial societies began to emerge.

The third model of why fertility falls is a variation of the second. In this case, the assumption is that people wanted to limit their families, but could not because they did not know how to. The appeal of this explanation is that it offers some reason why the educated upper classes generally controlled their fertility before the less knowledgeable lower classes. Likewise, it would also seem to explain why highly literate nations generally have much lower fertility than nations where the educational level is low. However, the evidence suggests that this model, too, may be invalid. In England in the seventeenth century, both peers and the peasants of Colyton were limiting the size of their families. While their motives may have been different than those of the peers, the residents of Colyton did not have to wait until the industrial revolution to share in the knowledge that births could be limited. Furthermore, among the Colyton residents and the Quakers of the middle colonies whom I have studied, the onset of family limitation was rapid. The speed at which family size fell seems to preclude any slow spread of the knowledge of birth control. I have found no evidence suggesting that the Quakers either gradually or suddenly became aware of methods of limiting births. In fact, the only specific mention of family limitation I have found suggested the adoption of an old method of restricting births (nursing) to a woman who had had a difficult pregnancy and wanted to avoid another. Regardless of the effectiveness of nursing as a long-term means of family limitation, the important point is that, in this instance, it was motivation for and not knowledge about birth control which changed.

The fourth model is very closely connected to the experience of the Quaker wife cited above. It assumes that most populations have at least some notions of how to control fertility (if not by contraception, then certainly by practicing abortion, infanticide, or abstention). Thus, fertility declines occur primarily because the motivation is strong enough for a people to practice one or more of these methods, rather than because they suddenly learn some new technique. Given the rapidity of change in Colyton and among the Quakers, and the fact that major declines in fertility had occurred long before rubber condoms or diaphragms (let alone pills or IUDs) became available, there can be little doubt that at least the initial stages of the demographic transition occurred because people began frequent use of traditional forms of family limitation. It is of interest to note here, incidentally, that Kingsley Davis, a prominent demographer, has issued a telling criticism of current birth-control programs, stressing that they are failing not because of lack of knowledge or techniques, but rather because people see no reason to reduce their fertility.

Emphasizing the importance of motivation in the reduction of fertility is certainly not in conflict with the theory of Demographic Transition. Where this essay does differ from the theory is in the suggestion that motivation to have few children did not result from the economic and social changes accompanying industrialization. Rather, I wish to hypothesize that fertility fell for reasons which *also* produced a decline in the death rate as well as changes in family structure and interpersonal relations and in economic development. Thus, industrialization and the demographic transition continue to be associated, but as two effects of the same cause, rather than one causing the other.

Central to this hypothesis is the assumption that human beings have sets of values which are generally well integrated. If this is true, then the demographic transition may be seen as only one manifestation of a major change in value orientation, a change which can conveniently be typified as the shift from a traditional to a modern world view.

The nature of this change in values has been portrayed effectively in an article by Laila El-Hamamsy entitled "Belief Systems and Family Planning in Peasant Societies." In an analysis of peasant cultures in both Egypt and Latin America, El-Hamamsy found that persons in such societies were generally characterized by a sense of powerlessness over their own lives and over the world around them. Both nature and human affairs were seen as capricious, hard, and uncontrollable. God had ordered the world according to some mysterious laws, and it was not within the province of men to interfere. As a result, most peasants either did not think about the future or else felt that the future will be the same as the past. Fear, fatalism, and a sense that contentment with the status quo is desirable to avoid disappointed ambitions had led most peasants to conclude that they could do little to alter the course of their lives. Within this framework, there was no apparent reason why few children would be preferable to many (in fact, interfering with conception might anger God), just as there is no apparent reason for altering any other social or economic traditions.

These views are strikingly different from attitudes (which we shall call modern here) which have emerged in Western European society since the sixteenth century. According to E. A. Wrigley, the best way to sum up modern attitudes is with the concept of rationality. Wrigley defines a modern society as one in which recruitment to roles is done on the basis of achievement rather than birth, social roles are more clearly and narrowly defined, and where the rule of law is substituted for arbitrary and capricious behavior. Furthermore, self-interest (or, at most, interest in the nuclear family) is seen as replacing any willingness by individuals to submit to broader social or institutional needs. Thus, in contrast to the traditional view, persons with modern values believe not only that the world is knowable and controllable, but that it is also to an individual's advantage to plan his or her life and attend to the future, as well as to the present and past. To merely avoid trouble is no longer enough (as it was in traditional society) for the modern individual; such a person wants to advance, and often measures advancement in terms of his or her material well-being.

It is easy to see how at least some demographic patterns and forms of family structure might readily have been altered once modern attitudes began to prevail. The reduction of mortality, for example, may well have resulted from the emergence of attitudes that misery did not have to be accepted after all. Such notions would have been conducive to both medical experimentation and the acceptance of new techniques. Similarly, in situations where children came to be seen as burdens, modern values might permit and promote the use of family limitation to protect or enhance one's position in the world. Likewise, the movement into cities, frequently seen as a cause of falling fertility, may actually only be another manifestation of modern attitudes. Urban immigrants may well have been those people who first came to believe that by individual actions (such as migration, or learning industrial skills) it was possible for a person to improve his lot. As we shall see shortly, attitudes toward both women and children changed during the course of the demographic transition, reflecting perhaps a modern emphasis on the worth of the individual and a denial of the unchangeable order of the world. Finally, industrialization and economic development may well be related to the demographic transition. But, instead of one causing the other, the habits of saving, investment, and experimentation and the adoption of new technology necessary to industrial society may have been responses to the sense that the future could be controlled, much as family limitation may have been a different reaction to the same concern for the future.

Certainly the relationships outlined here are plausible. The historical evidence that we have tends to support this line of argument. But before we turn to the data, one last point needs to be made. It is obvious that my argument rests on the assumption that values help to shape the decisions that individuals make. It is not, however, my contention that a shift in values alone will be sufficient to change behavior. Thus, while the hypothesis advanced here asserts that the demographic transition (and related phenomena) could only occur after modern attitudes appeared, it does not imply that such changes would have been an automatic result of the adoption of new ideas.

Having put forth a new hypothesis, it is now necessary to begin to test its merits. I shall attempt to do this by drawing on historical evidence for families in America. As was noted earlier, this focus on America is primarily because my expertise lies there. However, as I shall indicate from time to time, evidence from other countries also appears to fit the hypothesis advanced above.

The obvious place to begin is to show that modern ideas were emerging in America before the demographic transition or any of its economic or social correlates were apparent. Although some would say that the emergence of modern attitudes began as early as the sixteenth century, it is clear that at least some of the first colonists had attitudes which were similar to those found in the peasant societies discussed earlier. Edmund Morgan has found a remarkable fatalism and willingness to accept misery among the early settlers of Virginia. The Puritans who settled in New England also shared many traditional attitudes. Nature was seen as mysterious and fearful. Any deviance from the proper path could bring God's wrath upon individuals or a whole people. A theology which stressed predestination and order was certainly not conducive to notions of the individual improving himself. In fact, residents of Massachusetts Bay who were so bold as to advance ideas of human equality, the rule of the law, or the capacity of people to improve themselves were often accused of heresy and driven from the colony. To the extent that the early settlers worried about the future, they were concerned with the next world rather than this one. Life on earth was merely a brief prelude to an eternity in heaven or hell.

In some ways, the surprising thing about colonial society is how quickly modern attitudes began to appear. Richard Brown has recently shown that such values were clearly present in America by the end of the seventeenth century. By the time of the American Revolution, modern attitudes seem to have been quite prevalent in the colonies. According to E. A. Wrigley, "A government which ... levies large extractions arbitrarily and without due notice ... is incompatible" with modern, rational attitudes toward life. Thus, the American resistance to parliamentary interference stands as partial proof of the presence of modern values in society. The colonists were asserting not only constitutional principles, but also an attitude that life was controllable and misfortune need not be passively accepted. Anyone who reads the biographies of the Hancock or Otis families in Massachusetts, the Browns of Providence, Rhode Island, or the Beekmans in New York will certainly be struck by the fact that these people were concerned with this world and with controlling as much of their lives as possible. A man like Benjamin Franklin may have expressed the new ideas better than most of his contemporaries, but the values he articulated were shared by many others.

According to the hypothesis advanced earlier, the emergence of new attitudes should have had an effect on population in general and on the family in particular. Perhaps the earliest evidence of modern ideas affecting population trends in America was the adoption of smallpox inoculation in Boston and elsewhere in the colonies during the eighteenth century. It is possible to debate at length the motives and scientific attitudes which led Dr. Boylston and Cotton Mather to introduce inoculation in Boston in 1721. Nonetheless, the careful tabulation of statistics regarding the effectiveness of the treatment and the wholehearted adoption of inoculation after 1750 seems to be indicative of an attitude that disease could be understood and controlled, and that death need not be always accepted passively. In fact, the last quarter of the eighteenth century saw considerable interest in the scientific study of the patterns and causes of death. Richard Shryock has shown how professionalism, education, and scientific attitudes began to characterize the medical profession by the late eighteenth century. Although these changes did not have a significant impact on health until the nineteenth century, when accurate findings finally began to accumulate, they too reflect a modern outlook on the world.

As with the death rate, the Americans' growing sense of an individual's worth and his influence over his life may have affected family size and structure well before industrialization and urbanization played a prominent role in our society. About the time of the American Revolution, at least some Quaker couples living in the middle colonies began to limit their families deliberately. Although we cannot be sure, it seems plausible that these Friends were responding to the dislocations of wartime by postponing some of the births they might otherwise have had. At present we do not know why individual Quaker couples decided to limit their childbearing. We can suggest, however, that the military campaigns in the middle colonies, the pressure of being pacifists in a time of conflict, severe inflation, and the withdrawal of Quakers from political affairs after 1750 may have made the future uncertain for many Friends. In such a milieu, a reduction of childbearing would make good sense. It is of interest to note here that times of severe crisis seem also to have produced a similar response in Colyton, England, in the 1640s, in France at the time of her Revolution, and in Japan following World War II. It would be wrong, however, to assume on the basis of this evidence that catastrophies generally lead to a durable reduction of fertility. Without modern attitudes to give people the feeling that they need not passively accept their fate, and without a clear sense that a smaller family would improve prospects for the future, such change would not be likely to occur.

While the American Revolution may have triggered the adoption of family limitation among the Quakers, a crisis which evolved more slowly may have led other parts of the American population to reduce their fertility. In the early years of settlement, land had been abundantly available. But, by the middle of the eighteenth century, at least some of the older settlements were beginning to feel the pressure of population on natural resources. As a result, fertility began to change. Kenneth Lockridge has shown that overpopulation was becoming a legitimate concern in New England by the second half of the eighteenth century. Thus, it is of considerable interest to find that the proportion of children in the total population in New England in 1790 was generally lower than in the other states. The age distribution indicates clearly that childbearing was lower there than in any of the other colonies.

Increasing population density and declining economic opportunities may have led to reduced fertility in New England first. But by the early nineteenth century, the same phenomenon was appearing elsewhere. A recent book by Colin Forster and G. S. L. Tucker, *Economic Opportunity and White American Fertility Ratios,* has shown that between 1800 and 1860 substantial reductions in fertility occurred wherever farmland became scarce. This was true from one section of the United States to another. It was also true as a given region became more densely populated over time. Yet density alone may not have produced the change. Evidence from the present indicates that population density does not necessarily cause a decline in the birth rate. Thus, if my hypothesis is correct, it was not only greater density which mattered, but also the perception that reduced fertility would aid individuals in either protecting or advancing their economic well-being.

The ways by which fertility was controlled, at least in these early stages of the transition from high to low birth rates, are not certain. We do know that deliberate family limitation was practiced by at least one part of the American population by 1800. There is no reason why other groups were not capable of the same behavior given proper motivation. There can be little doubt that family limitation within marriage became widespread during the nineteenth century, but it is also possible that part of the reduction in the birth rate from about 50 per 1,000 in 1800 to 28.5 per 1,000 in 1900 was the result of altered marriage patterns. Etienne van de Walle has shown that in nineteenth-century France, both late marriage and family limtiation within marriage were used to control childbearing, though generally only one method or the other was used in a particular locality. Thus, it is plausible that both marriage patterns and marital fertility could have been altered by residents of the United States to ensure their future well-being by limiting births. Unfortunately, our knowledge of nineteenth-century marriage patterns does not allow us to determine which means of control was more prevalent at that time. Suffice it to say that both may be rational responses to a perceived problem and hence either means of control would fit the hypothesis as stated earlier.

The decline in the birth rate which began around 1800 (if not before) continued until 1933 when it leveled off. After several years of minor fluctuation, the birth rate began to climb slowly after 1938, and spurted upwards between 1940 and 1947. Had it not been for peculiarities in the age composition, the birth rate would have continued to climb until 1957, at which point it once again would have declined. This baby boom, which occurred primarily after World War II, has been extremely difficult for Transition theory to explain. At a time when America was more urbanized and industrialized than ever before, fertility should have decreased rather than risen. As the theory has been reformulated here, however, the baby boom makes more sense. Often reduced fertility involves the postponement of children who might be desired if circumstances permitted. In such a situation, any favorable change in the environment might lead to a sudden surge in fertility. As Richard Easterlin has suggested, this seems to be exactly what happened after World War II. For a variety of reasons, persons in the prime childbearing years were unusually prosperous. This alone might well have increased the birth rate, for the same reaction may have occurred in England in the late eighteenth and early nineteenth centuries as rising incomes were accompanied briefly by rising births, much to Malthus's dismay. However, the perception of well-being in post-World War II America must certainly have been accentuated by the contrast with the decade of the 1930s, a recent and vivid memory to those who had the boom babies. Why the boom came to an end is not clear, though we can surmise that a decade of high fertility was enough once again to emphasize the high costs of children even in times of prosperity.

So far we have seen how the modified version of Transition theory can help to explain variations in fertility patterns in American history which were inconsistent with the earlier theory. It is now time to turn our attention to the way in which the hypothesis advanced above may help to connect demographic change with altered kinship relationships and attitudes toward women and children.

Recall that traditional societies place an emphasis on order and stability. Everyone has a place in society and is expected to stay there until death. Human dignity and individual development are not considered important in such societies. In contrast, modern values place an emphasis on achievement (often monetary) and equality before the law. Although the evidence is scarce, it is possible to suggest that as modern values replaced traditional ones in America, attitudes toward family, women, and children altered significantly.

It is convenient to look first at the studies of colonial families in Andover and Dedham, Massachusetts, done by Philip Greven and Kenneth Lockridge, respectively. Both these works show that in the seventeenth century, families were well ordered and controlled. The ideals described by Edmund Morgan in *The Puritan Family* were being practiced there. Perhaps the most remarkable finding was the extraordinary authority exercised by parents over their older children. Of course, the desire to inherit the farm may have had some influence on keeping sons dutiful, but in a land of abundant acreage, it seems implausible that such control could have worked without a system of values which encouraged duty and suppressed any thoughts of individual advancement. Interestingly enough, in both Dedham and Andover control broke down in the eighteenth century, precisely the time when newer attitudes were emerging. John Demos's study of Plymouth indicates a rather high degree of mobility there, suggesting that modern attitudes may have emerged slightly earlier among the Separatists than among the Puritans. However, even among the Plymouth inhabitants authority within the family was important.

I have argued elsewhere that attitudes regarding the family had changed noticeably by the time of the American Revolution. No longer were marriage and life in a family deemed necessary for all individuals. Alternative roles and alternative living arrangements became more acceptable by the end of the eighteenth century. By the nineteenth century, family ties seem to have loosened even further. Mobility was common as a series of recent community studies have shown. No longer did individuals wait at home to inherit the family farm. Rather, Americans set out to improve their lot, and, if the evidence is to be believed, they kept on moving until they established themselves economically. Clearly, attitudes by this time favored individual advancement rather than passive acceptance of fate — a plot made famous by Horatio Alger. One hardly need add that migration for personal betterment is still a prominent feature of American life.

When we look at the actual structure of families, the evidence appears somewhat confusing as to whether nuclear or extended families prevailed. On the one hand, we find nuclear families common before 1800; on the other hand, kinship ties today are still important to many groups in our society. In the end, this debate over whether extended or nuclear families prevailed may miss the point. Instead of worrying over whether an individual had only immediate relatives or a large family to associate with, perhaps we should concern ourselves with the quality of those relationships. Michael Anderson has shown, for example, that in nineteenth-century Lancashire, extended families existed in towns, but on the basis of mutual aid and for calculated advantage. Families were to be used for protection and advancement. They were not designed to control an individual and keep him in his place. The kinship ties among various American ethnic groups seem remarkably similar to this pattern, encouraging rather than restricting individual advancement. However typical the Andover families of the seventeenth century may have been at that time, such relationships seem to have dissolved as modern values became more prevalent.

As traditional values gave way to modern, we might expect parental attitudes toward children to shift — and that they did. Studies of both Puritan and Quaker attitudes toward children show that before the middle of the eighteenth century, parents felt their main duties were controlling the child until he was responsible and trying to protect the state of his soul. Little emphasis was placed on the development of individuality; life after death was considered more important than life on earth. Gradually, these attitudes changed. Parents began to respect, rather than fear, the unique qualities of their children. Discipline remained important, but by the first half of the nineteenth century it was important to ensure success in this world rather than the next. Parents came to feel that they had a significant role to play in shaping their children's future; not all had been predestined or would be decided by fate. The child-rearing literature of the early twentieth century was much like that found a hundred years before, with one exception: in addition to being taught that they could influence a child's success, parents were told they could shape his health as well. In the 1830s death was still only partly predictable and controllable; by the 1930s disease was something to be prevented or cured, not endured. Thus, rather than viewing attitudes toward children as either cause or effect of variations in fertility or infant mortality, or as the result of an urban-industrial society, it seems more useful to see lower fertility, attempts to improve health, and notions of a child's unique qualities all as recognitions that the future on earth has some promise, especially if people work at improving it.

The role of women also seems to have evolved as modern values came to replace traditional attitudes. In the seventeenth century legal and social pressures combined to limit women's roles outside of marriage. By the time of the Revolution, however, legal changes began to indicate a recognition that women had equal rights before the law as property holders, an essential characteristic of modern society. Furthermore, attitudes toward marriage changed at the same time. No longer were unwed women oddities; those who married were able to choose a husband more on the basis of love, rather than for economic considerations. Individual happiness increasingly played a part in a woman's choices; in fact, women had choices by 1800 in a way they had not apparently had a century earlier.

The nineteenth century was a time of paradox for women in America. On the one hand, women joined in various reform movements as never before, expressing, it seems to me, the notion that the future could be improved. On the other hand, women were seen as the unchanging repositories of purity and virtue, who, among other things, suffered with great patience. This latter attitude sounds remarkably traditional, but given the extent of reform activity on the part of nineteenth-century women, it is hard to believe that they felt no chance to alter the future. Rather, I would suggest, many of the notions of purity and suffering were related to sex. Women were not supposed to enjoy sex, while at the same time they were to understand the animal drives of their husbands and sons, especially when they strayed to prostitutes. While these attitudes may seem strangely out of place today, they may have made good sense in the nineteenth century. At a time when people wanted to limit births but had only crude means available, it may have been useful to deny a woman's interest in sex. Coitus interruptus could not have been terribly satisfying to many women. Likewise, prostitution, whatever its evils, served as one means of reducing the risk of pregnancy for wives.

It is of interest to note that the admission that women, like men, have a sexual side corresponds to the development of more efficient and less obtrusive forms of birth control. The twentieth century has seen a greater concern for the development of a woman's full personality than ever before. It may well be that this has happened not only as a result of modern attitudes, but also because more effective birth-control methods have allowed these attitudes to prevail, whereas in the nineteenth century the desire to control fertility worked at cross purposes to any tendency to liberate women.

One last point deserves mention before we examine what future research on the family should entail. Not all parts of the American population have experienced changes in mortality and fertility at the same rate. Undoubtedly some of the variations can be explained by different preferences for the ideal family size, by different promises for the future, and by different access to the best birth-control methods. At the same time, at least parts of the population may simply have maintained traditional attitudes much longer than others. Blacks, for example, seem to have had levels of fertility and mortality in the late nineteenth century which were unchanged from the colonial period, when their experience was much the same as the whites. Undoubtedly some of this can be explained by the denial of medical services to blacks, but we should not overlook the possibility that under slavery and the Jim Crow laws there was little reason to hope for the future. For many blacks, the world was uncontrollable and uncertain, much as it is for many peasant cultures today. Interestingly, once blacks began to move out of the South (an action which in itself is indicative of a sense that the future can be improved) and into the cities, the demographic differences between the races narrowed noticeably. Although differences still exist, the trends since the 1930s have been remarkably similar, suggesting that many of the factors which determine fertility and mortality are color blind, even if much of the rest of our society is not.

In contrast to the black experience, the Hutterites, a religious group in the northern plains states, continue to have children at a rate that only the colonists could match. This is noteworthy because the religious values of this group are extremely conservative and very traditional. Order, discipline, and the submission of the individual are important values to these people. While they are aware that the future can be controlled, they are more concerned with the success of the group than with the development of the individual. Unlike immigrant groups that fostered kinship ties to protect and advance the individual, the Hutterites use kinship ties to subordinate individual success to the good of the whole, a very traditional attitude.

As projected here, the new version of the theory of Demographic Transition appears to make better sense of the historical facts of fertility and mortality changes. In addition, the emphasis on a revolution in values serves to integrate many of the disparate approaches to the study of families in the past. Nonetheless, what I have said here is only an hypothesis, and as such must be tested and presumably revised. It is my hope that historians of the family will find this task worthwhile, not only because it has some significance in a world faced with problems of implementing large-scale reductions in fertility, but also because this hypothesis can provide some unity to research on the family.

What needs to be done? First, we need to know more precisely when fertility, mortality, and migration patterns changed in the past. These patterns must be connected with the revolution in values I have assumed to have occurred. If modern attitudes do not predate or at least overlap with new forms of demographic behavior, then the whole hypothesis falls. Likewise, it is important to determine how the changes occurred. In part this is important because we need to know which changes were deliberate and controlled and which were accidental results of other changes in behavior. In the case of fertility, it is useful to know, for example, that a falling birth rate came from birth control rather than new marriage patterns, because the attitudes toward women and children and the future trends of childbearing may be determined by which method is used.

Of considerable interest here are comparative studies. Such comparisons would be cross-national, cross-cultural, or based on socio-economic differences within a society. The theory, as outlined here, seems to fit the American experience, but does it hold in Europe or

Japan? Furthermore, do regions which have still to experience the demographic transition all have traditional attitudes? Have recent declines in mortality been the result of the acceptance of modern attitudes, or have they been imposed from above by an imported medical technology?

Obviously most students of family history will continue to have more interest in one aspect of the family than another. This is understandable and is probably the most practical approach to the immediate problem of finding out what families in the past have been like. At the same time, I would hope that no longer would one definition of or approach toward the family be considered the only appropriate one. Studies of the family should no longer focus exclusively on kinship, *or* fertility rates, *or* child-rearing practices, *or* the role of women. Rather, they should seek to incorporate all relevant changes in values and behavior which may have affected the family. We must accept the idea that as a subject, the family is a complex but highly interrelated entity. A satisfactory approach to the history of the family must involve a study of all aspects of behavior within the family setting, as well as recognizing that family patterns are closely related to more general attitudes and behavior patterns of the society under study.

Selected Readings

Axtell, James. *The Indian Peoples of Eastern America: A Documentary History of the Sexes.* New York: Oxford University Press, 1981.

———. *The School Upon a Hill: Education and Society in Colonial New England.* New Haven: Yale University Press, 1974.

Beales, Ross W., Jr. "Anne Bradstreet and Her Children." In *Regulated Children/Liberated Children: Education in Psychohistorical Perspective.* Ed. Barbara Finkelstein. New York: Psychohistory Press, 1979, pp. 10-23.

Brobeck, Stephen. "Images of the Family: Portrait Painting as Indices of American Family Culture, Structure, and Behavior, 1730-1860." *Journal of Psychohistory* 5 (Summer 1977): 81-106.

Calvert, Karin. "Children in American Family Portraiture, 1670 to 1810." *William and Mary Quarterly* 39 (Jan. 1982): 87-113.

Cremin, Lawrence. *American Education: The Colonial Experience, 1607-1783.* New York: Harper and Row, 1970.

Demos, John. *A Little Commonwealth: Family Life in Plymouth Colony.* New York: Oxford University Press, 1970.

Earle, Alice Morse. *Child Life in Colonial Days.* New York: Macmillan, 1899.

Fleming, Sandford. *Children & Puritanism: The Place of Children in the Life and Thought of New England Churches, 1620-1847.* New Haven: Yale University Press, 1933.

Fraser, Walter J. "The City Elite, 'Disorder,' and the Poor Children of the Pre-Revolutionary Charleston." *South Carolina Historical Magazine* 84 (July 1983): 167-79.

Frost, J. William. *The Quaker Family in Colonial America.* New York: St. Martin's, 1973.

Greven, Philip. *The Protestant Temperament: Patterns of Child-Rearing, Religious Experience, and the Self in Early America.* New York: Alfred A. Knopf, 1977.

Hiner, N. Ray. "Adolescence in Eighteenth-Century America." *History of Childhood Quarterly* 3 (Fall 1975): 253-80.

———. "Cotton Mather and His Children: The Evolution of a Parent Educator." In *Regulated Children/Liberated Children: Education in Psychohistorical Perspective.* Ed. Barbara Finkelstein. New York: Psychohistory Press, 1979, pp. 24-43.

Hoffer, Peter C., and N. E. H. Hull. *Murdering Mothers: Infanticide in England and New England, 1558-1803.* New York: New York University Press, 1981.

Illick, Joseph. "Child-Rearing in Seventeenth-Century England and America." In *The History of Childhood.* Ed. Lloyd deMause. New York: Psychohistory Press, 1974, pp. 303-50.

Lewis, Jan. *The Pursuit of Happiness: Family and Values in Jeffersonian Virginia.* New York: Cambridge University Press, 1983.

Moore, Kathryn McDaniel. "The Dilemma of Corporal Punishment at Harvard College." *History of Education Quarterly* 14 (Fall 1974): 335-46.

Morgan, Edmund S. *The Puritan Family: Religion and Domestic Relations in Seventeenth-Century New England.* Revised edition. New York: Harper and Row, 1966.

Musto, David F. "The Youth of John Quincy Adams." *Proceedings of the American Philosophical Society* 113 (Aug. 1969): 269-82.

Reinier, Jacqueline S. "Rearing the Republican Child: Attitudes and Practices in Post-Revolutionary Philadelphia." *William and Mary Quarterly* 39 (Jan. 1982): 150-63.

Rutman, Darrett, and Anita H. Rutman. " 'Now Wives and Sons-in-Law': Parental Death in a Seventeenth-Century Virginia County." In *The Chesapeake in the Seventeenth Century.* Ed. Thad Tate and David Ammerman. New York: W. W. Norton, 1979, pp. 153-82.

Scholten, Catherine. " 'On the Importance of the Obstetrick Art': Changing Customs of Childbirth in America, 1760 to 1825." *William and Mary Quarterly* 34 (July 1977), 426-55.

Smith, Daniel Blake. *Inside the Great House: Planter Family Life in Eighteenth-Century Chesapeake Society.* Ithaca, N.Y.: Cornell University Press, 1980.

Smith, Daniel Scott. "Child-Naming Patterns and Family Structure Change: Hingham, Massachusetts, 1640-1880." *The Newberry Papers in Family and Community History,* Paper 76-5. Chicago: Newberry Library, 1977.

———, and Michael Hindus. "Premarital Pregnancy in America, 1640-1971: An Overview and Interpretation." *Journal of Interdisciplinary History* 4 (Spring 1975): 537-50.

Stannard, David E. "Death and the Puritan Child." *American Quarterly* 26 (Dec. 1974): 456-76.

Steffen, Charles G. "The Sewall Children in Colonial New England." *New England Historical and Genealogical Register* 131 (1977): 163-72.

Stone, Lawrence. *The Family, Sex, and Marriage in England, 1500-1800.* New York: Harper and Row, 1977.

Sutton, John R. "Stubborn Children: Law and the Socialization of Deviance in the Puritan Colonies." *Family Law Quarterly* 15 (1981): 31-64.

Thompson, Roger. "Adolescent Culture in Colonial Massachusetts." *Journal of Family History* 9 (Summer 1984): 127-44.

Vine, Phyllis. "Preparation for Republicanism: Honor and Shame in the Eighteenth-century College." In *Regulated Children/Liberated Children: Education in Psychohistorical Perspective.* Ed. Barbara Finkelstein. New York: Psychohistory Press, 1979, pp. 44-62.

Walsh, Irena S. " 'Till Death Us Do Part': Marriage and Family in Seventeenth-Century Maryland." In *The Chesapeake in the Seventeenth Century.* Ed. Thad Tate and David Ammerman. New York: W. W. Norton, 1979, pp. 126-52.

Walzer, John G. "A Period of Ambivalence: Eighteenth-Century American Childhood." In *History of Childhood*. Ed. Lloyd deMause. New York: Psychohistory Press, 1974, pp. 351-82.

Watson, Alan D. "Orphanage in Colonial North Carolina: Edgecombe County as a Case Study." *The North Carolina Historical Review* 52 (1975): 105-19.

Zucherman, Michael. "Penmanship Exercises for Saucy Sons: Some Thoughts on the Colonial Southern Family." *South Carolina Historical Magazine* 84 (July 1983): 152-66.

———. "William Byrd's Family." *Perspectives in American History* 12 (1979): 255-311.

Perfectible Children in an Imperfect World: Perspectives from Nineteenth-Century America

Introduction

There is almost complete agreement among scholars that a profound change occurred in adult attitudes toward children during the course of the nineteenth century. The Calvinist belief that the child was innately depraved, still strong in the early part of the century, was gradually replaced by a more benign view, which by the end of the century had been transformed into the modern cult of childhood, at least among the well-educated classes. Traditional attitudes toward children, however, showed remarkable persistence, and we should be careful not to assume that even when changes in attitude occurred, they necessarily resulted in changes in the way children were actually treated.

William McLoughlin provides a vivid demonstration of these issues in his article on child rearing in the Jacksonian Period. In October 1831, an anonymous letter written by the Reverend Francis Wayland (1790-1865), a prominent Baptist minister, author, teacher, and president of Brown University, was published in *The American Baptist Magazine*. Reverend Wayland explained in his letter how he starved his disobedient fifteen-month-old infant, Heman, into submission, and he offers this incident as a model for other parents and religious educators. Professor McLoughlin argues that this kind of severe discipline was a direct response to a breakdown of order and authority inherent in the Age of Jackson. He believes that this approach to child rearing produced reaction formations in the children who, when they had their own children, would repeat the pattern of authoritarian, repressive parenting. It should be noted, however, that Heman became a very successful adult by the standards of his day.

If Heman Wayland suffered from the excessive zeal of a loving, but authoritarian parent, many children of the poor had to grow up without the care and nurture of any parent. Under great stress from economic hardship and poor health, left alone by their lovers or husbands to care for their children, some women felt they had no recourse but to abandon the children. Paul Gilje reprints the court records of three cases of infant abandonment that occurred in early nineteenth-century New York. In his discussion of these cases, Gilje maintains that poverty, more than a concern for illegitimacy, was the cause of infanticide and child abandonment in the United States. He also notes the irony of the presence of child abandonment during a period when the status of both childhood and motherhood was being idealized by the middle class.

The most common fate of the abandoned, neglected, orphaned, and dependent children who appeared in distressingly large numbers in the nineteenth century was to be placed in orphanages or juvenile homes. Unfortunately, these institutions were usually dismal places, often dangerous to the health and well-being of the children who lived there. Foster care developed in the mid-nineteenth century as an alternative to this institutionalization. Priscilla Clement's article on families and foster care describes the work of agencies such as Philadelphia's Home Missionary and Children's Aid Societies, which were private charities that placed children out in country homes. Their purpose was to promote middle-class values, but they also served the needs of poor parents who found temporary relief from the burden of caring for their many children. Clearly not all approaches to child welfare in the nineteenth century were focused on institutions.

Another response to the increasing number of children who appeared in the nation's legal system was the development of the juvenile court. Ben Lindsey was perhaps the best known promoter of juvenile courts during the Progressive Era. A probate judge, he created his own court by bending a Colorado school law, and then became actively involved in the national movement to create juvenile courts in other states. Lindsey's own compassionate nature helped to win public acceptance of the court, but by personalizing the court, he left it open to future abuse by less compassionate judges and probation officers. D'Ann Campbell traces the founding of this very important juvenile institution and reminds us that while "social control" may have been the result of the juvenile court's operations, it was not necessarily the only or even the prime reason for its founding. The article also makes clear that not all innovations in the history of children and youth in America came from the Northeast.

The extraordinary changes witnessed by nineteenth-century Americans contributed to an intense interest, especially among middle-class parents, in the process by which their children, and the children of others, were being prepared to leave home and assume the responsibilities of adulthood. In his essay on this process of socialization in nineteenth-century America, Daniel Rodgers focuses his attention on the ways in which middle-class children were taught the work values that dominated nineteenth-century American life by analyzing three socializing forces: the routine of schools, child-rearing advice, and children's fiction. According to Rodgers, the nineteenth-century child often received mixed messages that reflected the confusion and anxiety of adults concerning the powerful economic and social forces that were transforming their society.

The family of the Reverend John Atwood, a Massachusetts minister. Painted in 1845 by Henry F. Darby. (courtesy of the Museum of Fine Arts, Boston, M. and M. Karolik Collection)

5

Evangelical Child Rearing in the Age of Jackson: Francis Wayland's Views on When and How to Subdue the Willfulness of Children

William G. McLoughlin

In October 1831, *The American Baptist Magazine* published an "anonymous" letter in which the noted educator, minister, and president of Brown University, Francis Wayland, explained how he subdued the willfulness of his fifteen-month-old son. This is one of the most unusual documents in the history of child rearing because few parents in the past have attempted to explain and defend their theory of child rearing with such a vivid description of their treatment of an infant. Following the document, Profesor McLoughlin provides a discussion of the response to Wayland's letter and a careful analysis of the possible implications of this approach to child rearing during this particular period in American history.

Mr. Editor,

I offer for the perusal of your readers, the simple narration of a trifling incident which has in a few days occurred in my own family. Although of but little importance to any one but those immediately concerned, I think it may be made to illustrate religious truths, and, if so, it will be valuable to all. It may be even specially useful from the part of its being of such a nature, as almost every parent is frequently called to witness.

My youngest child is an infant about 15 months old, with about the intelligence common to children of that age. It has for some months been evident, that he was more than usually self willed, but the several attempts to subdue him, had been thus far relinquished, from the fear that he did not fully understand what was said to him. It so happened, however, that I had never been brought into collision with him myself, until the incident occurred which I am about to relate. Still I had seen enough to convince me of the necessity of subduing his temper, and resolved to seize upon the first favorable opportunity which presented, for setting the question of authority between us.

On Friday last before breakfast, on my taking him from his nurse, he began to cry violently. I determined to hold him in my arms until he ceased. As he had a piece of bread in his hand, I took it away, intending to give it to him again after he became quiet. In a few minutes he ceased, but when I offered him the bread he threw it away, although he was very hungry. He had, in fact, taken no nourishment except a cup of milk since 5 o'clock on the preceding afternoon. I considered this a fit opportunity for attempting to subdue his temper, and resolved to embrace it. I thought it necessary to change his disposition, so that he would receive the bread *from me,* and also be so reconciled to me that he would *voluntarily* come to me. The task I found more difficult than I had expected.

I put him into a room by himself, and desired that no one should speak to him, or give him any food or drink whatever. This was about 8 o'clock in the morning. I visited him every hour or two during the day, and spoke to him in the kindest tones, offering him the bread and putting out my arms to take him. But throughout the whole day he remained inflexibly obstinate. He did not yield a hair's breadth. I put a cup of water to his mouth, and he drank it greedily, but would not touch it with his hands. If a crumb was dropped on the floor he would eat it, but if *I* offered him the piece of bread, he would push it away from him. When I told him to come to me, he would turn away and cry bitterly. He went to bed supperless. It was now twenty-four hours since he had eaten any thing.

He woke the next morning in the same state. He would take nothing that I offered him, and shunned all my offers of kindness. He was now truly an object of pity. He had fasted thirty-six hours. His eyes were wan and sunken. His breath hot and feverish, and his voice feeble and wailing. Yet he remained obstinate. He continued thus, till 10 o'clock A.M. when hunger overcame him, and he took from me a piece of bread, to which I added a cup of milk, and hoped that the labor was at last accomplished.

In this however I had not rightly judged. He ate his bread greedily, but when I offered to take him, he still refused as pertinaciously as ever. I therefore ceased feeding him, and recommenced my course of discipline.

He was again left alone in his crib, and I visited him as before, at intervals. About one o'clock Saturday, I found that he began to view his condition in its true light. The tones of his voice in weeping were graver and less passionate, and had more the appearance of one bemoaning himself. Yet when I went to him, he still remained obstinate. You could clearly see in him the abortive efforts of the will. Frequently he would raise his hands an inch or two, and then suddenly put them down again. He would look at me, and then hiding his face in the bedclothes weep most sorrowfully. During all this time I was addressing him, whenever I came into the room, with invariable kindness. But my kindness met with no suitable return. All I required of him was, that he should come to me. This he would not do, and he began now to see that it had become a serious business. Hence his distress

increased. He would not submit, and he found that there was no help without it. It was truly surprising to behold how much agony so young a being
could inflict upon himself.

About three o'clock I visited him again. He continued in the state I have
described. I was going away, and had opened the door, when I thought that
he looked somewhat softened, and returning, put out my hands, again requesting him to come to me. To my joy, and I hope gratitude, he rose up
and put forth his hands immediately. The agony was over. He was completely subdued. He repeatedly kissed me, and would do so whenever I commanded. He would kiss any one when I directed him, so full of love was he
to all the family. Indeed, so entirely and instantaneously were his feelings
towards me changed, that he preferred me now to any of the family. As he
had never done before, he moaned after me when he saw that I was going
away.

Since this event several slight revivals of his former temper have occurred, but they have all been easily subdued. His disposition is, as it never
has been before, mild and obedient. He is kind and affectionate, and evidently much happier than he was, when he was determined to have his own
way. I hope and pray that it may prove that an effect has been produced
upon him for life.

And now, Mr. Editor, let me say that I should not have taken the trouble
of writing, nor given you the trouble of reading this apparently trifling detail, but for some lessons of practical improvement, which it has suggested
to my own mind. If you will allow me briefly to lay them before your readers, I will make no further demands upon your patience.

I. From this incident, which is in every respect literal fact, without any
embellishment, parents may learn the intensity of the obstinacy of children.
When they find their children stubborn, they need not be surprised. Let
them hold out in a mild yet firm course of discipline until this obstinacy is
subdued. This is real kindness. There can be no greater cruelty than to suffer a child to grow up with an unsubdued temper. Let us strive, by the
grace of God, to cure the evil as early as possible. I do not make these remarks, by way of telling how much better I govern my family than other
people. I believe no such thing. Far from it. God has seen fit to call me to
bring up a child of unusually unyielding temper. I have related the effect of
this method of treatment, in the hope that it might be an encouragement to
those who may be required to undergo a similar trial.

II. But secondly, I could not avoid looking upon the whole of this little
incident, as illustrative of the several steps in the ordinary progress of a
sinner's conversion.

1. I remarked that my child was about 15 months old, and yet I had
never been obliged thus to treat him before. The fact is, I had never before
required anything of him, which was directly contrary to his will. Hence
there had never occurred anything to test the question, whether he was dis-
posed to consider my will or his own as of supreme authority. But as soon
as a case occurred, which brought him and myself into direct and naked

collision, his disposition was revealed in an instant. How unyielding that spirit of disobedience was, I have already related.

I have thought that this part of the incident illustrates the reason why so many sinners *are not,* and why some sinners are in a state of conviction. So long as they do not feel anything to be *immediately* required of them, which is at variance with their own wishes and pursuits, they are at ease in sin. They feel no distinct opposition to the law of God, and are not in fact *convinced* that they are sinners. Let God grant a sinner's desires, and require of him only external service, and he would be entirely content. But let the Holy Spirit present before him the law in all its broadness, let him see that he must submit his will unreservedly and universally to the will of God, and he is at once in open rebellion. He was living without the law before, but let the commandment thus come and his sinful disposition revives; that is, comes forth in its power, and he dies, that is, yields himself at once to its deadly influence. Thus the commandment which was unto life, that is, would have secured his happiness had he obeyed, is in consequence of his disposition found to be unto death. We see, therefore, why it is that men are not, when in a state of thoughtfulness, conscious of their enmity to God: namely, because they do not feel that his law is opposed to their will, and we see how it is, that their real character at once is revealed, when the real character of God is brought into immediate collision with their desires.

2. It will be remembered, that I offered my child food, and he would not take it. I offered to receive him to my arms, if he would renounce his hostility to me, and evince it by simply putting forth his arms to come to me. I would not force him to come, nor would I treat him with favor until he submitted. I was right and he was wrong. He might at any moment have put an end to the controversy. He was therefore inflicting all this misery voluntarily upon himself.

Here several things are to be observed.

1. The terms I offered him were perfectly kind. I was willing to pass by all that he had done, if he would only evince a right disposition.

2. I could offer no other terms. To have received him on any other terms would have been to allow that his will was to be my rule of action, and whenever he set out to have his own way, I must have obliged my whole family to have conformed in all their arrangements to his wishes. He must have been made the center of the whole system. A whole family under the control of a child 15 months old! How unjust this would have been to all the rest, is evident. Besides, my other children and every member of my family would have been entitled to the same privilege. Hence there would have been as many supreme authorities as there were individuals, and contention to the uttermost must have ensued.

Again, suppose I had subjected all my family to this infant's caprice, and had done so whilst he remained under my roof, how could I have afflicted him with a more grievous curse? He would soon have entered a *world where other and more powerful beings than he* would have opposed his will, and his disposition which I had cherished must have made him miserable as long as he lived.

Or again, if all this had been done, he could not have been made happy. He did not *know enough* to be able to secure his own happiness. Had I let him do as he pleased, he would have burnt and scalded himself a dozen times a day, and would very soon have destroyed his life. Seeking, therefore, his good, and the good of the family, I could do nothing else than I did. Kindness to him as much as to them, taught me not to yield to him on any other terms than a change of disposition.

On the contrary, by yielding to me, my whole family has been restored to order; he is happier by far than he has ever been before, and he is acquiring a disposition which will fit him for the wide world, which, if he lives, he will enter upon.

So, to apply all this to the case of a sinner, *God* can offer a sinner *no other terms than repentance.* To yield to the sinner's will, and save him without the unconditional surrender of his will, would be to make the sinner's will the center of the moral universe. How would you like amoral government founded on your neighbor's caprice? It would be to throw down the government of law, and make this universe a hell.

It would be unkind to the sinner himself. He does not know enough of the universe to secure his own happiness, if he were permitted to act without control. He would make a hell for himself, even if God left him entirely alone. It is, therefore, infinitely kind in God to resist him, for if he were not resisted, he would destroy the happiness of the universe and himself together. By resisting him, he only ruins himself.

To avoid all these evils, God only requires of him to surrender his own willful and wicked opposition, and be happy. Is it not exceedingly reasonable that he should do so? Is there anything to cause his pain but his own willful obstinacy? Does he not inflict all his misery upon himself? In one word, the creature is trying every possible means of escape from the wrath to come, except submission, and this it obstinately and most sensitively avoids. Ought we to tell a sinner in such a state to wait, to use the means or to submit to God, while yet he was holding out the sceptre of mercy?

3. Again. When very hungry, my child accepted of bread from my hand while yet his opposition to me was unchanged. Extreme distress produced a forced yielding, so far as to secure an immediate alleviation, but his heart was the same as ever.

Thus we fear it is with many a convicted sinner. He sees that eternal destruction is before him, and he must yield or perish. He yields as it were *to force.* He gives up this and that and the other external sin. He surrenders the objects on which his heart is set, rather than his heart itself. The stream is changed rather than the fountain. He gradually convinces himself that God has pardoned him, and settles down too frequently in a false hope. At other times God reveals to him again the deceitfulness of his heart with still greater clearness, and he is yet more distressed than ever. Happy are they who are thus led to surrender their whole body and soul and spirit a living sacrifice to their God and Redeemer.

4. The change, as I remarked, was instantaneous. He might have obeyed me as well twenty-four hours before. It produced an instantaneous change in his whole character.

So in the case of conversion. The sinner has only to submit himself to the righteous government of God, and accept of the Saviour's sacrifice, and the agony is over. There is no reason why he should delay. You may do it now, reader, whilst your eyes rest upon his trifling relation. The moment of your doing so, will introduce you to a new world. You will be filled with love to God. The peace that passeth understanding will be shed abroad in your heart. Your bosom will glow with love to the whole family of the redeemed on earth and in heaven. You will find that happiness can never be obtained by obeying your own will, but that it is obtained only by relinquishing it, and making God the center of your affections, the eternal rest of your soul.

I will close with a very few words of address.

1. We frequently hear persons declare that they are not opposed to God, and therefore need not a change of heart. My dear friend, should God set his law before you in the full exactitude of its enactment; should he cut you off from every thing you love until you obeyed his law, and loved him with all your soul, and mind, and strength, how would it be with you? How would you love such a God, and such a government? In such a condition you will soon find yourself. Is it not true then that you must be born again?

2. To the convicted sinner I would say, that all your distress results from the conviction that you must submit your will to God, or perish. Unqualified submission, is, to an unhumbled heart, the most grievous of all things. But I pray you consider that it is just. God's throne would be iniquitous unless he required it. You cannot be happy without it. You will be happy as soon as you do it. The whole redeemed universe will rejoice to welcome you to their family. *Submit yourself unto God.*

Not only is God just in this, he is infinitely compassionate. He gave his own Son to suffer, to render this offer possible. Now is his day of grace. He only asks you to be his dear child. His language during all your obstinate resistance to the strivings of his Spirit is, How can I give thee up, Ephraim? How can you resist so compassionate a Redeemer any longer?

3. But beware of a false peace. It is not giving up the objects of our regard, it is the surrendering of the will itself that is repentance. It is the renouncing our own will, and placing the will of God on the throne of our hearts. Let us pray for the searchings of his Spirit, that we may not, in so important a question, be deceived.

4. The evidence of this change is found in a life conformed to the will of God. If our wills are carnal and selfish, our lives will be so too. If the will of God rules in us, our lives will exemplify the holiness of his law. We shall love his society. We shall love to please and obey him. We shall love all holy beings, and derive much of our happiness from communion with the saints.

A PLAIN MAN
[Francis Wayland]

While historians have long recognized that subduing the willfulness of stubborn children was considered the first and foremost task of religious parents in the early republic, it is seldom that we find a detailed account by a parent describing precisely how this process was carried out. An anonymous letter to the editor of *The American Baptist Magazine* in October 1831 provides just such an illustration. Previous historians may have suspected that the account was fictitious and hence ignored it. However, by a fortunate circumstance we now know who the author was and which of his children was described in the letter. Furthermore, because the author was a man of some consequence in American educational and religious history, we have additional evidence to place the letter in context. The case also appears to have aroused some public notoriety at the time. Consequently, this description of child disciplining seems worth reprinting.

The parent was the Rev. Francis Wayland (1790-1865), D.D., LL.D., nationally noted Baptist minister, author, teacher, and educational reformer, and the fourth president of Brown University in Providence, Rhode Island. Not only was Wayland famous for his university reforms, but, as the author of two best-selling college textbooks (*The Elements of Moral Science* [1835] and *The Elements of Political Economy* [1837]), he significantly influenced two generations of college students during the golden age of American evangelicalism. The infant disciplined was to become the Rev. Heman Lincoln Wayland (1830-1898), minister, college teacher, Civil-war chaplain, Baptist magazine editor, and president of Franklin College. Perhaps the first and most significant fact pointed up by this apparently trivial incident is the apparent continuity between the generations (grandfather, father, sons) in their personal relationships, their value system, and their vocational careers.

President Wayland's father, also named Francis, was born in England in 1772. He came to New York with his young wife in 1793 and established himself in the currier business. A devout Baptist, the elder Wayland underwent a profound religious experience at the turn of the century (during what historians have called "The Second Great Awakening") which eventually led him to abandon business and enter the Baptist ministry. His son Francis and his grandson Heman followed him in this calling. Raised in strict conformity to evangelical piety and filial devotion, President Wayland followed the same pattern with his children. "My father was a man of very fixed ideas of family government," the president wrote, "and required of his children implicit obedience. I have no recollection of ever disobeying him deliberately but once." We know from Wayland's correspondence that throughout his life he retained close and reverent ties with his father, writing to him regularly, confiding in him, seeking his approbation until the old man died in 1849. This same pattern prevailed for the president's sons as we shall see from their correspondence.

President Wayland wrote a eulogistic memoir of his father after his death and the president's sons wrote a eulogistic memoir (in two volumes) of their father after his death in 1865. It would appear that evangelical children underwent a profound psychological experience when, at a very early age, they were forced to submit to their fathers' wills and give up their own. Freudian psychologists might see this as a "reaction formation" in which feelings of reverence and dependence were unconsciously substituted for those of anger and hostility in order to resolve the intense conflict. A student of Erik Erikson, reading the letters of President Wayland to his father and then of the president's sons to him (and to each other), might also conclude that far from developing a sense of autonomous self-reliance and individualism, these traumatic ordeals in childhood (considered so basic to child rearing among middle-class, pietistic parents) produced immense amounts of anxiety, self-doubt, and dependence. Children raised under such patterns of paternal discipline probably spent their lives trying to act consistently within them and looked to their fathers' approval long after they had reached maturity. Moreover, having repressed their own hostility toward their fathers, such evangelicals, when they became fathers, doubtless felt threatened by any refusal by their children to submit to their will.

If these assumptions have any validity, President Wayland's dramatic account of his method of subduing the stubborn will of his infant son may well have archetypal importance, not only in helping us to understand the dynamics of parent-child relations in the nineteenth-century evangelical home but also in helping us to understand the social (and political) behavior of American males when they felt themselves threatened by defiant gestures from allegedly weaker, infantile (certainly powerless) groups such as Indians, blacks, women, or ethnic minorities. That is, such defiance must be patiently but firmly (paternalistically) crushed for the good of the group concerned as well as for the good order of society and the advancement of God's will.

Historians of child rearing have long been aware of the various justifications for strict child rearing offered by middle-class evangelicals. Bernard Wishy, for example, has pointed out the particular fears of New England conservatives in the Jacksonian Era when so many of the old institutional controls and social patterns seemed to be failing: the established churches, the deference of the lower orders toward their betters, the steady habits of a stable, agrarian, small-town social system. He might well have cited President Wayland on this, for in his famous textbook on moral science Wayland made this point explicitly in his chapter devoted to parental training and duties: "That a peculiar insensibility exists [today, in 1835] to the obligations of the parental and filial relation is, I fear, too evident to need any extended illustration. The notion that a family is a society, and that a society must be governed, and that the right and duty of governing this society rests with the parent, seems to be rapidly vanishing from the minds of men. In the place of it, it seems to be the prevalent opinion that children may grow up as they please, and that the exertion of parental restraint is an infringement upon the personal liberty of the child." It was to stem this pernicious tide of public affairs in the Age of Jackson that Wayland wrote his book. Wayland, and those evangelical fathers who agreed with him, doubtless felt great personal anxiety when they observed others being disrespectful to authority or failing to observe traditional proprieties. Their strictness with their own children was a means of controlling themselves, though they saw it as a means of preserving good social order. Quoting the Bible and insisting that the laws of moral behavior were as universal, absolute, and scientific as the laws of physics or astronomy, Wayland offered as the first "Law of Parents": "The *right* of the parent is to *command;* the *duty* of the child is to *obey.* Authority belongs to the one, submission to the other." Furthermore, "in infancy the control of the parent over the child is absolute; that is, it is exercised without any due respect to the wishes of the child." Obviously then, Wayland's first "Law of Children" is *"Obedience.* By this I mean that the relation between parent and child obliges the latter to conform to the will of the former *because it is his will. . . ."* The other principal duties of the child were "reverence" to the parents and "filial affection." Such a theory implicitly demands reaction formation.

While Wayland spoke of "parental duties," the personal pronoun invariably used for the parent was "his" — "his duty," "his right," "his authority," and "his child." That this was not merely a grammatical rule common to the time can be seen in his using the terms "parental" and "paternal" interchangeably. Wayland specifically mentions the general absence of the father from the home "on business" as one of the prominent reasons for the breakdown of family discipline: "The father who plunges into business so deeply that he has no leisure for domestic duties . . . is equally to be pitied and to be blamed." Periodicals written for parents in these years frequently echoed the same sentiment. There was no substitute for the father's authority.

God-fearing parents looked to evangelical ministers and educators like Wayland for guidance for other reasons in the Age of Jackson.

The waning of the old doctrines of Calvinism, like the waning of the colonial social order, posed new problems in child rearing. While new Arminian doctrines softened the notions of predistination and original sin which had condemned Puritan children dying without grace to "the easiest room in Hell," they also fostered an increasing insistence upon the freedom of the will. Both of these new outlooks placed an additional burden upon parents. As God's sovereignty lessened, parental responsibility increased. It was not divine determination nor Adam's fall which placed children who died unconverted in Hell; at a very early age the child began to assert its free will and at that very early age the parent acquired the obligation to bring that child into harmony with God's laws. Evangelical parents did not share the optimism of romantic Transcendentalists who were coming to believe, like Wordsworth, that children came into this world directly from heaven — pure and undefiled. Hence they had no use for those educational reformers, like Bronson Alcott, who thought that the basic duty of parents was simply to cultivate or elicit the innate goodness of the young. Evangelicals of all denominations continued to believe that children still had much of the old Adam in them — they had sinful propensities which must be checked. "Inasmuch as the present state of man is morally imperfect, and every individual [young and old] is a sharer in that imperfection, it is the duty of the parent to eradicate so far as is in his power the wrong propensities of his children. He should watch with ceaseless vigilance for the first appearances of pride, obstinacy, malice, envy, vanity, cruelty, revenge, anger, lying . . . and strive to extirpate them before they have gained firmness by age or vigor by indulgence." The problem became a matter of timing: at what age should a parent begin to assert authority over a child? When did infants begin knowingly to sin and thereby endanger the future of their immortal souls (as well as of parental souls who failed to do their religious duty in time and who might be punished by being eternally parted from their children in the next world)?

This question does not seem to have received any precise answer either in theoretical works like Wayland's *Moral Science* or in practical guides, like the multifarious parental guidebooks and periodicals of the day. The closest approximation I have discovered appeared in a journal entitled *The Mother's Assistant and Young Ladies Friend:* "A worthy matron being asked to disclose the secret by which she had successfully reared a large family of children said, 'I am accustomed to *obey* them during the first year of their existence and ever after to *exact the most implicit obedience from them.*'"

Some evangelical ministers, like the Reverend Nathaniel W. Taylor of the Yale Divinity School, believed that infants became "morally accountable" to God for their actions after six months. Probably most parents first began to pay serious attention to child discipline when their children were old enough to walk and say their first words, somewhere between one and two years of age. While disciplinary training varied with individual children, it appears that boys were likely to be disciplined earlier and more severely: "Boys are more difficult of management than girls," wrote one evangelical minister in a parents' magazine, "because they are naturally less tractable."

Francis Wayland, in seeking to discipline his son at the age of fifteen months, seems to have been well within the norm of evangelical practice in his day, though he may have been the first to publish an exemplary account of it, and his determination to have it over and done with in one supreme test of wills probably involved more time, patience, and perseverance than most fathers could muster. From his account of the ordeal he appears to have been especially pleased that he did not resort to corporal punishment; perhaps he was breaking new ground here. It is unfortunate that we do not have more precise details about child rearing in the Wayland family. We know nothing of the training of Wayland's other children nor of the role their mother or nurses played. Wayland obviously felt that this child, his third, "was more than usually self willed" and that "several attempts to subdue him had thus far been relinquished from the fear that he did not fully understand what was said to him." But we do not know what these earlier attempts consisted in nor who made them. When Wayland says, "I had seen enough to convince me of the necessity of subduing his temper," we get the feeling that he had previously simply observed the ineffective efforts of the nurse or the mother and suddenly decided to demonstrate his own superior ability in this line. Yet the fact that the child cried violently when his father took him from the nurse might indicate that father and son had previously engaged in some battles of the will and the infant suspected what was coming. Nevertheless, all this is speculation. Wayland chooses to concentrate wholly upon the details of this single incident, and of course, we see it only from the father's perspective.

To fill in what bare facts we do have, Wayland was married in Boston on November 21, 1825, while pastor of the First Baptist Church there. The following year he was offered a professorship in moral philosophy at his alma mater, Union College, and in 1827 he accepted the presidency of Brown University. Though never a wealthy man, he was able to employ maids, nurses, and servants for his growing family. His first child, also named Francis, was born August 26, 1826. His second, Emma, was born in 1827 but died at the age of fifteen months (a point which Wayland mentions in his account and which may be relevant to his sudden concern over the moral status of his third child at the same age). Heman Lincoln Wayland, the subject of this account, was born April 30, 1830, and brought to account for his stubborn temper in July or August 1831. While none of the extant letters of Wayland in the Brown University Archives throws any light upon his relationship to his children prior to 1831, there are two letters in 1834 and 1835 which contain significant remarks. The first was written to his father on December 22, 1834, eight months after his wife's death: "I find that in this state [as a widower] I feel my own responsibility to my family more. I am more useful to my little boys and have a greater influence over them, am more attentive to them, as well as they to me, and I learn my duty as a parent better and I hope I gain something more than I otherwise should in patience and gentleness. These I greatly need and these the care of children is I think greatly calculated to foster so that there are blessings emanating from bereavement. . . ." The second excerpt is from a letter he wrote to "My Dear Little Boys" from New York City on April 22, 1835: "I am very sorry that Frank [Francis, Jr.] has not yet answered my letters as I have been very anxious to hear from you. I hope you are very good boys and mind Mary and Emeline and that above all you strive to love and serve the blessed Saviour. Do not neglect to say your prayers and to read the Bible. You must remember that you are the only comforts I have left in this world, and it will grieve me very much if you are naughty and wicked boys and like those boys who do not know anything about God."

The parental relationship revealed in these letters is probably not atypical of evangelical families though it is obviously heightened by the recent death of the mother. Wayland remarried in 1838 and had another son, Howard. We do not know what his first two sons thought of this marriage though from the letters quoted below it would appear that they did not have a very close attachment to their stepmother. The letters of Francis, Jr., and Heman (which begin in the 1850s) indicate that Frank was for many years the black sheep of the family. He did not undergo the conversion experience expected of all evangelical children in puberty. Moreover, he became a lawyer and dabbled in politics in his early manhood. Neither of these professions seemed wholly respectable to his father. Heman, hwoever, was converted in his college years (both sons attended Brown University where they had to attend their father's classes). After joining the Baptist church, Heman was ordained for the ministry and became (like his father) a college teacher and later a college president. Frank moved from the bar to the bench and then to the lieutenant-governorship of Connecticut, but he too ended his career as a college teacher at the Yale Law School, finally becoming the dean of that institution.

In order to point up the intense filial piety of these two sons and their inordinate respect and reverence for their father, it is worth quoting from a few of the letters which Heman wrote to his brother in the years 1852 to 1866. I have selected a few quotations which seem to be evidence of a reaction formation that might have originated in the psychological encounter between the father and son in 1831, though it would be difficult to assert that these quotations could not have occurred in the letters of any evangelical children in this era. But that, in a way, is the point of this essay.

Heman, though the younger son, seems to have dominated Frank — in large part because he was always in his father's favor and Frank was not. Both sons lived in awe of their father and yearned constantly for his affection and approval in all they did and thought. Much of their correspondence deals explicitly with their relationship to their father. One particularly striking letter from Heman to his brother came at the time of their father's fifty-sixth birthday in March 1852.

Father is 56 [on March 11]. Another year nearer is that time of inevitable separation which must issue one day. I almost fear to write to him. I used to look forward to Birthdays of myself and others with glee, but I no longer do. Father is two and a half years older than Aunt Stone [who died recently]. Do you ever, Frank, look forward to that time when we must part from Father? I can hardly bear to do so and yet I sometimes for a moment have done so. It is sad to think of standing by his bedside or having him stand by ours and bidding him goodbye for the last time. But how much sadder it is to think of being parted from him forever! Frank, think for a moment of what is said about the "great gulf" [between the saved and the damned in the Bible]. Unless you are converted, that gulf is between you and Father forever.

One wonders why Heman suddenly reversed the fear of standing by his father's deathbed to suggest that perhaps the father might be standing by his deathbed? Knowing the tactic which his father utilized to subdue his will at fifteen months, we are certainly tempted to see these fears of separation as part of that repressed trauma.

Among the many typical statements of Heman's "reverence" for his father is this from a letter of November 18, 1952: "I cannot express to you the manner in which I regard Father. As Gen. (Somebody, I forget who) wrote of Washington, 'He is my eyes *the Great* and good man.' Hence any one who says a word against him makes an enemy of me at once." Even in private correspondence with Frank, Heman feared to say anything which might offend his father and instructed his elder brother, "One point relative to our correspondence. I hope we shall avoid writing anything of a nature which we should want secret from Father. He is, I need not say, our best Earthly friend and I think we should find it best to adopt the rule to write only that that we would be willing to have Father see." Somehow the two boys dared not put on paper any doubts, hostilities, or fears they may have had.

After Heman left Providence to live in Rochester, New York, he asked Francis, who lived nearer home, to write anything their father might say about him: "Write so far as may be all of Father's conversations, remarks, etc. Let me merely suggest that as I value Father's opinion above that of any other human being (and the opinion of others chiefly as it furnishes an indication of his) I should receive with interest any remarks which he might make upon his jnr. [junior] son. I do not want to hear what any one else says of me." Words of praise from their father were evidently rare, however: "Father does not say much and hence what he does say is of value. When I like to know what Father says about my success here, I really do not think it is from vanity but I sometimes rather am in want of some encouragement. For the general run of criticism, favorable or otherwise, I think I do not care much. Father's I value." This was in 1853 when Heman was starting his first job, teaching at Rochester University.

Such thoughts might not be too unusual for a son following in his father's footsteps. Sometimes his dependence on his father's approval appears as a desperate longing for the mother who abandoned him shortly after the traumatic incident with his father as an infant: "Dear me, what hours of care and regret we cost Father," he wrote to his brother in 1854. "Yes, Frank, as you suggest, the Blackest day in our lives, the day that more than any other or any 1000 others we may regret was the 3rd of April, 1835. It is impossible to estimate what a dark day that was to us. . . . Had Mother lived this life had been another place for me and I another man than I am or shall be." Since Frank raised the issue, perhaps he, who was eight when their mother died, was more "mother's boy" in contrast to Heman, who was all father's. In another letter Heman confessed of his mother, "I remember nothing whatever of her." His sorrow over her death may have stemmed less from any memory of her kindness than from her absence and his fear of his father's displeasure with him. Or possibly memories of her were so painful as to be repressed.

Heman and his brother seem rather early in life to have sought some way to express their mixed feelings toward their father in a public way, as though people would not see how truly great their reverence was. In 1853, while their father was still vigorously pursuing his career as president of Brown and while they were still in their twenties, Heman wrote to his brother (after they had both visited home):

During my journey [from Providence back to Rochester] on Monday, I devoted some time to thought on the topic we spoke of one evening at home, namely the Life of Father. We at that time thought we saw no one who was qualified in all ways for the work and saw no alternative but that if we survived Father it must come to us. Reflection does not lead me to alter that opinion. I propose then to you that we should regard it as a settled matter that we hence forth use every means to prepare ourselves for that work. . . . The memory of a man like Father should not be lost for want of care and labor and his memory and fame may perhaps with a peculiar fittingness be entrusted to guardianship to those for whom he had done so much.

Did they fear that other biographers might criticize their father and endanger their respect for him, or was this but another manifestation of the psychological dynamic established in their infancies? Quite possibly Heman's visit home evoked the old threat and produced this "reverent" response.

Twelve years later, when their father died, the two brothers at once set to work to enshrine his memory. Within two years after his death their two-volume memoir appeared. It contained very little about their own relationship with him, but much about his greatness as a man, a father, a husband, a writer, a theologian, and an educational reformer. Yet despite its unabashed filial pietism the book does not reflect the full dimension of their love/hate relationship. To guard against unconscious hatred, they could only find him faultless. "It is not so much that we have lost, as you say, so dear a friend and counsellor," Heman wrote to his brother shortly after the funeral, "but the words are nothing, that we have lost one whom no human language can describe. Oh, what can I say?" And a few days later: "To you and to a *very* few others I can speak without fear of being seemed extravagent. Did you ever remark the resemblance between his character and that of Jesus of Nazareth? I speak with reverence. His unselfishness, his care for others, his courage, for righteousness and justice, his sympathy for the suffering, his pity for the fallen, his prayerfulness. How few characters will bear close inspection, but his perfectly." President Wayland was, of course, a man of eminence whom everyone respected. He was not, however, a great champion of the oppressed. He took a decidedly conservative stand upon the issue of slavery and strongly opposed the great political rebellion in Rhode Island which sought to extend the suffrage. He was a Whig, not a Democrat, and his sons followed his conservative political position as they did his evangelical one.

Heman suggested that on his father's tombstone should be placed a text from John 17:24 indicating the longing of the brothers to rejoin their father even beyond the grave: "Father, I will that they also whom

thou hast given me, be with me where I am." The words are those of
Jesus to his heavenly Father and on the tombstone represent the
sentiment of Francis Wayland asking that his family be allowed to
join him in Heaven. The choice of that text, however, was made by
a son who could not bear the thought of permanent separation from
his stern, forbidding father.

Two final aspects of the principal disciplinary incident should be
considered in order to place it in context: what did the episode mean
to Francis Wayland, the father who wrote it for publication, and what
impression did it make upon the contemporary public for whom he
wrote it? The fact that Wayland signed it "A Plain Man" rather than
with his own name as president of Brown University may indicate
that he had certain doubts about its reception. Perhaps more significant, the fact that he wanted to publish it at all may indicate that
he felt some qualms or guilt feelings about what he had done and
sought public exoneration for it. Did his wife or other members of his
family who knew about it consider it unnecessarily cruel? He calls it
"a trifling incident," but it was obviously much more than that to
him. It was also a "trial" — a "task I found more difficult than I had
expected." He writes, it seems to me, defensively, as though to fend
off charges that he was unduly harsh with his infant son.

It is not clear whether Wayland or the editor of the magazine gave
the title "A Case of Conviction" to the piece, but Wayland's effort to
lift the particular case into a general paradigm for evangelical behavior
is certainly noteworthy. He, the human father of a willful, stubborn,wicked child, has done no more than what God the Father of all
mankind does with all his earthly children. To do one's duty as a
parent, however harsh it may seem, is not only for the betterment of
the child but also for the glory of God — not to mention the good
order of society. "There can be no greater cruelty than to suffer a
child to grow up with unsubdued temper." Not only would it spoil the
child and place the whole family under the dominion of its malicious
will, but when the child entered the outside world, "a world where
other and more powerful beings than he" refused to submit to his
will, then he would suffer even more. Thus even a plain man might
see that Wayland's conduct has been justified at all levels — parental
government, duty to the child, obligation to society, and respect for
the will of God. The thrust of the piece is thus turned away from
Wayland, the parent, and toward the sinner who reads it. To cast
blame upon Wayland would be to flout all authority, justice, and benevolence. This is a common characteristic of evangelical sermons
which, to those outside the faith, may seem self-righteous but to those
inside are self-justifying.

Fortunately we have some evidence of how the contemporary public responded to this incident, though it may stem from those outside the faith. In the Brown University Library there is a copy of this article by Wayland to which Sidney Rider, the noted collector of nineteenth-century tracts and pamphlets, attached this note: "On page 296 of the pamphlet within is the celebrated account written by Dr. Francis Wayland of his starving an infant son 15 months old into obedience. It is anonymous, being signed *A Plain Man,* but it was written by Francis Wayland. In the *Literary Subaltern,* a newspaper, there are two severe criticisms upon this paper. They were in the issues for Dec. 1st and 30th, 1831."

The *Literary Subaltern* was a weekly newspaper published in Providence, Rhode Island, by Sylvester S. Southworth. Whether it was Southworth who wrote the "severe criticism" or not we do not know since neither article is signed, but they fill many long columns. Whoever wrote the articles (and they may have been written by the same person) claimed not to know who the cruel parent was. But it is strange that the first article was titled "Analogy of Brutality" when Francis Wayland had, on September 7, 1831, published a striking address before the Phi Beta Kappa Society of Rhode Island entitled "A Discourse on the Philosophy of Analogy." The most significant parts of the article of December 1 are these:

The subject of Analogy of Brutality, like the subject of Analogy of Philosophy, was never taken up by a grown man till the middle of the nineteenth century if we may believe the assertions of a man of science, and one like the other is full of the most unequivocal and enduring interest.

In the October number of the Baptist Magazine, a periodical that is published in the city of Boston and patronized by many worthy individuals of the city of Providence, there is a paper written, we know not by whom, which we and some hundreds have read and consider with emotions that we will not undertake to describe. The paper is headed "A Case of Conviction" but as it is not analogous with the caption or the text, we have, as we think, appended to it very appropriately, the title of Analogy of Brutality.

The paper, undoubtedly, is from the pen of a *philosopher* — from a man who has been enabled to arrive at that state of feeling which prepared him to starve and chastise in a philosophical manner, an infant boy, only fifteen months old, and frighten him into a state of passive obedience. Such discoveries in Philosophy should command the especial admiration of the world and gain for the discoverer a wreath of *imperishable glory.* It seems that the infant child, though only *fifteen months old,* had the hardihood to refuse a piece of bread from the hands of its philosophical father; and what is more outrageous than all this, when a cup of cold water was given it to drink, it refused to place its little hands on the sides of the unoffending vessel that contained it! For these most flagrant outrages upon all kinds of decency and philosophical rule, the vile infant boy *"fifteen months old"* was philosophically shut up alone, in a vacant apartment or prison, where it was kept thirty-six hours without partaking of any kind of nutriment to sustain its existence. That every man of sense and feeling may have a fair view of this most wonderful performance in philosophy, we copy the paper alluded to from the Baptist Magazine. . . .

After printing the first part of the article, the writer continued:

The remainder of the article we have omitted because it has no connexion with the story of the father towards an infant child only fifteen months old and is only a *philosophical* discussion of unmooted points to prove that God makes saints out of sinners by taking bread from them and shutting them up six-and-thirty hours in a "dark closet." The arguments are too philosophical for us and as we believe they would not be acceptable to our readers, we decline laying them before the public. . . . Be he who he may, he is but little better than a brute and should not be allowed to preside over the destinies of infants. His own acknowledged brutality towards his own offspring should gain for him the anathema of the public and the indignation of every parent. We say this without entertaining any feeling of hostility towards any one; and as the writer of the offensive article is unknown to us, we certainly cannot be accused of indulging in feelings of personal ill will; our only object is to hold up to public contempt an anonymous writer who, in the face of the world, boasts of his unnatural treatment of that offspring to whom he gave existence and whom he punished with the most wanton cruelty because it was guilty of the monstrous crime of refusing to take a piece of bread from that parent, who is not entitled to the love of his infant. The writer of the article not only publishes the story of his own inhumanity, but exults in the recital of the transaction as if it were an act of unperishable glory.

It would seem that of late parents and guardians and school masters have ventured in one grand scheme to make a display of their cruelty. But a few weeks since a school master in Boston whipped one of his infant scholars till death had nearly relieved the sufferer from torture; and from the following account, it appears that a *Reverend* gentleman schoolmaster of one of the towns of New Hampshire has been guilty of a similar and if possible a more brutal transaction.

Here the writer printed an article about the Rev. Samuel Arnold of Ossippee, New Hampshire, who had adopted a young boy and then one day beaten him almost to death for the boy's inability to pronounce the words "utter" and "gutter" to his satisfaction.

The article of December 30 in the *Literary Subaltern* was a poem ostensibly translated from a mysterious Chinese document written in Sanskrit. The poem, which reads like some of Lewis Carroll's parodies of Engish school rhymes, was heavily footnoted to give it a learned appearance. The footnotes were in many respects more revealing than the poem.

I have a little churlish brat,[1] it was not very old,

And yet the idle chap would cry and fret and scold,
And I resolved to conquer him with stripes and kicks and blows,
And when he wouldn't mind me, well I pulled his little nose.

And as I went home one day and stroked his little head,
He cried aloud and long at me and[2] threw away his bread:
I said to him, you naughty boy,[3] I'll conquer you I vow,
Such things in you are very bad and such I'll not allow.

At that he looked most wickedly[4] and made a naughty face,
He looked just like a naughty man,[5] all destitute of grace:
And so I locked[6] him up one day and left him all alone.
And bade him pick his little nose, and like a sinner moan.

My little boy looked sadly then and shook his little head.
But still refused to[7] kiss his Pa, or take his father's bread;
Says I, my boy, I'll teach you how to cut up such a shine.
You'll have no supper when I eat, no beef steak when I dine.

My little boy was naughty still and[8] yet he'd sob and sigh,
Says I, my lad, you still may whine, and whisk about and cry,
If I don't conquer you,[9] my boy, before I go to dinner,
Philosophy I will forego, and own myself a sinner.

Just fifteen months had rolled away since my bad boy was born,
And blest my happy bridal bed, one blessed Sunday morn,
He's fifteen months of age today, and yet he's very sad,
I vow that I will conquer him[10] and starve out all that's bad.

Imprisoned within the closet walls — I kept him many an hour,
And hop'd that I should make him good with my paternal power.
But still he'd sob and cry aloud, bemoan himself and wail,
And then to stop his noise and[11] din, I spanked his little tail.

And then I shut him up again to try his little spunk —
Exhausted nature soon gave way and he began to[12] flunk,
And then quite starved and wan and faint, he begged me for his supper,
And as I'd carried all my points,[13] I gave him bread and butter.

Oh, how rejoiced was I to find my boy had been redeemed
From Satan's ways and ugliness new hopes within me beamed.
And then unto myself I said, my plan doth well accord
With all my philosphic[14] plans — and now I'll praise the Lord.

For what I've done, and mean to do, to every wicked boy.
And tell the tale to all the world and fill men's souls with joy;
And now my darling boy has got the means of grace,
I'll let him look upon the world[15] and scorn the human race.

For his dear heart is now so changed — he looks just like a saint,
All dressed so fair in swaddling clothes — a beauty without paint;
And I will give him[16] little strings to tie his little hose,
Oh, he shall have more gingerbread — a 'kerchief for his nose.

> A cap with tassels he shall wear — *Philosophy* he'll learn.
> Phi Beta Kappa's[17] he shall love — The Delphi's he shall spurn.
> And when unto some handsome maid, the boy shall go to woo,
> He shall be cock of all the walk[18] a cock-a-doodle-doo!

Some of the footnotes were simply quotations from Wayland's article (though the source was listed facetiously as *Oriental Magazine* rather than *American Baptist Magazine*). But some of the other notes are significant:

5. "The obstinacy of infants, of such I mean as are not of the elect, bears a strong resemblance to the obtuse hearts of those sinful men who are destitute of grace" (Bishop Butler).
9. "The best way to conquer a restive horse is to take him to the stalls at an early period after breakfast and there confine him and beat him above the ears with a hickory club till dinner time. If he does not then knock under, the better way is to knock him down" *(Lessons for Grown Horsemen).*
10. "If the spannel still refuses to set the game and will flush, you may be assured that he is fed too high. To correct him successfully, you shall confine him to his kennel and *starve out* the bad qualities and, my word for it, he'll flush no more" *(London Sporting Magazine).*
11. "Excessive punishments in the nursery are not commended. Whipping may sometimes be useful if the child be old enough to appreciate the objects of punishment. Nurses, however, should be careful where they inflict flagellations and in no case should strike the head. A slight *spanking* on the *tail* of the little urchin has often been known to be productive of valuable results" *(Mrs. Crompton's Lessons to Nurses).*
13. "When you have carried all your points and subdued the natural obstinacy of the child, and he begins to beg, it is a good plan to kiss him and give him some light diet, such for instance as bread and butter" *(Mrs. Wiggins to Her Kinsfolk).*
18. "My son is a snorter, a very fine lad, The pattern and image of his very dear dad: He goes with the best people their darters to woo; He's a rip-snorting stayer, a cock-a-doodle-doo" *(Poems of David Crocket, M.C.).*

Presumably the author of this satirical poem, by lumping together in these footnotes parodies of advice on training children and animals as well as philosophical and evangelical wisdom (not to mention the poetry of Davey Crockett), was speaking in the language of anticlerical Jacksonians. Sylvester Southworth, if he were the writer, must have known that many of his readers in Providence would sympathize with this ridicule of a pious evangelical father whose philosophical cant seemed simply a mask for cruelty and self-righteousness. While we lack evidence to explain why Wayland's article aroused public outrage, we might speculate that he was either somewhat outdated in his rigor or that he was simply more thorough in his practice than most fathers. The outrage could be that of persons who, while they had experienced considerable domination from their fathers, had not been so completely subjugated as to develop a reaction formation. These individuals would appreciate the conflict and humiliation of the son and, contrary to Wayland's expectations, would take his side. Perhaps this helps to explain the psychological dynamic which leads Americans to identify with the underdog.

We have no record of Francis Wayland's reaction to these articles though he must have been aware of them. Doubtless they simply reinforced his belief that too many people in the Age of Jackson were not practicing the proper methods of child rearing.

It would be unfair to leave the reader with the impression that Francis Wayland was so cruel and tyrannical as Southworth believed or as a twentieth-century reader of Wayland's piece might assume. He was capable of unbending at times in play with his children. Nor did he mind if some thought him undignified when they found him indulging them in his home or in public. His sons, describing the behavior of their father toward them in the years 1834-38, wrote: "Often, as they [Frank and Heman] met him on the college green returning from his study, he would carry them home on his shoulders much to the amusement of those who witnessed this exhibition of parental affection." And, "many a visitor was surprised when calling upon the president at his residence, to find him stretched at full length upon the floor engaged in a frolic with his boys and abundantly enjoying their wild delight when they were allowed to believe that they had conquered their father."

They had not, of course, conquered him, and never did. But neither did his conquest of them prevent them both from having full and successful careers according to the standards of their day. It would be interesting to know what steps Francis and Heman Wayland took with their children when they first engaged in a contest of wills. We have no accounts, but we can guess. Child-rearing patterns tend to have a long persistence, especially within devout evangelical families. Historians need to consider more carefully the relationship between child-rearing patterns and American social and political behavior.

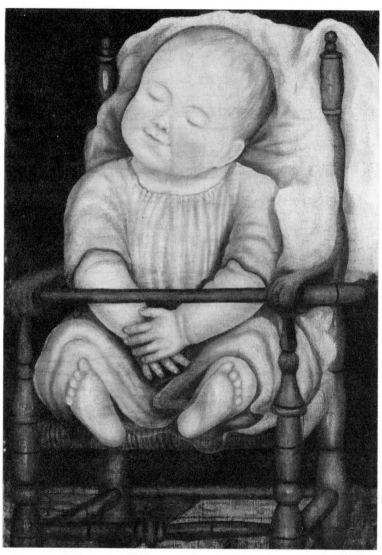

Baby in Red Chair, 1800-1825. Artist unknown. (courtesy of the Abby Aldrich
Rockefeller Folk Art Center, Williamsburg, Va.)

6

Infant Abandonment in Early Nineteenth-Century New York City: Three Cases

Paul A. Gilje

Infanticide and infant abandonment are both ancient practices. Greeks and Romans had few qualms about murdering unwanted babies, and most non-Western societies have countenanced some infanticide. Though the Judeo-Christian tradition views destruction of an unwanted child as a crime, for centuries impoverished or unwed mothers in Europe occasionally killed their offspring because they feared the drain on family resources or were unable to face the ignominy of having an illegitimate child. Many another woman took the less severe step of abandoning her baby on a doorstep in the hope that the infant would receive better care in a different home.

European historians have diligently examined the phenomena of abandoned and murdered babies. There are recent studies of foundlings in Renaissance Florence and eighteenth- and nineteenth-century France and of English infanticide from the Middle Ages to the nineteenth century. There is an interesting comparative study on infanticide in England and New England from 1558 to 1803, but for the most part American historians have not addressed the problem.

Infanticide and infant abandonment, however, occurred in America from the colonial period onward. During the eighteenth century in New England there were several well publicized cases, which prompted local ministers to expound upon the necessity of a virtuous life and the miseries of "that soul Sin of Uncleanness," or fornication. Four of these sermons were published, and each highlighted both the repentence of the young mother who murdered her illegitimate child and the severity of judge and jury. After the American Revolution babies were still murdered or abandoned by desperate mothers; newspapers and court records readily attest to this. Reports occurred intermittently of newborn infants who were found floating in rivers, who were left exposed to the elements in the cold winter, or who were strangled, cut, and even mutilated. Notices of abandoned babies also appeared — a less sensational crime, perhaps, but still offensive to sentimental notions of motherhood.

The legal system frowned upon both infanticide and abandonment of babies. Triggered by concern over the social discord during the Elizabethan era, prosecutions for infanticide increased in the late sixteenth and early seventeenth centuries. A law passed in 1624 strengthened this trend; it stipulated that when a single woman concealed her pregnancy and later gave birth to an infant that died, she was obligated to prove she had not murdered the child. Although this statute was rigidly enforced at first, there is evidence suggesting that by the eighteenth century the letter of the law was more severe than the practice. Peter C. Hoffer and N. E. H. Hull argue that the decline in the conviction rate for infanticide during the eighteenth century in the Anglo-American world was connected to the emergence of affectionate parenthood among the elite, making it increasingly difficult for judge and jury to believe that a mother would willingly murder her offspring.

Yet it was not until the end of the eighteenth century that the new liberal attitudes led to changes in the law. England dropped the provision that concealment of an illegitimate child was proof of guilt in 1803. Several American legislatures acted sooner. After the Revolution the notion that mothers were the best guardians of the republic's virtue reinforced the romanticization of motherhood, and it became even harder for lawmakers to believe a woman could harm her child. Massachusetts altered the infanticide law in 1784, and Pennsylvania passed a bill in 1787 placing the burden of proof on the prosecution. Other states, however, took longer to act. New York, in the absence of a statute to guide the courts, lacked any precedent until 1818 when a judicial decision clearly established that, unless proven otherwise, the court had to take the word of a mother who stated that her child was born dead. Yet, despite the transformations in attitude and law outlined above, infanticide remained an atrocity condemned by magistrates and the public.

Likewise, in the eyes of the law, abandoned babies were viewed as outcasts. English poor laws, followed in early America, ensured a harsh welcome to foundlings by making the local parish responsible for supporting any individual born within its precincts. Unwanted children thus taxed the entire community. By the early nineteenth century in the United States, there were calls for the establishment of foundling hospitals to house and raise discarded children. Those who advocated setting up such institutions, which already existed in Europe, argued that the hospitals would cost less money than other forms of relief and that infanticide would also be decreased. But most people's attitudes did not change that radically, and there was only limited sympathy for both mother and child. Many opposed creating a public home for abandoned babies, claiming that it would encourage sexual license and illegitimacy. Both those for and against foundling houses agreed that women who murdered or abandoned their infants were unwed mothers wishing to hide their shame from the world.

Why *did* mothers want to get rid of their children? Historians who rely mainly on literary evidence basically agree with the traditional view that single women were attempting to protect their reputations. There is some support for this position in the court records of infanticide cases in England and New England, but such records indicate only the cases brought before the magistrates, and they contain a built-in bias. The infanticide law of 1624 was geared toward prosecuting the mothers of illegitimate children. It was much more difficult to obtain evidence and prosecute a married woman who might claim that she had accidently smothered or "overlaid" her infant. Another perhaps more compelling reason for infanticide and abandoning children was poverty. Studying the records of abandoned children in eighteenth-century France, Claude Delasselle states that as many as 20-30 percent of foundlings were legitimate and concludes that there was a positive correlation between grain price increases and the number of abandoned babies in Paris. This statistical evidence is supplemented by letters of parish priests attesting that the parents of abandoned children were incapable of providing for them.

Poverty was also a cause of infanticide and abandonment of children in the United States. There was a sharp increase in the number of such cases reported in 1819 and 1820, a period when economic panic created intense hardship for the poor. An unusual and extended comment on the subject appeared in a New York newspaper in June 1820. The author complained that "almost every week" there were reports "from the coroner of an inquest held on the body of some infant born alive, but cruelly exposed to die in some neglected part of our city and suburbs." Periods of economic depression, however, were not the only times when hard-pressed Americans felt compelled to commit infanticide. In Schenectady, New York, a free black woman was charged with infanticide in 1810. In her confession she asserted that she had murdered the child because "she thought it would be happier out of the world than in it, where its mother had a hard lot and it would have the same if alive." Such direct evidence from mothers is rare.

Three sets of documents from 1818, 1820, and 1822 in the New

York City Municipal Archives, however, outline the reasons why some women were willing to abandon their babies. These records represent only a small sampling of all the infant abandonment cases in New York City, but they are among the few pieces of detailed testimony available for the period. Surprisingly, none of the women claims to be hiding the shame of an illegitimate child. Two of the women assert that they were married and were unable to provide for the infants because their husbands were absent. All three cases remind us of the inadequacies of early nineteenth-century poor relief. The Irish woman, whose handwritten note is still kept with the records of the case, feared the Protestant upbringing of the public almshouse and wanted to leave the child at the Catholic bishop's home. The other married white woman, Catherine Archambeau, describes how she was shunted from one boardinghouse to another before the birth of her child. Her baby was born in the almshouse, but within three weeks she moved out to yet another boardinghouse. While there she decided to leave her infant burden at the door of a total stranger. The third case, involving a black woman, was somewhat different. The child was avowedly illegitimate. The mother insisted that she knew who the father was and that the only reason she left the child in a cellar entry was to have it sent to the almshouse. There, she felt, city officials would investigate the matter and legally bind the father to pay her for the support of the child.

As with all historical documents, it is possible to question the truth of the testimony. Only a woman in a desperate situation would abandon a newborn infant, and, when confronted by disapproving authorities, she might feel compelled to invent a husband or to claim that she was only trying to coerce the father to pay child support. Whatever the truth, the magistrates recognized that these women needed assistance and not punishment. The cases were handled leniently and, as in many similar circumstances, they were not pursued very far. The vulnerability of these mothers as poor women is evident in each case. Saddled with children they could not support, faced with an economic system that had no place for them, left by men who had no time for them, these women took the most humane course available: they left their offspring to others, in hopes that the children might somehow find better lives.

That these cases occurred at a time when the status of both motherhood and childhood was rising is especially noteworthy. In the years after 1800, middle-class moralists relentlessly underscored the importance of mothers to the nation's stability. Women were the ones, in Catharine Beecher's estimation, who would provide the moral ballast for weathering the "storms of democratic liberty," who would

educate the next generation of republican statesmen, who would civ-
ilize the untamed West. Mothers would also, through carefully regulated nurturance of children, create sober, industrious, self-controlled
citizens while simultaneously providing a refuge from the hurly-burly
of the marketplace. This charge, then, was the heavy responsibility
entrusted to women — a responsibility many accepted, as evidenced
by the involvement of middle-class women in various temperance,
church, maternal, and reform organizations.

But beneath this middle-class world of idealized moral saviors lay
another realm, a realm inhabited by poor women who were less ballast
for democratic storms and more a part of the storm itself. If the rise
of a market society created the necessary preconditions for the separation of male and female spheres in the middle class, if that process
brought on the re-evaluation of womanhood and motherhood noted
above, that same process also left poor women subject to the fickle
winds of economic change. More and more people began to move from
place to place adjusting to variable economic conditions; some searched
for opportunity, others merely struggled for survival. Within this
changing world poor women had the fewest options. The cases below
show clearly that, although all three women had enjoyed some geographic mobility, they had made few economic gains. Moreover, an
impoverished woman's position worsened with a pregnancy that placed
new constraints and restrictions upon her. In such circumstances the
middle-class ideals of motherhood were impossible to maintain. The
early nineteenth-century poor relief rolls, which contain countless
women left or abandoned by husbands, suggest that thousands of
women shared experiences similar to those of the women documented
here. While these three women are not necessarily representative of
all women left by husbands and lovers, or of all women in nineteenth-
century America who felt compelled to abandon their infants, their
cases do reveal an underlife in New York and the plight that all too
many women faced.

Frances Black & Theresa Wardlow v. Bridget McGlone

City of New York
April 1, 1820   *Hibbin's Watch*

City of New York ss. Frances Black No 204. Elizabeth Street & Theresa
Wardlow of No 204 Elizabeth Street being duly sworn say that between 9 &
10 Oclock last evening in the Bowery they met with the woman now here
present calling herself Bridget McGlone with a young child in her arms
which she said she was going to Bishop *Connolly* with — that deponents
told her that they would shew her the *Bishops* House & she Bridget followed these deponents to the Bishops House which is in the Bowery nearly

opposite to Rivington Street in the 8th ward & there she Bridget halted & lay the child down on the stone in front of the door & then knocked at the door & then started & ran off that she was directly afterwards pursued & overtaken & then denied knowing any thing about the child & still denies it to be hers.

Frances Black
Theresa Wardlow

Sworn the first day of April 1820
    Chas. Christian-
      Justice

Catherine Gelson and Ann Broaden each of 94 Banker St. being sworn, each for herself says — that the female infant child this morning shown them in the old Alms house is the child of Bridget McGlone who resides in the same house with deponents (occasionally) has frequently seen her give it suck.

their
Catherine "X" Gelson
Ann "X" Braden
marks

Sworn before me
    Chas. Christian
Further witness, Henry Abell, Alms House

New York March the 27th 1820
To the care of the Revd Bishop Connolly this baby kind Sir it is poverty and hardship that occations my intruding on you. I am the Mother of the baby I cant earn a living for myself and the baby four children I have beside this one I am going to the Country and in the course of a few months when please god I recover myself I will come to town and, Sir i will make myself known to you she is Cristian by the Cathelis priest her name is Alice McGlone I dont know whether her father is living or not he is gone from me since before she was born and since that I have no house or home nor any of earning to live by I trust my poor forsaken infant to the kind mercy of god and your goodness and dont let it go to the Alms House as I would not like it to be brought up to the religion the[y] have there Although I am at present a poor member of the roman Church I hope the Almighty will pardon me as it was severe hardship that compels me to take this step I remain With thanks to my kind benefactors and lord will bless both and them

Bridget brot out of prison in the afternoon & admits the child to be hers & of having left it as above states that she has no regular place went last week to the Mayor for relief & he gave her an order to go to the Commissioners — She has three children now in the Alms House — She got a little drunk yesterday on Beer

Taken herein 1st of April 1820

The mere circumstances of leaving the child on the Biship's stoop — *with intention* that he should take care of it. — is not an indictable offence. if any injury had happened to the child it might be but this woman appears to be reduced to the extreme of wretchedness & I do not see any good purpose to be answered by any further persecution of her —

V.W.

Dismissed.

The People v. Catherine Archembeau

City of New York
November 24, 1818

Catherine Archembeau brought up charged with having exposed her infant child to perish being examined says — that she was born in Portland, State of Massachusetts — that she has resided within the State of New York about two years. That she was married on the seventh of May 1817 to Charles Archembeau a baker — that he left her last March to go to France with intention to return — that at that time they both boarded at Mrs Jones's in Roosevelt St — that immediately after her husband went to France she went to service at Mr McGowan's, tavern keeper, Fly Market. Staid there about four week's, then went to live with Mrs Ely, Liberty Street; Staid there six weeks; when she left Mrs Ely's went to the Alms house and was there delivered of a female child on the second of this month, November, Left the Alm's house about a week ago and went to board at Mrs. Palmer's No ten Ferry St — Left Mrs Palmer's yesterday morning and went to Mrs Ely's in Liberty St where she slept last night — On last friday night, 21st inst, left Mrs Palmer's about dusk, took her child with her, it being then nineteen days old, went to a street, which she thinks is called Harrison St, went into the gate way of a house, and left the said infant on the back stoop of said house, the name of the inhabitants of which house she does not know, nor had any acquaintance with them. Having so left the infant she returned to Mrs Palmer's and told her she had left it with a woman to nurse. Did not return to the house in Harrison Street, nor heard nothing of the child or what became of it until this day. She was called by Mr. Abell. Don't know what has become of the child, or who has it.

Catherine Archambeau

Taken by me
24 November 1818
Chas. Christian

Witness — Sarah Palmer No 10 Ferry St
Mary Bond, a servant
No ten Harrison St
Halbert Rene, a Baker
Maria Osborn — No 12 Harrison St
Elenor Elwood, corner of McDougul and King Streets
   Each of the above are necessary to this chain of testimony.
Dismissed

People v. Mary Anderson Exposing her child in the street & abandoning it

11 Feby 1822

City of New York ss: Eunice Kagland of No 44 Henry, St being duly sworn
says that Susan Mann and Milley _____two black girls living No ____
Chapple St between Anthony & Thomas St had an infant child aged about
four months in their care, said to be the child of Mary Anderson a black
woman living at Doct Jacques in Broadway which child is said to have
been left exposed in the Street & from there taken & brot to the Alms
House. On deponents making enquiry of said Milley this day about the
child she was told that it was given to the mother last evening.

Sworn the 11th of
Feby 1822   Eunice Ragland

City of New York ss: Mary Anderson a Black being Examined says that she
is 30 years of age was born in Baltimore & there married & after her husbands death she came on to this city where she has been five years — she
lived at Mechanic Hall & there got take for child & Jno Battis a b[l]ack at
Mechanic Hall & father of the child sent her to NewBurgh to lay in where
the child viz a female child was born on the 11th of Oct last after she got
well she returned to the City & put the child to board with Amelia Dawson
the yellow woman now here with whom it remained till last evening when
Exs [Mary Anderson] & said Amelia went in Duane St & there Amelia laid
the child in a cellar entry — It was laid there so that it might be taken to
the Alms House & the father made to support it as he refused to do any
thing for her & she was not able to do for that & one other child that she
has — She told Battis that she would do so & then he would have to take
care of it.

Taken the 11th of
Feby 1822

Amelia Dawson says that she had the child to live with her & last evening
took it to the mother Mary Anderson who said that she would lay it at
some gentleman's door — Exs [Amelia Dawson] left Mary so in the street
alone by where she handed her the child & Exs [Amelia Dawson] walked
about the streets alone till Mary returned saying that she had put the child
at a door where it would be taken care of — & from there Ex [Amelia Daw-

son] & Mary went to an oysterstand corner of Warren & Broadway. Exs [Amelia Dawson] did not see *Ann Johnson* from the time she parted with her at the corner of Duane St & Broadway previous to handling the child to the mother, till this morning.

Amelia "X" Dawson
her mark

Taken the 11th of
Feb 1822

The Commissionors wish to have the persons removed from the County[—] doubt whether an indictment in this case would be necessary.

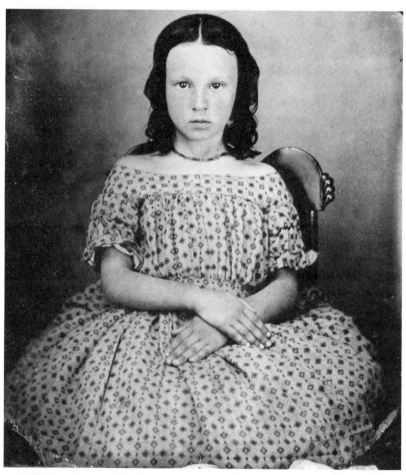

Alice E. Foh (?), age 7, 1860. Photographer unknown. (courtesy of the Museum of Modern Art, New York City)

7

Socializing Middle-Class Children: Institutions, Fables, and Work Values in Nineteenth-Century America

Daniel T. Rodgers

Nothing is more certain or important about childhood than the leaving of it. Ultimately the protective layers of dependency essential to infancy must be stripped away, swaddling clothes exchanged for new roles and costumes, and children propelled into adulthood. Above all, the propensity to play must somehow be supplanted by a willingness to assume those burdens which by common consent form a society's work. These processes of leave-taking are not incidental to childhood; to a great extent they form its very core, shaping children from their earliest years to anticipated adult consequences. The essential history of childhood is thus not so much the story of a stage of life as the story of the ways in which the young have been hurried out of it and shoved and socialized into adult roles and responsibilities.

Central as that socialization process is to the shaping of culture, its history remains largely unwritten. A good deal of the story has been fragmented along institutional lines. Excellent histories of schools, of the public treatment of dependent and delinquent children, and of family structure crowd the shelves, but histories of the ways in which these and other child-shaping institutions have impinged as a whole on children are much rarer. The issue has been clouded in another part by the conventions of progress which still run strongly among students of the family and which have tended to subsume questions of the changing social expectations of children under a more limited concern to demonstrate the steady amelioration of child life. In the one reading of childhood, issues of structure and power prevail; in the other, the slow eclipse of cruelty by kindness. But socialization itself remains a surprisingly neglected question in the history of childhood and with it are neglected the critical processes by which cultural norms are perpetuated across the expanse of time and generations.

What might the outlines be of a history of child socialization in nineteenth-century America, written with an emphasis on one of the period's most central and conspicuous values, that of work? What notions of duty and responsibility did those entrusted with the shaping of children strive to impart, through what configuration of pressures and institutions, and with what effect? How, in short, did a work-obsessed nation undertake to reproduce itself in its children?

Any such history would clearly be multiform, for chasms of class and geography ensured that children of differing backgrounds came upon work and lessons in work in radically different ways. But no group stands in a more critical relationship to these questions than the Yankee bourgeoisie. Its hold over nineteenth-century institutions of learning, its ability to shape the canons of respectable values, and its control over the shifting nature of work itself have been generously documented. If the perpetuation of work took place, always with a large dose of necessity and coercion, in the nation's shops, farms, and factories, the perpetuation of the peculiar *valuation* of work which often seemed to characterize the nation began elsewhere — in the schoolrooms and nurseries in which northern middle-class children were handed on, albeit sometimes in importantly transformed ways, the convictions of their parents.

The discussion that follows focuses on three of the socializing forces which bore with particular weight and particular historical visibility upon such children: the routine of schools, the child-rearing advice pushed upon book-reading parents, and the fiction written to shape and satisfy the imagination of middle-class youngsters. These are bookish matters and that their history reflects corresponding shifts in the actual experiences of children is clearly open to question. Descriptions of nineteenth-century classroom practice are scarce, while the voluminous statements of educational intent with which historians traditionally fill the gap are far from trustworthy guides to what children in fact experienced in their schools. Culling the most widely printed and presumably widely read family-management guides from the chaff of more ephemeral opinion, essential (and neglected) as it is as a first step, does not touch upon the much more knotty question of the relationship between printed exhortation and family practice. Still more murky is the relationship between the imaginative world of children and the deliberate attempts of adult story writers to stock their daydreams with proper materials.

In the end, the classroom hours endured and the gallons of ink didactically expended may have counted for far less in such children's lives than the historically much more elusive influence of peers and unwritten parental example. But it would be rash to think that nineteenth-century teachers, family counselors, and story writers were wholly wrong in giving their work the immense moral force they so strongly assumed it had, or that it was a simple matter for a middle-class child wholly to escape their reach.

At the least the schools, child-rearing guides, and children's fiction — taken together, as they impinged upon the young — can tell us a good deal about changing adult expectations of children, and that history is not one of steadily accumulating progress. What these measures suggest, rather, is a series of major shifts in the definition of work and, by implication, adulthood as they were formally taught to northern middle-class children over the course of the century. Conflicts between systematization and sentiment played an important role in this process. More critically, so did a series of nervous doubts about the directions of social change. Formal child-shaping agencies did not always act in concert; at times, in fact, they fell conspicuously out of step, thrusting contradictory messages at their charges. But together they produced a series of quiet but crucial transformations in the formal socialization of northern middle-class children, successively recasting the meaning of work and adult responsibility in ways that served both to bind the generations together and to wedge them apart.

The first of these transformations was a rationalizing one. It emerged with striking speed in the 1830s; a generation later, though its geographic domain would continue to expand, the outlines of that transformation were virtually complete. Everywhere it intruded into a society in which the socialization of children had been relatively informal, unsystematic, even to a degree haphazard.

Not that earlier generations of Americans had been indifferent to the rearing of children to a clear sense of adult duties. But even in New England, where Puritan legacies of diligent upbringing in a calling retained a good deal of force, caring fell considerably short of sustained, systematic training. If wills were often broken at a very tender age in early nineteenth-century America, they were also indulged in what seemed to later writers an irregular and all too impulsive pattern. The same elements of contest and irregularity dominated much of schooling and apprenticeship as well, as youngsters oscillated between long stretches of fear-induced obedience and bursts of outright rebellion. As for work, if it came early in children's lives, it, too — even in the shops and counting houses of the middle class — was uneven in tempo and dominated by the often explosive quirks of personality. Work and obedience, service and mastership, remained intricately tangled together in early nineteenth-century America, and the socialization of children followed suit in its preoccupation not with system but with submission and authority.

The child shapers who moved rapidly onto the scene after 1830 were impelled, by contrast, by a strikingly different conception of work, marked not by obedience but by self-control, and induced not through fear as much as through the systematic inculcation of habit. The implications of that transformation were clearest in the rationalizing assault launched against the schools in the middle third of the century. That attack took place on many fronts, but from a child's point of view its most important manifestation was the breaking up of the traditional mixed-age schools into new, age-segregated classrooms. Age-grading did not change the essential technique of instruction; in the new schools as in the old, rote learning remained the rule, despite the pleas of some of the school reformers. But age-grading helped work a major revolution in classroom discipline. Even in the most strictly managed of ungraded schools, a child spent most of his school day reading his lessons in relative neglect and only a fraction of it reciting at the front of the schoolroom under the teacher's immediate scrutiny. As the century wore on, however, visitors to urban, graded classrooms brought back reports of a fundamentally different schooling regime in which entire classrooms of children passed as one through a common set of exercises: rising and falling in unison, reciting together in choral sing-song, or conning their common lesson with their bodies locked in precisely the same posture. What age-grading made possible was the introduction into school children's lives of a much more consistent behavioral scrutiny than ever before and a much tighter, habit-ingraining behavioral regimentation.

The most vivid descriptions of the new classroom management methods, it should be admitted, come from schools catering primarily to children of the working class and the poor, and there is little doubt that school superintendents faced with masses of such youngsters were particularly quick to seize upon the quasi-military possibilities inherent in the reorganization of education. "Soft-line" reformers like Horace Mann harbored much more ambivalent attitudes toward regimentation and a much more exalted notion of a teacher's impressive moral force. But their reservations do not seem to have much affected the practical thrust of classroom management. If the discipline imposed upon northern middle-class children was doubtless less severe than that imposed on the children of the poor, there is every reason to believe that in the generation after 1830 these children, too, found themselves increasingly subject to the same desire to rationalize classroom methods, the same growing obsession with orderly and consistent behavior, and the same new psychological faith that disciplined habits systematically laid down in childhood would ultimately bear fruit in the habitual self-control which mid-nineteenth-century writers praised as "character."

Certainly the child-rearing advice and children's fiction absorbed by middle-class households in the generation after 1830 were shot through with these assumptions. Both genres expanded very rapidly in the second third of the century, flooding the presses with stories explicitly for children and counsel explicitly for parents where there had been only a trickle before. Not all the new books clothed new advice. Several of the most widely read child-rearing guides of the second third of the century continued to push the theme of submission, insisting (much as traditionalistic schoolmasters insisted on the point of swift, vigorous response to schoolroom insubordination) on the paramount obligation of parents to steel themselves for the battle of wills by which children were to be decisively broken to obedience. But just as classroom management shifted from contest to system, family counsel took the same tack. In place of what now seemed a haphazard pattern of neglect punctuated by efforts at wrenching behavioral conversion — or "fondness by fits and starts," as Lydia Maria Child put the indictment of impulsiveness so central to the new advice — the majority of the most widely circulating mid-nineteenth-century child-management guides tried to inspire parents with an ideal of far more orderly family governments, constructed out of kindly but consistently enforced punishments and carefully graded, habit-forming lessons in industry, duty, and restraint.

Finally, through their new storybooks children found themselves directly besieged by much the same advice. The nascent children's fiction industry, which grew rapidly after 1830 on the efforts of Jacob Abbott, Samuel G. Goodrich, Lydia Child, and others, was built on tales consciously shorn of the dramatic and fanciful elements on which a child's restless imagination was feared to fester. Instead children's story writers filled their stories with deliberately commonplace events, a pervasive reasonableness, and insistent moral choices. Painstakingly, storybook heroes learned to set aside play for the deeper satisfactions of perseverance, just as they painfully learned to resist the temptations laid everywhere in their path by their more reckless peers. Child readers drawn into such stories found idleness locked in war with industry, desire set against patience, grandiose daydreams in contest with sober, everyday duties — all the temptations of impulse pitted against a code of habitual self-control.

Even if one grants a good deal of slippage between the printed word and the actual lives of children, the result of these developments was to surround those northern middle-class children who grew up in the second third of the century with a set of socializing pressures and

interlocking moral injunctions critically different from those impressed upon children before them. The common themes which ran
so insistently from schoolrooms to storybooks flowed in part from the
fact that the rationalizers of child life were to some extent an interlocking set of persons, Whiggish in social outlook for the most part,
intellectually stirred by the still vital currents of the moderate En-
lightenment.

But the most important foundation of commonality was a set of
widely shared assumptions about the nature and ends of moral education. Moral training, the most influential child shapers increasingly
insisted after 1830, was to begin with habit — with systematic enforcement of what William T. Harris later called for the schoolmen
the "semi-mechanical" virtues of industry and regularity — drummed
in by the regular discipline of schools and school-modeled homes,
reinforced by didactic storybook example, and finally apotheosized in
the overblown rhetoric of school declamations until habits became
second nature. The expected upshot was not only a firmly internalized
moral code but a highly cautious one. Its "key words became control,
self-discipline, and restraint," Michael Katz writes, and its expected
result was an adult imbued with a firm sense of duty, a deep distrust
of impulse, and an ingrained capacity for patient, self-denying industry.

For all its coherence, however, this remains a surprising faith,
launched as it was at the onset of a headlong regional plunge into
economic growth. What expansive, mid-nineteenth-century capitalism
presumably needed most from its white-collar children was managerial
skill, entrepreneurial adventurousness, perhaps even a dash of reck-
lessness. Yet what such children were taught was diligence, self-discipline, and restraint, and the resulting contrast between economic
needs and highly cautious moral aims is a measure of the power of
nineteenth-century child-shaping matters to concentrate anxieties,
particularly those concerning social change. If optimism and economic
calculations helped fuel the calls for the rationalization of child life,
so still more did fear: a nervous distrust of the destabilizing effects
of economic expansion and an intense desire to isolate children from
what seemed to be the increasing disorderliness of social life.

These nervous elements were particularly clear among writers for
children, whose distrust of the shifting economic order was explicit
in their warnings against ambition, their strenuous cautions against
peer example, and their repudiation of the city in favor of isolated,
village settings. Among nineteenth-century educators the mixture of
confidence and anxiety was more complex. But for all the school
reformers' willingness to compare their schools to smoothly running
machines, to stress the economic advantages of classroom lessons in

regular and punctual habits, and to equate economic and moral advance, their faith in progress was qualified, and it frequently shattered into nightmares of social breakdown. To the child shapers the evidence of disorder often seemed omnipresent: in the failures of family discipline, in the swelling and often riotous populations of the cities, in the scrambling of social relations, and in the overheated competition for place and advancement. Even as they tried to socialize the young, the child shapers found it hard to see children and society other than in opposition. In the end, their hopes for tightly disciplined schools and families which would armor children with habits of self-control were inverted reflections of their apprehensions of chaos.

For all the child shapers' efforts to inject a new ethos of restraint into child life, and thence into northern society, their success should not be exaggerated. There were important rifts among those charged with the socialization of children, and everywhere there was resistance to the systematizing advice. From old-fashioned district schools, to old-fashioned evangelical tales designed to wrench children's hearts to conversion, to old-fashionedly impulsive parents — alternately shoving their children forward under the noses of astonished European visitors and punishing them severely — there remained a vast amount of the older, unrationalized world into which a child could escape. But the effect of the first of the nineteenth-century revolutions in child socialization was, nonetheless, to inject a new set of values and institutions into northern middle-class child life and, in so doing, to mark off the potential experience of a generation of children from the experience of those who had preceded and those who would follow them.

The first link in this structure to give way was that which at first glance seems least consequential: the fiction aimed at middle-class children. By the 1850s the simple didactic story formulas of the 1830s and 1840s had already been transformed by a major infusion of melodrama and sentiment. Forty years later, when the revolution in the children's fiction aimed at middle-class households was complete, the old stories, with their insistence on work as discipline, had virtually disappeared under an avalanche of new stories which often talked of work in the same terms but showed it as an act of heroism. Jacob Abbott's six-year-old children, painstakingly learning to sort nails and straighten their desks under the watchful supervision of parents and teachers, were displaced by youngsters who leapt aboard runaway trains, thwarted bank robberies, melted adult hearts, and redeemed aged misers. This shift from a code of restraints to one of heroic impulse was a quiet, almost unnoticed revolution. But if children's fantasies have any relation to the materials they are offered, it represented the collapse of the mid-nineteenth-century child shapers' work in a particularly strategic part of children's lives.

Two central fantasies dominated fables for middle-class children by the last third of the century. Storybook figures, if boys, found themselves swept away from adult help and suddenly called to acts of single-handed heroism. If girls, they found themselves confined by a set of emotionally constricted, often much too hard-working parental surrogates whom they won over to their purer, more sentimental creeds of spontaneous love. Few of the children's story writers who worked these veins were fully aware how deeply subversive their stories were of the authority of adults or the ethics of habit-built restraint. Yet the fact remains that beneath the late nineteenth century's earnest talk about discipline, book-reading children were being drawn into dramatic fantasies of heroism. Even as children were admonished to repress their desires, they were being quietly stoked with daydreams of conquest. In children's fiction in the last third of the century, rationalism was all but swept away by a flood tide of impulse and sentiment.

In less dramatic ways in the last third of the century, sentiment made inroads into the other child-socializing agencies as well. Among educators, the kindergarten movement, Francis W. Parker's much heralded reforms at Quincy, Massachusetts, and Edward A. Sheldon's equally famous proselytizing of the "object method" at the Oswego, New York, normal school — all of which caught fire in the late 1860s or 1870s — represented a widely noted pedagogical revolt against drill and memory in the name of a more natural, child-centered education. Similarly, in many of the most widely circulated child-rearing guides published after 1860 the familiar complaint of parental inconsistency gave way to a new alarm at the over-forced pace of schools and the excessive restrictions of households, a new concern with parental coolness, and fervent praise of a mother's quickly responsive love.

Perhaps the most dramatic sign of the new drift in child matters was the decision of the American Sunday School Union in 1894 to put its authority behind a massive distribution of Elizabeth Grinnell's *How John and I Brought Up the Child,* a romantic, markedly permissive account of the manner in which a child could be raised virtually on the strength of love alone — never made "victim to regularity," virtually never punished, never set to tasks except those stripped of their forbidding character by transformation into play. In advice such as this, work as traditionally conceived retreated (as in children's stories) to the vanishing point. "Let every child, before going to bed, hold a high court of revelry . . . devoted to romp, to dance, to shout, to sing, to riot, and to play," one of the most widely used home pediatrics manuals of the late nineteenth century advised. The spontaneity of childhood was not to be cut short by abrupt adult intrusion but preserved, extended, even turned into a model for emotion-cramped parents themselves.

In ushering tasks and habits so cavalierly out of children's lives, writers in the new vein did not mean to lessen the elements of moral training; rather, they urged the preeminence of the imagination in the shaping of children. In his introduction to Felix Adler's widely used *The Moral Instruction of Children* (1892), William T. Harris could reiterate the still familiar case for systematic discipline, but Adler's own primary concern was to demonstrate the efficacy of myth and heroic literature in infusing a child's mind with ethical impulses, ready to spill over into everyday life. For all Adler's preference for ancient fable over concocted melodrama, that was precisely the rationale with which children's story writers justified their turn toward more heroic, imagination-compelling plots, just as it sanctioned the rapidly growing place of games and play in child-rearing advice. By the 1890s, book-reading parents could hardly miss the argument that training in restraint was less essential than the encouragement of a child's moral will and active moral energies. It was not drill that made the man, one heard, but a vigorous, ethically-stocked imagination.

This striking shift in ideas does not seem to have been the product of any major shift in the social composition of the child shapers. Even the children's fiction writers, through whom the sentimental and heroic possibilities of childhood were raised to their highest pitch, fit as comfortably into the region's moral establishment as had their mid-nineteenth-century predecessors. If a Horatio Alger or an Oliver Optic borrowed heavily from the dime and nickel novel literature which swirled below the threshold of middle-class respectability, they were as orthodox in their political and economic values and as tightly enmeshed in a network of Sunday schools, child-saving agencies, and business patrons as a Horace Mann or a Jacob Abbott before them.

What had changed were not the social origins of the child shapers but the nature of their anxieties about society itself. Economic dislocation and specters of urban chaos had helped push child shapers after 1830 into systematic antidotes to disorder. But as mercantile capitalism gave way in the last third of the century to its industrial successor, and farms and shops were pushed aside by factories, machinery, batteries of clerks, and tighter work discipline, many of those nervous about change grew increasingly nervous about systematization itself. Drawn particularly to child matters, they turned their fears into idyls of pre-machinery childhoods where children's spirits had not

been ground under by the drill of Gradgrindish schoolmasters or crushed
by premature labor. Child shapers who worked the sentimental veins
were as anxious as their predecessors to segregate children from a
world they distrusted, but they tried to do so by carving out not refuges
of order but oases of the imagination where drama and spontaneity
could rule unhindered by systematization run to excess. The result
was a literature which served at once to train children and to enlist
them in a web of adult fantasies — to project upon children, and thus
lay bare, much of the covert restlessness and half-disguised anxiety
within late-Victorian America. As childhood was made over into the
antithesis of the machine, one can watch the thrust of middle-class
nervousness shift, towing children in its wake once more.

From a child's point of view, however, the direction of change may
have been less important than its unevenness. Schools, child-rearing
guides, and children's fiction moved at markedly different rates in the
last third of the century, the schools apparently most slowly of all.
Despite the attention granted the innovations at Quincy and Oswego,
they seem to have made only a minor dent in conventional classroom
practice. Kindergartens were absorbed into public school systems only
through the jettisoning of most of their romantic ideological under-
pinnings, while object teaching, initially designed as a way to draw
the interests of children into the learning process, quickly degenerated
into a complex rote pattern of its own. Normal school educators and
an occasional progressive superintendent might decry the ubiquity of
drill and memory, but classrooms seem to have proved highly resistant
to change. The inroads of sentiment into the child-rearing guides, as
the American Sunday School Union's action showed and the women's
magazines reaffirmed, was much more complete. Yet well after the
turn of the century, there remained a markedly defensive tone to the
newly permissive counsel and a sense of major resistance from parents.
Only in children's stories were the older, disciplinary notions of growth
into adult responsibilities abjectly routed.

But the result of this unevenness was to thrust upon many children
a markedly contradictory set of injunctions: classroom lessons in system, discipline, and restraint on the one hand, and storybook codes
of heroism, impulse, and spontaneous love on the other. Certainly
fantasy and everyday life have never coincided for children, nor have
they ever found the way to adulthood unequivocally charted. But the
fact remains that northern middle-class children who grew up in the
last third of the century found formal child-shaping agencies considerably more out of step, the chasm between adult-encouraged daydreams and adult-imposed discipline vastly wider, and the meaning
of work far more ambiguous than had the children who had preceded

them. Between schools and storybooks, the creed of system and creed of sentiment, the experience of a generation of children was fractured in a particularly visible and distinctive way.

Finally, at the turn of the century the configuration of socializing forces bearing on northern middle-class children rapidly shifted and broke up once more, slowly to settle into yet a third pattern, and redraw once again the essential meaning of work. Part of what occurred — and the development has made the years immediately after the turn of the century particularly difficult to characterize — was simply a vigorous eruption of the contradictions implicit in late nineteenth-century child training. With regard to older children, romantic attitudes swelled rapidly, spilling out of juvenile fiction in striking new forms. In child study, instinct theory pushed aside old assumptions of exercisable mental faculties; an organized play movement gathered sudden strength, pushing playground games and a host of team sports into the normal experiences of children; a new generation of child-centered educators simultaneously began to inject a number of seat-unlocking curricular reforms into the schools. No authority drew these new emphases together with more influence than G. Stanley Hall's *Adolescence* in 1904, and within a decade boy-rearing guides were shot through with its themes of recapitulative instincts, the imperatives of play and hero-acting, the irresistible swell of the group spirit in adolescence, and the need for tolerance of irregular, organic growth.

Yet at the same time that themes of instinct and activity burgeoned with regard to older children, infant-rearing advice turned in precisely the opposite direction: toward alarmist complaints of sentiment and indulgence gone to excess, a reassertion of the primary role of habit, and an insistence on new forms of calculated, aseptic, and highly scheduled infant care. L. Emmett Holt's immensely popular nursery handbook of 1894, *The Care and Feeding of Children*, set the tone for the new rationalistic advice which quickly saturated the child-rearing handbooks and women's magazines. Such recommendations derived their authority in large part from the widespread end-of-the-century alarm at the extent of infant mortality among the malnourished and presumably overdosed babies of the urban poor. But the upshot was to shoulder a new set of public health authorities and hospital doctors into the ranks of the experts bearing on middle-class families and to impress on anxious book-reading mothers a new set of routines essentially derived from hospital practice: pure food at carefully timed intervals, vigorous, antiseptic scrubbing, and tolerance of a great deal of crying.

Beneath the unreconciled debates between experts, however, the more important turn-of-the-century development was an explosion of interest in the social aspects of child life. Boys' fiction broadcast the new emphasis on groups and teamwork in an outpouring of sports stories, school stories, and scouting stories after 1900, which all but eclipsed the single-handed heroes characteristic of late-nineteenth-century fiction and injected a new, explicit insistence on conformity into child life. The profession of youth work grew with equal speed, spawning Epworth Leagues, scouting troops, and youth clubs of all sorts to organize the tangled world of peer relations. Somewhat more slowly, but still more consequentially, the burgeoning public high schools moved in the same direction to offset the self-centeredness of traditional education through an array of athletic and extracurricular activities, mock governments, and civics lessons gathered together under the banner of "social education." In the process, early twentieth-century child shapers recast once more the essential lesson in work as it was to be formally inculcated in northern middle-class children — no longer as discipline, nor as heroism, but as socially cooperative teamwork.

The accomplishment was accompanied by a fanfare of hope. Progressive child shapers wrote optimistically of their achievements in preparing children for a world grown rapidly more complex and interdependent. But that optimism did not wholly disguise the legacy of nervousness so central to nineteenth-century child shaping, nor did it reduce the importance of the debates over child socialization in revealing the shifting currents of middle-class social anxiety. In their rapidly rising concern to cultivate the social impulses of the young and to turn schools and youth groups into models of the team spirit, progresive child shapers were moved not only by dreams of a more cooperative (or, as others had it, more corporate) social order but by a deep concern that twentieth-century America had badly wrenched its traditions of social cohesion in its spectacular leap from village to city. Fears of social atomization — of economic and political selfishness run amuck in blatant corruption, of adolescent delinquency and family breakdown, particularly among the immigrants cast abruptly into turn-of-the-century American cities — haunted many of the most prominent progressives who took part in the child-shaping debates. Nervously displaced upon the largely middle-class youngsters closest at hand in the new high schools and youth organizations, fears such as these helped provide a cutting edge for the aggressive organization of adolescent free time and the calls for social education.

Perhaps the clearest manifestation of anxiety, however, was the child shapers' uncertainty as to whether the essential thrust of their efforts should be to integrate children into society or to preserve them from it. In vocational training for working-class children, progressive child shapers leaned heavily toward the side of integration, trying to tie adult occupations and child life far more tightly together than ever before. But with regard to middle-class children their aims were far more ambiguous, and the most important upshot of their efforts to forge the young into model social republics was probably not to ease the passage into adult work roles but the reverse — to isolate middle-class children in an age-segregated world of peers and social clubs, sports and scout hikes, from which the exits were by no means immediately obvious.

Certainly the theme of insularity grew increasingly pronounced in writings for and about children. It pervaded boys' story writing as the old codas in which boys were formally ushered into an adult world of jobs and marriages were lopped off, leaving heroes in timelessly suspended adolescence. Child-rearing counselors quietly endorsed much the same segregation of youth and age in their recommendations of an isolated, rarely disturbed nursery, a regular adult-free play time, or a backyard shed exclusively reserved for a child's gang. Progressive child shapers envisioned child life as a series of deliberate rehearsals for adulthood. But anxiety about the directions of social change helped make it seem logical that those rehearsals should take place increasingly removed from adulthood itself — that preparation for the world and segregation from it should go hand in hand.

In all these ways, progressive child shaping repeated themes common to almost a century of formal child socialization: the critical role of social anxiety in generating designs for children, the repeated displacement of fears rooted elsewhere onto the children of the middle class, the continued tension between the impulse to educate children into adult mores and to seize on them as a corrective for adult faults.

How much all of this really mattered in children's lives, how deeply schools and stories and a sprinkling of advice shaped character and values, is a much more difficult question. The analytical temptations are abundant: to see some of the essential ingredients of cautious late nineteenth-century Victorianism as emanating from childhoods spent among the books and schools and injunctions of mid-nineteenth-century child shapers; to see something of the new restlessness that marks northern middle-class culture after the turn of the century in the peculiar contradictions of late nineteenth-century child socialization and its escalated stakes of sentiment and adventure; perhaps to see one of the roots of William H. Whyte's organization man in the social transformation of the twentieth-century high school. Such may be the stuff of half-truths at least, and perhaps a few useful hypotheses, when the history of childhood and the history of adulthood are pieced back together.

But what seems clearest about formal child shaping is the fact of repeated change — sometimes strikingly abrupt, always more complex in its directions than progressive theories of family history would have it. From the campaign to systematize child life, to the quieter efforts to stake out childhood as a refuge from industrialism, to the drive to organize adolescents into models of social cooperation, waves of reform rolled over nineteenth- and early twentieth-century children. If those successive assaults on social ills through an attempted reformation of society's children did nothing else, they shifted the configuration of formal institutions pressing upon children, exposed them to altered formal canons of value, and redrew (particularly through the schools) some of the normal parameters of child life. In fashioning children for the society that adults envisioned, the child shapers cut off children in important ways from the society that adults made. And in doing so they helped to divide children themselves into generations of distinctly different experience. When the full history of child socialization is written, that process should be central to it.

Untitled photograph of two girls, c. 1900 New York, by Gertrude Kasebier. (courtesy of the Spencer Museum of Art, University of Kansas, gift of Mrs. Hermine M. Turner)

8

Families and Foster Care: Philadelphia in the Late Nineteenth Century

Priscilla Ferguson Clement

In 1883 Mrs. S. and her children Ella and John, ages three and thirteen, respectively, made their home in the streets of Philadelphia. Her husband deceased and herself unemployed, Mrs. S. tried desperately to keep her homeless family together. Another impoverished mother gave up trying to care for her youngest child, seven-week-old Ethel D., in 1894, and left the girl a foundling in the streets of the city. Officials of the Children's Aid Society who took charge of Ethel eventually traced her mother's identity and discovered that, although the woman had abandoned her infant daughter, she continued to support her two older children with earnings from her labor as a servant in "houses of ill fame."

Children from indigent families such as these provoked a growing concern among many urban Americans by the third decade of the nineteenth century. In cities like Philadelphia, impoverished vagrant youngsters were highly visible. As numerous historians have observed, child vagrancy can be accounted for by the operation of such forces as urbanization, industrialization, and immigration. Moreover, scholars of the subject have generally agreed that the thousands of poor children wandering about city streets (Charles Loring Brace estimated their number in New York to be between 20,000 and 30,000) so distressed many middle-class urban dwellers that they began to expand and alter existing child welfare services.

In Philadelphia and other American cities in the eighteenth and early nineteenth centuries, public welfare officials routinely assisted indigent infants by paying their mothers or wet nurses to care for the children at home. Older impoverished children entered the almshouse, where they remained until they could be indentured out to live with families and learn trades. In this era private charitable organizations concerned with children also commonly assisted them in their own homes or, if they were homeless, in institutions temporarily until they could be indentured. However, beginning in the 1820s and 1830s and continuing for most of the rest of the century, institutionalization of children in public or private asylums grew increasingly popular. It seemed to many to be the ideal answer to the question of what to do with the thousands of dependent and delinquent children in cities. Still, home care for the indigent young was never wholly abandoned and gained such vocal supporters as Charles Loring Brace of New York and Samuel Gridley Howe of Massachusetts. Brace, in particular, urged foster care and founded the Children's Aid Society in New York, which in the late nineteenth century placed thousands of poor city children in private homes in the country. Stimulated by Brace's success, reformers in Philadelphia and other cities founded comparable foster care agencies.

In recent years a number of historians have singled out for particular emphasis one of the goals of the child welfare reformers of the mid- to late nineteenth century: their desire to morally reform and socially control poor children. Whether they placed children in institutions or in country homes, the reformers stressed removal from "immoral" city streets and placement in a more controlled, disciplined environment where the youngsters could learn middle-class values. Although this social control argument seems equally useful in explaining the motivations of both the advocates of institutionalization and those who favored placing out in families, it has been applied almost exclusively to the former. Few studies of nineteenth-century foster care agencies have been made. In addition, advocates of the social control thesis sometimes explicitly, but more often implicitly, assume that the new child welfare practices of the nineteenth century served only to oppress indigent youngsters. Few historians have suggested that institutions for children and foster care agencies in the last century may have served a necessary social function.

In this essay I shall describe foster care, the noninstitutional method of caring for poor children, as it was practiced in one city in the last decades of the nineteenth century. Although in these years fewer children were placed out in families than were institutionalized, foster care increased in popularity, and by the mid-twentieth century had become the most prevalent method of assisting poor dependent children outside their own homes. I shall approach the subject by examining two foster care agencies in Philadelphia between 1880 and 1905 — first from the perspective of their middle-class administrators and then from that of their lower-class wards. In this fashion I hope to suggest the social functions these charitable organizations served in the urban community. The two foster care agencies are the Home Missionary Society of Philadelphia (today called the Inter-Church Child Care Society) and the Children's Aid Society of Pennsylvania.

Members of the Methodist Episcopal Church originally founded the Home Missionary Society not to care for dependent children but, rather, "to promote the extension of the Redeemer's kingdom by means of preaching, prayer, exhortation, and by the establishment of Sabbath schools, distribution of Bibles, Testaments, Tracts, and other books of a religious nature." The history of the Home Missionary Society closely parallels that of other city missions founded by members of evangelical religious groups in New York and elsewhere: their original purpose was to spread the gospel among the poor, but gradually they began to supply the needy with food, fuel, and clothing as well. About mid-century, members of the Home Missionary Society, as they performed their religious and relief-giving duties among the poor, increasingly observed children "of parents who were either too poor or too vicious" to care for them properly. As a result, about 1854 the Home Missionary Society of Philadelphia assumed the added task of placing poor dependent children in "good Christian homes" in the country.

Unlike the Home Missionary Society, the Children's Aid Society of Pennsylvania had always cared for children exclusively and never had any direct religious affiliation. It was organized in 1882, about three decades after Charles Loring Brace founded the first Children's Aid Society in New York. Like its predecessor, the Philadelphia agency sought to place all street and institutionalized children in private homes so "they might lose the mark of pauperism."

Not surprisingly, the leaders of both the Home Missionary Society and the Children's Aid Society were substantial middle-class citizens. Most of the men on the Home Missionary Society Board of Managers were prosperous businessmen or professionals, while the leaders of the Children's Aid Society were women of good social standing.

The middle-class leaders of both these child-care agencies expected to save both souls and money by placing poor children in good homes. The degraded surroundings in which dependent children lived corrupted their morals and sent them to "drunkards' graves" or to "the prison or almshouse." The "degradation and the corrupting influence of the city" also failed to prepare the child for an independent, useful life and instead kept him dependent on charity — an expensive business. "The best way to fit a child for an active, industrious, wage-earning life is to place it in an active, industrious wage-earning family." These arguments reflect both a deep fear of "pauperism," which to nineteenth-century Americans meant immorality, laziness, and excessive reliance on charity, and a pervasive optimism that such "pauperism" could be eradicated. Leaders of both agencies confidently predicted that the destitute city children they placed in good homes in the country would either be adopted or would become (or marry) self-sufficient farmers, ministers, doctors, or businessmen. The agency directors planned to transform their lower-class wards into responsible middle-class citizens through the placing-out system.

As they defended family placing, logically enough the leaders of both the Home Missionary Society and the Children's Aid Society argued strongly against permanent institutionalization. Agents of both societies used institutions for temporary care, although they preferred to keep their wards in families at all times. The directors of the Children's Aid Society in Philadelphia warned, much as did the members of their sister society in New York, that children raised in institutions were trained to be dependent. An institutional regimen failed to prepare youngsters for self-sufficiency in the outside world.

Whether they were defending the family plan or attacking institutionalization of children, it is clear that the leaders of both agencies were most concerned about the amelioration of social ills. Improper environments, whether urban or institutional, were the focus of their concern. Rescuing children from such environments and placing them in more healthy ones was for them a social and moral reform. Although traditional humanitarianism remained one of the motivations for their child-placing work, it was not the primary one. They were concerned less with the individual, personal problems of the child than they were with the social and moral problems he or she posed in the larger community. The objectives of these agency leaders seemingly confirm the arguments of the social control theorists.

While the leaders of the Home Missionary Society and the Children's Aid Society utilized the family plan in order to achieve moral and social reform, they implemented it in different ways. The major difference was that the Home Missionary Society placed out with indentures, and the Children's Aid Society did not. Under the Home Missionary Society system, the parent or guardian of a child first indentured him or her to the agency, and in doing so officially relinquished all right to visit and to correspond with the youngster. Then the society indentured the child to a responsible family until the age of eighteen or twenty-one, when he or she returned with one of his foster parents to the society's office and there received $25 or $50 (depending on how the indenture read) in the presence of the society's agent. While the indenture agreement said nothing explicit about a work relationship, implicit in the contract was the understanding that the child would work for his foster family in return for his food, clothing, education, and the monetary payment that concluded the indenture. After 1882 the society began to place a small number of children without indentures. The agency simply directed parents to foster families in the country; the mother or father of the child and the foster parent then made their own agreement.

Children's Aid Society officials refused to use indentures because of their inflexibility; since an indenture contract was permanent, it was difficult to do what was often necessary for the safety of the child: remove him or her on the mere suspicion of ill-treatment. Flexibility in removal was an advantage of the Children's Aid Society program of placing children without indentures, either with families that agreed to care for them without charge or with foster parents who accepted payment for the youngsters' board. From 1882 to 1893, agency officials placed most children in "free" homes where they probably worked for their "caretakers." However, after 1893 the new, young, innovative Children's Aid Society agent, Homer Folks, substantially increased the number of children placed in "board" homes (where payment was made for the youngsters' care) in order to prevent them from being overworked.

As for the methods of selection of foster homes, the Home Missionary Society's procedures appear to have been the most haphazard. Probably any well dressed person who appeared in the agency's office could get a child within hours. For a time the Children's Aid Society's procedures were comparable: it found homes simply by advertising in newspapers and by "keeping an open office." However, after 1890 the society, prodded by Homer Folks, required prospective foster parents to fill out an application that dealt with their "material fitness" (e.g., how much property or livestock they owned). A questionnaire sent to six neighbors and a personal investigation of the "caretaker's" home by the Children's Aid Society agent provided information on the family's "moral fitness."

Once a child was placed out, both agencies required that his or her foster parents report twice a year in writing on the child's progress as well as admit an agency visitor to see the youngster alone. The Children's Aid Society also requested pastors and teachers of agency wards to send quarterly reports to the society, and after 1900 the Home Missionary Society did likewise.

In the years between 1880 and 1905 the two agencies sought to keep in contact with the approximately 5,400 children they placed out. Of this number, the Home Missionary Society was responsible for 1,400 and the Children's Aid Society for 4,000.

In all probability, most of these children were born in the Philadelphia area. The records of the Home Missionary Society agent indicate that a majority of the children aided by that agency were born in or near the city, and there is no reason to suppose that the birthplaces of youngsters assisted by the Children's Aid Society were substantially different. On the other hand, neither agency bothered to note the birthplaces of the parents of children placed out; of course, these mothers and fathers may have been foreign born. It is certainly surprising to find these social agencies so little interested in the ethnic backgrounds of their wards, and this in an era when many welfare officials expressed concern about immigrants and the social problems they allegedly created.

Although both agencies were avowedly nonsectarian, probably the majority of those they placed out were Protestant. The evidence about the religious background of the boys and girls assisted by the Children's Aid Society is the most explicit. When the society was first founded, it did not care for any but Protestant children largely because of the remonstrations of Catholic church officials. They feared that the society might seek to convert Catholic youth by placing them in Protestant family homes. Later church leaders relented and agreed to agency placement of a few Catholic children in Catholic family homes exclusively. Catholic officials never commented on the foster care program of the Home Missionary Society, and since that agency obtained much of its support from Protestant churches and employed as its chief agent a Protestant minister, it seems likely that it cared primarily for Protestant children. On the other hand, in view of the evangelical nature of the Home Missionary Society, it may have occasionally taken charge of Catholic youngsters in order to place them in Protestant country homes. Nevertheless, with only a few exceptions, it appears that the Children's Aid and Home Missionary societies generally assisted Protestant youths, while the Catholic welfare agencies in the city probably aided most needy Catholic youngsters.

The majority of children in the care of both agencies were native-born Protestants, and, in addition, about 90 percent were Caucasian. Still, there is no evidence that either society deliberately discriminated against nonwhites. Actually the opposite may have been true since both agencies cared for a higher percentage of blacks than their proportion of the city's population would warrant. Between 1870 and 1890 the number of blacks in Philadelphia hovered at just under 4 percent of the total population, while 10 percent of the boys and girls assisted by the Children's Aid and Home Missionary societies were black. The extreme poverty of the city's nonwhite population in the late nineteenth century, which has been well documented elsewhere, many in part account for the relatively significant minority of black youths in the care of the two agencies.

Most of the largely native, white Protestant children in the care of these two agencies were old enough to work, yet still young enough to need family supervision. Three-quarters of the Home Missionary Society children and one-half of the Children's Aid Society wards were between the ages of six and fourteen. Such boys and girls could render useful service in the home or on the farm, but they probably were too young to be able to obtain a wage-paying job in either place. In all likelihood, children over the age of fifteen could find regular jobs. Very few such adolescents (3 percent) entered the care of the Home Missionary Society because they no doubt preferred to be paid for their labor rather than be bound by indenture to work for nothing till age eighteen or twenty-one. The Children's Aid Society aided more older children: about 19 percent of its wards were over fifteen. This agency probably placed out more teenagers because it permitted them to work for wages in homes approved and supervised by the agency. There were very few young children in the care of either society: just 18 percent of the Home Missionary Society wards and 28 percent of the Children's Aid Society wards were under the age of five. Such children were too young to work, and perhaps the Home Missionary Society turned them away because the farmers and householders who sought cheap laborers through the society's indenture system specifically requested older boys and girls. The Children's Aid Society may have been more willing to accept very young children because of its boarding-out system: a foster parent could be paid to care for a child until he or she was old enough to earn his or her keep, whereupon the youngster could be transferred to a "free" home.

Thus the "typical" child in the care of both agencies was a native-born Protestant white boy or girl between the ages of six and fourteen. Customarily parents or other relatives brought such youngsters to the Home Missionary Society or to the Children's Aid Society. Over 90 percent of the children who entered the Home Missionary Society's office and two-thirds of those who approached the Children's Aid Society came accompanied by relatives. Only the latter agency established contact with a sizable minority of its wards (one-third) through the intervention of charity workers, public welfare officials, the courts, or the police. Since the Children's Aid Society deliberately cultivated relationships with the city's various welfare agencies, it is understandable that this agency received many referrals from such groups. Nevertheless, what is really significant is that most children entrusted to the care of both agencies were not vagrants picked up by the police nor indigent children removed from their homes by budding social workers, but youngsters whose families deliberately relinquished them to child care agencies.

The economic and social conditions of the families who entrusted their sons and daughters to the two agencies explain much about their motivations. Their occupations alone indicate that most were poor. In the Home Missionary Society Indenture Books, all the parents whose occupations were noted worked at low-paying jobs, the fathers as laborers and the mothers as servants or seamstresses. Many others were unemployed. Not only occupational evidence but the comments made by the parents themselves confirm their indigence. The most common reason given by all parents for relinquishing their children to the Home Missionary Society was poverty. For example, Mr. S., a widower, worked as a hostler at a New Jersey hotel, where he earned $10 a month. On such wages he could not afford to support both his aged parents and his three children, and consequently he relinquished the youngsters to the Home Missionary Society.

Mr. S.'s plight exemplifies another characteristic of the parents of agency wards: most were trying singlehandedly to raise their children. Almost 60 percent of the Children's Aid Society wards and over 90 percent of the Home Missionary Society wards were without one or both parents. Most lived in single-parent households. The Home Missionary Society records indicate that in just one-third such families fathers like Mr. S. were the sole breadwinners, but in the remaining two-thirds mothers alone were responsible for the support of several children. All such indigent single parents faced the difficult problem of caring for their youngsters while they themselves were at work, or, if they were ever unemployed, providing for the children at all. The cases cited at the beginning of this essay serve as illustrations of these difficulties so often faced by single parents. Mrs. S., unemployed and homeless, could not care adequately for her son and daughter, and so she placed them with the Home Missionary Society. The case of Ethel D.'s mother reflects the special problems of poor working women in this era. Child-care expenses were particularly burdensome for them because as servants and seamstresses, almost the only jobs open to women in this era, they generally earned even less than did the lowest-paid male laborers. Ethel's mother, a servant, managed to support two children, but she could not care for a third and so abandoned the infant to the care of the Children's Aid Society.

Thus the pattern emerges of desperately poor parents, many of them without spouses, trying unsuccessfully to support large families. In the absence of public relief as we know it today (most of which now goes to the very same groups that were in the nineteenth century so often in need: female-headed, single-parent families), indigent parents in the last century turned desperately to child welfare agencies. Such agencies promised to do what poor parents could not: feed, clothe, and educate their children in a family setting.

While many impoverished parents voluntarily relinquished their youngsters to the Home Missionary Society or to the Children's Aid Society, most viewed foster care not as a permanent solution to their child care problems but simply as a temporary expedient. Thus over half of the children placed with both agencies remained in foster care for three years or less — most of them for only a few months. When children left the care of these agencies, they typically went back to live with their families. Fully 55 percent of those who left the care of the Children's Aid Society and 47 percent of those who emerged from the Home Missionary Society placing-out program returned to live with relatives. Here the examples cited at the beginning of this paper are again instructive. The case of Ethel D. is exceptional, for she did what both agencies hoped their wards would do: she lived many long years with a foster family which eventually adopted her. In contrast, Ella and John S. followed the typical pattern of agency wards: they stayed in foster care for a few months and then returned to live with their mother.

Thus foster care provided temporary relief from the burdens of child support for many poor families. Once indigent parents improved their economic situation, they asked the agencies to return their children. Both agencies apparently complied, although they often did so grudgingly. According to Children's Aid Society officials, thirteen-year-old Martin D. had "worthless" parents, but, nevertheless, the agency returned him to them within a year of his placement because Martin was "homesick" and his family anxious to have him home.

While children were in the care of these agencies, whether for a few months or many years, agency officials saw to it that they received some schooling and employment experience. Visitors for both agencies noted that almost all children attended Sunday School regularly and public school for the six-month term characteristic of farm communities. Thus most agency wards obtained the rudimentary elementary and spiritual education that Children's Aid and Home Missionary Society leaders, in common with most Americans, valued. As for employment experience, most children placed out by the two agencies labored as servants or farm laborers — girls as the former and boys as the latter. Since foster families generally treated agency wards as hired help, they did not provide them with any sort of professional training as they might their own children. Thus foster children did not enter typically middle-class occupations as child-care agency leaders hoped they would. However, the youngsters did acquire in their temporary country homes some skills which may well have proved useful to them once they left the care of these agencies.

Typically, foster children assisted by these agencies acquired their education and work experience in not one but several foster homes. This is particularly true of boys and girls assisted by the Children's Aid Society: officials transferred them frequently from one foster family to another. Youngsters in the care of this agency for less than a year averaged three placements (two transfers) apiece, and those with the agency over a year averaged between five and ten placements (four to nine transfers) apiece. In contrast, children who remained wards of the Home Missionary Society for less than a year usually stayed in one home and were not moved about at all. Youngsters who were in the care of this society for longer periods of time were customarily transferred just once or twice on the average.

The placement policies of the two agencies explain why one moved children about more than the other. The Children's Aid Society policy appears to have been to board a child in family after family until finally one agreed to keep him or her on without payment. This policy inevitably produced more transfers than did the Home Missionary Society program of making each foster parent firmly agree, by indenture, to keep a child until he or she was of age. Although the indenture plan was disadvantageous in that it made the removal of children from unsatisfactory homes difficult, conversely it did discourage frequent, casual transfers of children and thus minimized the number of major disruptions in their lives. In all probability every transfer from one family to another was a disruptive experience for a child. He or she had to adjust to new surroundings and new authority figures. Thus, while foster care in late nineteenth-century Philadelphia may have provided many needy children with useful skills, it did so in the context of an uncertain and insecure environment.

The family environments in which foster children dwelt were not closely scrutinized by either agency. Both placed their wards in homes fairly close to Philadelphia, so distance did not make frequent visiting impossible. However, budget limitations did adversely affect the visitation programs of both agencies. It was costly to employ persons to travel about visiting children. The Children's Aid Society, which had greater financial resources than did the Home Missionary Society, managed to pay employees to visits each of its wards just twice yearly between 1883 and 1905. In contrast, the Home Missionary Society was unable until 1891 to employ agents to visit all of its wards even once a year. It seems unlikely that one or two visits a year were sufficient to ensure that each child was well placed and well treated.

Still, visitors for both agencies noted that roughly two-thirds of the children they talked to personally were doing well in their foster homes. "Doing well" typically meant that the child was "bright," "happy," "useful," or a "hard worker," and occasionally that he or she had been adopted or was "treated as own." Of course, the visitors were somewhat biased: as employees of the agencies they were probably inclined to report what the managers of the Children's Aid and Home Missionary Societies wanted to hear — that most poor city children profited from the placing-out system. Nevertheless, while the visitors emphasized "success stories," they did not entirely ignore "failures" (children who lied, stole, absconded). The characteristics of children in both categories are revealing. They indicate that the youngster most likely to be content in a country home was a boy or girl who entered the care of the agency under the age of ten and stayed in foster care for four or more years. Probably younger children were the most pliant, and when they remained in country homes for several years, their new families had the greatest opportunity to mold them. On the other hand, the child who most frequently rebelled against foster care was a boy who became a ward of the agency when he was eleven or older and stayed in country homes for three years or less. It is not surprising that older boys who were probably accustomed to the casual freedom of city street life did not take kindly to the more orderly, restrained atmosphere of the country homes where agency personnel placed them. They quickly departed such homes before their foster families had much opportunity to reshape their lives. This pattern of foster child success stories and failures is not unique. In the same era, the New York Children's Aid Society also found that younger children were most likely, and older children least likely, to adapt successfully to the foster homes to which the agency sent them.

The success stories as well as the failures of the Philadelphia Children's Aid Society and the Home Missionary Society bring us back to their basic goals, for agency leaders labeled as successes those who achieved these goals and as failures those who did not. As we have seen, the intent of the middle-class managers of both societies was to remove children, at as young an age as possible, from unsavory urban environments and place them instead in salutary country homes where they would acquire proper moral values and useful skills. Such objectives tend to confirm the arguments of the social control theorists. The affluent leaders of these two foster care agencies did indeed seek to exert social and moral control over lower-class children by removing them from "bad" environments to "good" ones. Humanitarian concerns were of secondary importance to these agency leaders. Moreover, in the long run, the managers of the Children's Aid Society and of the Home Missionary Society achieved much of what they set out to do: by providing most of their charges with religious and elementary education as well as with job experience, they accomplished some moral and social reform.

On the other hand, certain policies of the agencies affected foster children in ways that their managers did not anticipate. Thus the frequent transfers of children from home to home and infrequent visitation by agency employees meant that agency wards led a disjointed existence in a variety of foster homes where they were little protected from ill treatment.

Although these early foster care programs certainly had weaknesses by late twentieth-century standards, these should not be overemphasized. After all, foster care provided needy youngsters with the basic necessities of life when their parents temporarily could not. Short-term emergencies, such as unemployment or illness, plagued poor families and were particularly troublesome for single parents. Those who migrated to Philadelphia from nearby farms or from distant countries could not rely on a network of relatives to assist them during temporary emergencies. To cope with such crises, long before the federal government inaugurated aid to families with dependent children, at least some needy parents in late nineteenth-century Philadelphia turned to foster care agencies. Thus these agencies allowed for new social adjustments to be made in an urban environment. And, as we have seen, they also permitted middle-class Philadelphians to exert social control over lower-class youth. These various functions were not incompatible. The Home Missionary Society and the Children's Aid Society were founded and administered by persons interested in social and moral control, and they were sustained by indigent parents who voluntarily relinquished their sons and daughters to the agencies during temporary family emergencies.

Lewis Hine, "Breaker Boys Working in Ewen Breaker." Mine in S. Pittson, Pa., Jan. 10, 1911. Records of the Children's Bureau (102-LH-1941). (courtesy of the National Archives)

9

Judge Ben Lindsey and the Juvenile Court Movement, 1901-4

D'Ann Campbell

In 1888, nineteen-year-old Benjamin Barr Lindsey had reached his full height of five feet five inches and his maximum weight of ninety-eight pounds. Since the death of his father three years earlier, he had struggled to support a family of five. Finally, weighed down by premature family responsibilities and despondent over his small stature, Ben locked himself in his room, in Denver, Colorado, placed a loaded revolver to his head, and pulled the trigger. The cartridge failed to explode. Suddenly overwhelmed by the realization of what he had just attempted, Lindsey "went back" to his life "with something of a man's determination to crush the circumstances that had almost crushed me." Soon, his chance came. While clerking in a law office and studying for the bar, Lindsey became acutely interested in the plight of children sentenced to prison for minor offenses and sought to champion their rights. Appointed county judge in 1901, he launched a personal crusade to establish a special court — a juvenile court — where young male offenders might be placed on probationary status and given a chance for rehabilitation. The philosophy and procedural techniques he developed during these years played a major role in promoting the highly successful juvenile court movement that subsequently spread across the nation and made Lindsey a prominent figure in American life.

Ben Lindsey was born in Jackson, Tennessee, in 1869. Soon after, Ben's family moved to Denver, Colorado, because his parents, reared in Presbyterian households, had converted to the Catholic faith. As Ben later explained, "In a southern town like Jackson, to be a Catholic was to be almost ostracized." Because no Catholic high school existed in Denver, Ben soon left to enroll in the preparatory department of Notre Dame University. Two years later his promising career as a scholar, theologian, and orator was cut short by the news that his father, quite ill, was no longer able to finance his son's expensive education. Ben returned to Jackson, Tennessee, to live with his Presbyterian grandparents, who placed him in Southwestern Baptist University, where he took courses in the prepatory school. Forced to defend his religious beliefs, both at school and at home, Ben developed a fighting spirit that remained with him throughout his life. After two strenuous years, Ben graduated from Southwestern and returned to Denver, determined to become a top lawyer.

Young Lindsey was shocked by the condition of his family. His father was deeply in debt, and poor health made it impossible for him to support the family. Instead of entering high school, Ben joined his brother Chal in securing jobs to help out. Several months later, the elder Lindsey committed suicide, slashing his throat with a shaving razor. Suddenly, at the age of eighteen, Ben was the head of a poverty-stricken family of five. To help his mother feed his younger brothers and sisters, he took on three poorly paying jobs at once and lived on a diet consisting mainly of gingerbread and molasses. The next year, with the world closing in on him, Ben attempted to end his life.

Following his abortive suicide attempt, Lindsey found a respectable job as a law clerk with Denver attorney R. D. Thompson. Shortly after going to work, he discovered that Thompson's firm had been appointed by the county court to defend two twelve-year-old indigents accused of burglary. Lindsey, in charge of preparing the brief, visited the "clients," and found them playing poker with their cell mates, a professional safecracker and a horse thief. By talking with the boys, he learned that children could be placed in jail for picking coal off the tracks or for invading a farmer's pigeon coop near their school — the kinds of things Lindsey as a child had probably done repeatedly! Shocked, he finally arranged to have the boys released in his custody. Almost by accident, Lindsey became the first probation officer in Colorado.

Determined to become an attorney, Lindsey studied law and in 1894, at the age of twenty-five, he was admitted to the Colorado bar. He formed a partnership with Fred W. Parks and the firm soon made a local reputation by winning a series of victories as defense lawyers. In 1899 Ben was appointed public administrator, or guardian of orphans and dependents of deceased persons, in Arapahoe County by Charles S. Thomas, the candidate he had actively supported for governor. Now he was able to concentrate on helping children. For the next two years Lindsey acted as guardian of orphans and other wards of the county. While powerless to stop most of the injustices, he witnessed the varying misfortunes of children. Such memories increased his determination to lead a crusade to help children. Appointed county judge in January of 1901 to fill an unexpired term, Ben Lindsey finally had his chance.

Not long afterwards, Judge Lindsey sat listening to a case involving "some musty old mortgaged furniture," when an assistant district attorney interrupted the proceedings to ask a favor. Would the judge take just a moment to dispose of an open and shut case of theft? Lindsey consented and the public official brought a trembling teenager, Tony Costello (a pseudonym), before the court. Caught in the act of stealing coal off the railroad tracks, Tony offered no defense. Lindsey, having no legal choice, sentenced the boy to a term at the state reform school. Upon turning his attention back to the mortgage suit, he suddenly heard "the most soul-piercing scream of agony that I ever heard from a human throat." Tony's mother was hysterical. Startled and alarmed, Lindsey and the assistant district attorney hurriedly conferred and agreed to suspend the boy's sentence and release Tony in his mother's custody.

Unsure about the legality of his decision, and concerned about Tony and his mother, Lindsey set out to investigate the entire affair. He began by visiting the Costello home, a filthy two-room shack. Stretched out on the only bed, the father lay dying of lead poisoning which he had contracted while working twelve hours a day in a smelter. In Lindsey's words, the Costello family was "damned by poverty, going down in slow starvation." The judge realized that Tony had taken the coal to heat his home. After seeing these squalid conditions, Lindsey vowed to save the Tony Costellos of Denver.

Lindsey searched for a legal basis for granting children special treatment. Digging through the state laws, he came across the School Law of April 12, 1899. Section four stated that children under fourteen, or those between fourteen and sixteen who could not read or write the English language or were not holding full-time jobs, "shall be deemed a juvenile disorderly person and be subject to the provisions of this act" if they got into any trouble.

While the law was intended only for the disciplining of school children, the unorthodox judge realized its wider implications. Lindsey explained his discovery: "A juvenile disorderly person! Not a criminal to be punished under the law but a ward of the state to be corrected as *parens patriae.*" He immediately called the office of District Attorney Henry A. Lindsely, reported his discovery, and requested that all children's cases be transferred to his county court. Because Lindsely knew that most justices did not like to handle these troublesome cases, he willingly agreed to make the adjustment. Thus, in an irregular, informal manner began the Denver Juvenile Court.

Only 10 percent of the juvenile delinquents in Denver between 1901 and 1904 were girls. Lindsey apparently did not feel he could handle these "more difficult" problems, as he referred to them. Consequently he arranged for a female probation officer to sponsor their rehabilitation. Lindsey kept promising that someday he would write an article with the title, "Why Girls Go Wrong." His only such attempt was a one-page analysis published in the *Ladies' Home Journal* in 1907. It was not very enlightening.

Lindsey recognized that he must build a broad base of support to accomplish his goals to help wayward boys. To win the respect and cooperation of the "juvenile delinquents" became his first important task. As juvenile judge, he had two choices: 1), he could place a child on probation; or 2), he could send him to reform school. In 80 percent of the cases, Lindsey opted for probation and developed an intricate program to rehabilitate children. Every other Saturday morning approximately 200 boys on probation attended an informal conference, a "snitching bee." Lindsey explained to his boys that they could "snitch" on themselves and still not violate the boys' code of never tattling on others. Using slang terms, he cloaked his lectures in "boyville" language. Winning their attention, interest, and respect, Lindsey also encouraged the boys to seek summer jobs and become responsible citizens. He even arranged for some of them to work in the local beet fields during the summer to earn extra money. Both businessmen and boys profited from these experiments.

To each Saturday session, the probationers brought a report card, on which their teachers had ranked their performance in school as excellent, good, fair, or poor. Lindsey congratulated the boys who received excellent and good ratings, tried to build confidence and strength in the ones whose performance had been ranked only fair, and placed those receiving a poor rating on the 5 o'clock docket. After the others left, Lindsey met all boys listed in the poor category on an individual basis. Trying to understand each boy from "heart to skin," Lindsey developed an uncanny talent for discovering the root of a child's problem.

While Lindsey gained a great deal of satisfaction and success from his probation experiment, he knew that he also needed the cooperation of the boys sent to the state reform schools as well as of the city gangs. Not until he had exhausted every other possibility would Lindsey send a boy to reform school. When a delinquent was sent, the judge tried an "honor system." He offered the boy a "square deal," gave him commitment papers, and sent him unescorted to the reform school. In some cases the juvenile had to travel through town and ride the bus. In other cases the experiment involved a train ride. Never did Lindsey inform the warden to expect the delinquent. All arrived at their destination.

Especially interested in gang psychology, Lindsey scoffed at reformers for trying to break up gangs. He divided gangs into two groups: good and bad. Only bad gangs, Lindsey felt, caused the law officials trouble. To prove his theory, Lindsey called in two probationers, the only members of a particular gang caught stealing coal. He asked the pair to round up the other boys for a talk — no strings attached. He wrote the city gang a note stating that the boys delivering his message had not "snitched," but that Judge Lindsey needed to talk to all of them. The following morning, the entire gang reported.

Lindsey explained that if the boys would not help him, he could not help them. "Kids, we are all in the same boat, and if anybody swipes anything again, I am going to get fits, and the first thing you know, you will be getting a new judge up here that will hike you all up . . . ," he stated. Then and there he organized a Little Citizens League; its members pledged they would clean up the streets. Rule number one stated that if a boy broke a law, he should come to Lindsey for help. In the next three years, over 200 volunteered to talk with Lindsey and became members of his snitching bee. In addition, every boy tempted by an adult to engage in an activity prohibited to minors (i.e., smoking, drinking, gambling, robbing, playing hookey) immediately reported the incident to Judge Lindsey.

By acting as a teacher, minister, physician, and judge, by addressing his boys in a paternal, at times even fraternal manner, Lindsey won the trust of his boys and the respect of many community members. Several members of humanitarian and charity organizations, surprised by Lindsey's rapid success, publicly endorsed his efforts. School officials, pleased with the drop in truancy, decided to cooperate with Lindsey by filling out report cards and arranging a series of night classes for boys working full time. Policemen, marveling at Lindsey's ability to stimulate gangs to patrol the streets and crack down on crime, applauded his achievements. Several businessmen, astonished and relieved to discover a reduction in robberies and petty thefts, wrote Lindsey that they no longer needed as many daytime detectives to watch the railroad tracks and department store merchandise. Finally, taxpayers learned that Lindsey had actually saved the state money under his experimental program. Governor James H. Peabody, addressing state legislators, stated that Lindsey — by cutting down on the number of official trials and by letting boys travel unaccompanied by a law officer to reform schools — had saved the state $88,000 over the preceding three years. It was no small wonder that journalists and newspaper reporters throughout the nation began referring to Ben

Lindsey as "The Kid's Judge," "The Just Judge," or "The Denver Boys' Best Friend."

Lindsey was acutely aware of the value of good press relations. "The press is of exceptional service if one's work can be dramatized," he once stated. His probation system, snitching bees, honor system, and Little Citizens League captured the interest of the four Denver newspapers. His experiments and picturesque episodical adventures as the "Kid's Judge" provided material for many human-interest stories. Under headlines such as "Bad Boy Reforms," "Judge Makes It a Personal Matter with Incorrigible Boy," Lindsey explained the Denver Juvenile Court system and its goals. He recounted stories of boys living in vermin-ridden cells with hardened criminals, simply because they had stolen coal to keep their families warn. He told of his practice of putting these "desperate criminals" on his lap and having a chat with them. These newspaper stories stimulated interest, generated public sentiment, and obtained for Lindsey invitations to speak at churches, schools, and various community functions. Lindsey seized the opportunity to deliver ringing, stirring speeches. The newspapers printed the laudatory comments, and more citizens requested that Lindsey address their organizations.

Lindsey had succeeded in winning the devotion of his boys, the admiration of the community, and the support of the press. However, he realized that his achievements were mere palliatives; ultimately, the boys returned to the same environment. He realized that he must publicize his proposals until he galvanized the entire community into action. The fight would not be easy: Denver had a national reputation for its gambling halls, saloons, and brothels. The alliance between criminal Denver and the municipal government appeared strong and mutually beneficial. Yet many townsmen, tired of widespread corruption, were willing to help clean up the Queen City of the Rockies. Reform-minded citizens organized clubs which began advocating measures such as the secret ballot and home rule and protesting against fraudulent elections and other forms of government corruption.

In 1901, Lindsey saw a chance to help local reformers and gain their support for his crusade. Reform-minded citizens had launched a campaign against "wine rooms" — dives with back rooms used for a variety of "sinful" activities — and were appealing a local court ruling. Like justices before him, Judge Peter L. Palmer had dismissed a case against Daniel Cronin, a downtown saloon owner arrested for violating the city ordinance against wine rooms. Lindsey asked to hear the case on appeal and reversed Palmer's decision. For days Lindsey's daring ruling dominated front-page headlines. The Anti-Saloon League, the Women's Christian Temperance Union, the Good Government Association, the Law and Order League, and the Methodist, Episcopal, and Baptist churches, all grateful to Lindsey, rallied to his side.

Not content to let the incident drop, Lindsey published a letter in the newspapers pointing out the evil example set for children by wine rooms and gambling dens. He related that he had pleaded with Police and Fire Board members on several occasions to close down the offending enterprises, but that they had not cooperated. When the board members denied his accusations, maintaining that he exaggerated the problem, the judge publicly invited the members to visit his court the following Saturday.

The commissioners arrived to discover a room filled with boys and reporters. Possessing a dramatic flair, Lindsey made the most of his opportunity by inviting the commissioners to sit in the jury box. "I have asked you gentlemen to come here and look at these boys ... ," he said. "You knowingly permitted them to run in violation of the law," Lindsey continued, "yet the child is punished and disgraced. You and the dive keeper, the real culprits, you go scot-free." Having set the stage, Lindsey asked several of his probationers to "testify" or describe the temptations and conditions of the wine rooms and gambling halls. The newspapers published the shocking stories. One paper printed both a front-page cartoon, depicting the board members sweating in the jury box, and an editorial feature story entitled "The Wine Room Is the Gateway to Hades." All four newspapers made the most of the sensational material. Looking back on the affair, Lindsey later observed that sometimes it became necessary to "grand stand with a megaphone."

By the hundreds, citizens began writing and calling Lindsey to ask how they could help. A deft public relations man, the judge organized committees and allocated assignments. Prominent among the committees were the Woman's Non-Partisan Juvenile Court Association, the Denver Christian Citizenship Union, the Juvenile Improvement Association, and the Playground Commission. He also drafted help from the Ladies of West Side Neighborhood Home, the Denver Woman's Club, and the Denver Chamber of Commerce, plus prominent physicians and reformers. His immediate goals were to install baths in the basement of the courthouse; distribute copies of leading boys' magazines; provide exams by physicians and alienists for special cases; establish playgrounds, gymnasiums, fresh air camps, and boys' clubs; and promote trade schools, night classes, and the hiring of boys for permanent and summer jobs.

Within eighteen months, substantial progress had been made in each of these areas. Lindsey's fundamental belief was that the home, the school, the church, and the state should *all* accept responsibility for raising children. His court did not replace the family, but rather supplemented and strengthened it. Parents must be compelled "to do their duty when they are careless" and "to ask for assistance when they are helpless."

Lindsey's reversal of Judge Palmer's decision secured for him the support of the general public but the enmity of machine politicians, members of the Police and Fire Board, and their underworld connections. Because his term would expire at the end of 1902, Lindsey started campaigning without delay. Recognizing Lindsey's popularity with the public, the Democrats reluctantly renominated Lindsey but actively campaigned for his opponent. "The Machine," "Big Mitt," "The Establishment," or "The Beast," as the old-style organization was called, underestimated Lindsey's appeal to the voters. Women could vote in Colorado and several prominent women's clubs fully endorsed Lindsey's efforts. That November, he won the election by 5,000 votes, polling 2,000 votes more than any other Democratic nominee. Lindsey interpreted his victory as a mandate to continue his campaign on behalf of children.

Confident that a majority of Denver citizens would back him, Lindsey began looking for ways to formalize and legitimize the Denver Juvenile Court and its novel methods. He realized that his beloved children's court rested on shaky legal ground and that the machine politicians would soon challenge its constitutionality. While looking for precedents, Lindsey discovered a copy of the *Juvenile Record,* a monthly publication promoting the Chicago Juvenile Court. Lindsey wrote Judge Timothy Hurley of Chicago for advice, and was in turn invited to the 1902 National Conference of Charities and Corrections, which was to be held shortly in Detroit.

Lindsey accepted the offer and appeared at the conference. There he learned about the provisions and problems of the Chicago Juvenile Court. In return, he described his Denver experiences. He astounded his colleagues by explaining that Denver had first established a court, and just now had started building its legal bases. Impressed with both his conviction and intelligence, several juvenile court enthusiasts invited Lindsey to speak in their home states. These invitations served several purposes. Besides gathering ideas and promoting his Denver work, Lindsey established connections with nationally influential figures, such as Theodore Roosevelt, Lincoln Steffens, and Timothy Hurley. Moreover, newspaper reporters pointed out to Denver voters that Lindsey was now moving in national circles and widely publicizing both the city's achievements and its weaknesses. The judge's campaign to establish a Denver Juvenile Court profited greatly from the added publicity.

Armed with data and ideas, Lindsey designed a three-part program. He would ask his fellow county judges — all were afraid by now to refuse to help him — to draw up bills establishing a juvenile court system, a set of complementary and supplementary laws, and a restructuring of the probate laws. Lindsey prefaced his suggestions by asserting, "No juvenile court system can be complete unless there is back of it a compulsory school law, an equitable child labor law, provisions for a detention home for children and an adult delinquency or negligence law." Major elements of his proposals included properly establishing a Denver Juvenile Court system; granting it original jurisdiction in all cases involving children; providing for paid probation officers and court physicians; stipulating that no child under age eleven could be thrown in a city or county jail; and expanding the definition of a juvenile delinquent. Under the suggested definition, the distinction between a juvenile delinquent and a dependent (ward of the court) virtually disappeared. According to Lindsey, it was a short step from stealing coal to stealing groceries, to robbing the till, and finally to committing major crimes. He intended to stop this process during the first stages of its development.

The so-called Lindsey bills used the Chicago statutes as a model but strengthened and expanded these laws to the point of actually changing their nature in two key respects. Lindsey's Colorado law greatly extended the definition of a delinquent and abolished courtroom trials for such offenders. He substituted instead discretionary sentences based on the juvenile judge's (i.e., Lindsey's) assessment of a person's social background and individual needs. Apparently his goal in the second measure was to avoid the stigma and drama of a courtroom trial and a criminal record for his boys. At the time he did not realize that, by so personalizing judicial decisions, he left the youngsters open to abuse by less humane and less sociologically minded justices who decided such delicate matters on the basis of a different set of criteria. For better or worse, however, future juvenile court laws generally followed the Lindsey pattern.

Designing and drafting proposals had been time-consuming but relatively straightforward work; securing their passage promised to be a more difficult assignment. While many members of the state legislature favored the Lindsey bills, the machine politicians were determined to block their passage. Senator William Adams, brother of the president of the Denver Police and Fire Board, announced that the bills would never reach the floor of the legislature. Harry Wilbur, a *Rocky Mountain News* reporter, told Lindsey that the judge's only chance would be to arouse public sentiment by dramatizing the situation.

Lindsey took the advice and began setting the stage by arranging for Wilbur to interview him the following day. The reporter asked Lindsey if his juvenile offenders complained about the conditions of the Denver jail. Lindsey answered that his youngsters had been subjected to kangaroo courts, sadistic jailers, and sexual perversion. The *News*, serving as Lindsey's megaphone, printed the grim story. The Denver Police and Fire Board again denied his charges. Demanding a full investigation, Lindsey invited the governor, the mayor of Denver, and several prominent ministers and members of the Denver Police and Fire Board to a Saturday session of his juvenile court. All three board members claimed previous commitments, but the others came and played right into Lindsey's hands. At first, the guests tried to challenge a boy's testimony. The attempts only revealed further damaging evidence. From then on, these men listened quietly to the accounts until one pastor, nauseated, left the courtroom. Others soon followed. Opposition to the bills ceased.

Lindsey's next goal was to maintain public interest and support in order to ensure the "active, persistent, and earnest enforcement" of his laws. Without proper enforcement, all previous achievements would seem of little consequence. Two local elections would test the strength and endurance of the Denver Juvenile Court system. In the first election, every member on the Denver School Board faced re-election. Without cooperation from the school board, Lindsey maintained, the juvenile court effort might be jeopardized. Losing no time, he devised a two-part plan of attack. He arranged for a reporter from each paper to ask him to evaluate the candidates. Next, Lindsey requested that several prominent Denver women actively campaign in their own communities. As a result of these efforts, every member elected to the school board had publicly pledged to back Lindsey's juvenile court.

The second election, held in 1904, proved more complicated and time-consuming. Late in 1903, Denver citizens ratified a home rule amendment. Because the city and county of Denver were to be carved out of Arapahoe County, new elections were necessary. To continue as juvenile court judge, Lindsey had to be properly nominated and elected as Denver city and county judge. Lindsey's enemies successfully blocked his nomination as the Democratic candidate. His chances seemed dim until several powerful Republicans, delighted to upset any Democratic plan, nominated Lindsey as their candidate. Startled, but not to be outdone, the Democrats now also endorsed Lindsey. Suddenly, seven political parties (all but the Socialist party) nominated the judge, assuring his election that May.

All the elections, however, were contested and many leaders of both major parties had second thoughts about their action. Alarmed, Lindsey called a meeting of leading Democratic and Republican reformers. As a result, Thomas Patterson, owner of the *Rocky Mountain News* and *Denver Times,* threatened to fight the entire Democratic ticket through his newspapers unless his party endorsed Lindsey. In addition, Senator Thomas Wolcott and a handful of young Republicans filibustered during the Republican convention and refused to stop their activity unless Lindsey was renominated. Just to be sure he would win, Lindsey also called a meeting of prominent women, ministers, teachers, doctors, lawyers, charity officials, reformers, and reporters, and pleaded his case and asked for their support. The Woman's Club volunteered to ring doorbells and distribute pamphlets. The ministers promised to deliver sermons on the value of Lindsey's work with children. The reporters offered to write a series of feature articles to keep Lindsey's name in the news. Others arranged for Lindsey to address their groups in a series of honorary banquets. Even his boys, sensing the danger, added to the effort by composing and chanting "Lindsey cheers" throughout the city. Lindsey's victory was overwhelming.

Having built a solid foundation of support, Lindsey had assured his re-election as Denver Juvenile Court judge for the next twenty-five years. His Denver experiences and success also provided the necessary stepping-stone for his advancement to the national arena and the international spotlight. Within a decade, Ben B. Lindsey became the leading proponent and the best-known judge of the juvenile court movement.

Lindsey's qualifications for leading a nationwide juvenile court movement were effectively illustrated during his campaigns in Denver. His impulse was to act first, on an emotional level, and afterwards find a legal basis for his decisions. Consequently, he experimented with a juvenile court system and learned its strengths and weaknesses before drafting a juvenile court law. As finally designed, the Colorado Juvenile Court Law was more extensive and comprehensive than any previous measure. Moreover, Lindsey's all-encompassing involvement and dedication to his crusade, at times becoming almost an obsession, gave the juvenile court movement a full-time leader. Without this total commitment, the juvenile court movement in Denver might have been blocked at a number of critical stages. In addition, Lindsey's innate talent for dramatizing and publicizing his campaigns gained him a tremendous following by Denver citizens. The bitter fights during the local elections highlighted the importance of a wide base of support. Luckily for Lindsey, many community improvement clubs were organized in Denver and available for assistance. Lindsey, however, was particularly effective at tapping the energy and enthusiasm of a variety of reformers and at organizing dynamic campaigns.

For many Denver citizens, Lindsey embodied the Juvenile Court Movement and the essence of Progressivism. He was imbued with a sense of mission, his was a holy crusade to help children, and he was certain that God had given him the talents necessary to ensure its success. The right man, at the right time, in the right city, Lindsey's campaigns touched the hearts of hundreds and galvanized them to work at changing the environment and at making it a better place for adults as well as children.

By thoroughly personalizing the juvenile court system, however, Lindsey left these youngsters open to abuse in the future. Not all probation officers would have Lindsey's benevolent attitude or even his all-consuming interest. Indeed, such abuses ultimately led to the United States Supreme Court's decision *in re Gault* (1967) and the restructuring of the juvenile court system in the late 1960s and 1970s. But in 1904, the juvenile court advocates were not even sure that their campaign would gain nationwide support, or that, once accepted, juvenile courts would prove successful. In fact, only one thing at this time appeared predetermined: Judge Ben B. Lindsey, megaphone in hand, was ready to help organize, dramatize, and popularize the new humanitarian crusade which would extend far beyond the immediate child in distress and into the realms of family relations, educational institutions, and general social conditions surrounding children.

Selected Readings

Albert, Judith. "Transcendental School Journals in Nineteenth-Century America." *Journal of Psychohistory* 9 (Summer 1981): 105-26.

Allmendinger, David J., Jr. *Paupers and Scholars: The Transformation of Student Life in Nineteenth-Century New England.* New York: St. Martin's, 1975.

Barenholtz, Bernard. *American Antique Toys: 1830-1900.* New York: Harry N. Adams, 1980.

Ben-Or, Joseph. "The Law of Adoption in the United States: Its Massachusetts Origins and the Statute of 1851." *New England Historical and Geneological Register* 130 (1976): 259-72.

Bloch, Ruth. "American Feminine Ideals in Transition: The Rise of the Moral Mother, 1785-1815." *Feminist Studies* 4 (June 1978): 101-26.

Boylan, Anne M. "The Role of Conversion in Nineteenth-Century Sunday Schools." *American Studies* 20 (Spring 1979): 35-48.

———. "Sunday Schools and Changing Evangelical Views of Children in the 1820's." *Church History* 49 (1979): 320-33.

Brenzel, Barbara. "Domestication as Reform: A Study of the Socialization of Wayward Girls, 1856-1905." *Harvard Educational Review* (May 1980): 196-213.

———. "Lancaster Industrial School for Girls: A Social Portrait of a Nineteenth-Century Reform School for Girls." *Feminist Studies* 3 (Fall 1975): 40-53.

Brumberg, Joan Jacobs. "Chlorotic Girls, 1870-1920: A Historical Perspective on Female Adolescence." *Child Development* 53 (1982): 1468-77.

Cavallo, Dominick. *Muscles and Morals: Organized Playgrounds and Urban Reform, 1880-1920.* Philadelphia: University of Pennsylvania Press, 1981.

———. "The Politics of Latency: Kindergarten Pedagogy, 1860-1930." In *Regulated Children/Liberated Children: Education in Psychohistorical Perspectives.* Ed. Barbara Finkelstein. New York: Psychohistory Press, 1979, pp. 158-83.

Censer, Jane Turner. *North Carolina Planters and Their Children, 1800-1860.* Baton Rouge: Louisiana University Press, 1984.

Clark, Dennis. "Babes in Bondage: Indentured Irish Children in Philadelphia in the Nineteenth Century." *Pennsylvania Magazine of History and Biography* 101 (1977): 475-86.

Cott, Nancy. "Notes Toward an Interpretation of Antebellum Childrearing." *The Psychohistory Review* 6 (Spring 1978): 4-20.

Cremin, Lawrence. *American Education: The National Experience, 1783-1876.* New York: Harper and Row, 1980.

Demos, John, and Virginia Demos. "Adolescence in Historical Perspective." *Journal of Marriage and the Family* 31 (Nov. 1969): 632-38.

Duffy, John. "School Buildings and the Health of American School Children in the Nineteenth Century." In *Healing and History.* Ed. Charles Rosenberg. New York: Science History Publications/USA, 1979, pp. 161-78.

Elson, Ruth Miller. *Guardians of Traditions: American Schoolbooks of the Nineteenth Century.* Lincoln: University of Nebraska Press, 1964.

Farber, Bernard. *Guardians of Virtue: Salem Families in 1800.* New York: Basic Books, 1972.

Finkelstein, Barbara. "In Fear of Childhood: Relationships Between Parents and Teachers in Popular Primary Schools in the Nineteenth Century." *History of Childhood Quarterly* 3 (Winter 1976): 321-35.

———. "Pedagogy as Intrusion: Teaching Values in Popular Primary Schools in Nineteenth-Century America, 1820-1880." *History of Childhood Quarterly* 2 (Winter 1975): 349-78.

Fitts, Deborah. "Una and the Lion: The Feminization of District School Teaching and its Effects on Students and Teachers in Nineteenth-Century Massachusetts." In *Regulated Children/Liberated Children: Education in Psychohistorical Perspective.* Ed. Barbara Finkelstein. New York: Psychohistory Press, 1979, pp. 140-57.

Fuller, Wayne. *The Old Country School: The Story of Rural Education in the Middle West.* Chicago: University of Chicago Press, 1982.

Glenn, Myra. *Campaigns Against Corporal Punishment: Prisoners, Sailors, Women, and Children in Antebellum America.* Albany: State University of New York, 1984.

Gregg, Edith Emerson Webster. "Emerson and His Children: Their Childhood Memories." *Harvard Library Bulletin* 28 (Oct. 1980): 407-30.

Greven, Philip, ed. *Child-Rearing Concepts: Historical Sources.* Itasca, Illinois: F. E. Peacock, 1973.

Hardy, Stephen, and Alan Ingham. "Games, Structures, and Agency: Historians on the American Play Movement." *Journal of Social History* 17 (Winter 1983): 285-301.

Hawes, Joseph. *Children in Urban Society: Juvenile Delinquency in Nineteenth-Century America.* New York: Oxford University Press, 1971.

Heininger, Mary, Karin Calvert, Barbara Finkelstein, Kathy Vandell, Anne MacLeod, and Harvey Green. *A Century of Childhood, 1820-1920.* Rochester, N.Y.: Margaret Woodburry Strong Museum, 1984.

Hiner, N. Ray. "Children's Rights, Corporal Punishment, and Child Abuse: Changing American Attitudes, 1870-1920." *Bulletin of the Menninger Clinic* 43 (May 1979): 233-48.

Holl, Jack M. *Juvenile Reform in the Progressive Era: William R. George and the Junior Republic.* Ithaca: Cornell University Press, 1971.

Horlick, Alan Stanley. *Country Boys and Merchant Princes: The Social Control of Young Men in New York.* Lewisburg, Pa.: Bucknell University Press, 1975.

Jones, Kathleen W. "Sentiment and Science: The Late Nineteenth-Century

Pediatrician as Mother's Advisor." *Journal of Social History* 17 (Fall 1983): 79-96.

Kaestle, Carl F. *Pillars of the Republic: Common Schools and American Society, 1780-1860.* New York: Hill and Wang, 1983.

————. "Social Change, Discipline, and the Common School in Early Nineteenth-Century America." *Journal of Interdisciplinary History* 9 (Summer 1978): 1-17.

————, and Maris A. Vinovskis. "From Apron Strings to ABCs: Parents, Children, and Schooling in Nineteenth-Century Massachusetts." In *Turning Points: Sociological Essays on the Family.* Ed. John Demos and Sarane Spence Boocock. Chicago: University of Chicago Press, 1978, pp. 39-80.

————, and Maris A. Vinovskis. "From Fireside to Factory: School Entry and School Leaving in Nineteenth-Century Massachusetts." *Transitions: The Family and the Life Course in Historical Perspective.* Ed. Tamara K. Hareven. New York: Academic Press, 1978, pp. 135-85.

Katz, Michael. *The Irony of Early School Reform.* Cambridge, Mass.: Harvard University Press, 1968.

Kelly, R. Gordon. *Mother Was a Lady: Self and Society in Selected American Children's Periodicals, 1865-1890.* Westport, Conn.: Greenwood Press, 1974.

Kett, Joseph. "Curing the Disease of Precocity." *American Journal of Sociology* 84 (Supplement 1978): S183-S211.

————. *Rites of Passage: Adolescence in America, 1790 to the Present.* New York: Basic Books, 1977.

Kuhn, Anne L. *The Mother's Role in Childhood Education: New England Concepts.* New Haven: Yale University Press, 1947.

Larkin, Jack. "The View From New England: Notes on Every Day Life in Rural America to 1850." *American Quarterly* 34 (Bibliography 1982): 244-61.

Lerner, Gerda. "The Lady and the Mill Girl: Changes in the Status of Women in the Age of Jackson." *Midcontinent American Studies* 10 (1969): 5-14.

MacLeod, Ann Scott. *A Moral Tale: Children's Fiction and American Culture, 1820-1860.* Hamden, Conn.: Archon Books, 1975.

Mennel, Robert. *Thorns and Thistles: Juvenile Delinquents in the United States.* Hanover, N.H.: University Press of New England, 1973.

Merriam, Eve, ed. *Growing Up Female: Ten Lives.* New York: Dell Publishing Co., 1971.

Modell, John, Frank K. Furstenburg, and Theodore Hershberg. "Social Changes and Transitions to Adulthood in Historical Perspectives." *Journal of Family History* 1 (Autumn 1976): 7-32.

Nasaw, David. *Schooled to Order: A Social History of Public Schooling in the United States.* New York: Oxford University Press, 1979.

Novak, Stephen. *The Rights of Youth: American Colleges and Student Revolt, 1798-1815.* Cambridge, Mass.: Harvard University Press, 1977.

Pickett, Robert S. *House of Refuge: Origins of Juvenile Reform in New York State, 1815-1857.* Syracuse: Syracuse University Press, 1969.

Platt, Anthony. *The Child Savers: The Invention of Delinquency.* Chicago: University of Chicago Press, 1969.

Raichle, Donald. "School Discipline and Corporal Punishment: An American Retrospect." *Interchange* 7 (1977-78): 71-83.

Rapson, Richard. "The American Child as Seen by British Travelers, 1845-1935." *American Quarterly* 17 (1965): 520-34.

Rettew, Gayle, William Siener, and Janice Wass. *'Behold the Labour of My Tender Age': Children and Their Samplers, 1780-1850.* Rochester, N.Y.: Rochester Museum and Science Center, 1983.

Riblett, Jane Wilkie. "Social Status, Acculturation and School Attendance in 1850 Boston." *Journal of Social History* 11 (Winter 1977): 179-82.

Romanofsky, Peter. "Saving the Lives of the City's Foundlings: The Joint Committee and New York City Child Care Methods, 1860-1907." *New York Historical Quarterly* 61 (Jan.-Apr. 1977): 49-67.

Ronda, Bruce A. "Genesis and Genealogy: Bronson Alcott's Changing Views of the Child." *New England Historical and Genealogical Register* 85 (Oct. 1981): 259-73.

Ryan, Mary. *Cradle of the Middle Class: The Family in Oneida County, New York, 1790-1865.* New York: Cambridge University Press, 1981.

Ryerson, Alice Judson. "Medical Advice on Child Rearing, 1550-1900." *Harvard Educational Review* 31 (1961): 302-23.

Schlossman, Steven. *Love and the American Delinquent: The Theory and Practice of "Progressive" Juvenile Justice, 1825-1920.* Chicago: University of Chicago Press, 1977.

Schultz, Stanley K. *The Culture Factory: Boston Public Schools, 1789-1860.* New York: Oxford University Press, 1973.

Slater, Peter. *Children in the New England Mind: In Death and Life.* Hamden, Conn.: Archon Books, 1977.

Soltow, Lee and Edward Stevens. *The Rise of Literacy and the Common School: A Socioeconomic Analysis to 1870.* Chicago: University of Chicago Press, 1981.

Stambler, Moses. "The Effect of Compulsory Education and Child Labor Laws on High School Attendance in New York City, 1898-1917." *History of Education Quarterly* 8 (Summer 1968): 189-214.

Stansell, Christine. "Woman, Children, and the Uses of the Streets: Class and Gender Conflict in New York City, 1850-1860." *Feminist Studies* 8 (1982): 309-35.

Strickland, Charles. "Paths Not Taken: Seminal Models of Early Childhood Education in Jacksonian America." In *Handbook of Research in Early Childhood Education.* Ed. Bernard Spodek. New York: Free Press, 1982, pp. 321-40.

———. "A Transcendentalist Father: The Child-Rearing Practices of Bronson Alcott." *Perspectives in American History* 3 (1969): 5-73 (also in *History of Childhood Quarterly* 1 [Summer 1973]: 4-51).

Strong, Bryan. "Toward a History of the Experiential Family: Sex and Incest in the Nineteenth Century." *Journal of Marriage and the Family* 35 (Aug. 1973): 457-79.

Tyack, David. "The Tribe and the Common School: Community Control in Rural Education." *American Quarterly* 24 (Mar. 1972): 3-19.

————, and Michael Berkowitz. "The Man Nobody Liked: Toward a Social History of the Truant Officer, 1840-1940." *American Quarterly* 29 (Spring 1977): 31-54.

Vinovskis, Maris A. "Quantification and the Analysis of American Antebellum Education." *Journal of Interdisciplinary History* 13 (Spring 1983): 761-86.

Weiss, Bernard, ed. *American Education and the European Immigrant.* Urbana: University of Illinois Press, 1982.

Welter, Barbara. "The Cult of True Womanhood, 1820-1860." *American Quarterly* 18 (1966): 151-74.

Wishy, Bernard. *The Child and the Republic: The Dawn of Modern American Child Nurture.* Philadelphia: University of Pennsylvania Press, 1968.

Zelizer, Viviana. "The Price and Value of Children: The Cost of Children's Insurance." *American Journal of Sociology* 86 (1981): 1036-56.

Zuckerman, Michael. "Children's Rights: The Failure of Reform." *Policy Analysis* 2 (Summer 1976): 371-85.

Part III

Growing Up Red and Black in White America

Introduction

The historical experience of minority children often differed radically from that of the children of the majority. Slave children in the antebellum South, for example, obviously had very different experiences, were subjected to profoundly different expectations, and were provided with vastly different opportunities for development than were middle-class children in New England. These differences usually acted to the very great disadvantage of the minority children. Even so, David Wiggins's essay on the play of slave children demonstrates how children, even those severely disadvantaged or oppressed, can to some extent modify and structure the meaning and content of their experience in order to satisfy some of their own emotional or developmental needs. Wiggins says that one of the most important aspects of slave children's play took the form of role-playing and the re-enactment of events. The roles and events the children incorporated into their own play were often drawn from black culture and slave society rather than from white society. An interesting feature of the various games slave children played was the absence of any games which required the elimination of players. Wiggins regards this practice as a reaction to the possibility that members of the slave community might be sold suddenly and as a confirmation for the strong sense of community which characterized slave society.

The end of slavery did not automatically produce an immediate improvement in the daily lives of black children. Rebecca Scott traces the struggle between former slave owners and black families over efforts to bind black children to apprenticeships during Reconstruction in North Carolina. The role of the Freedmen's Bureau, caught in the middle, is the focus of her account. This article shows that the bureau and the North Carolina courts rarely considered the interest of the children and illustrates the continuing hardship and deprivation faced by black children after the Civil War.

Melvin Williams examines the life histories of two black men who grew up in a Pittsburgh ghetto, including the details of life in an inner city neighborhood, what the men did as children and how they entered into adolescence. The theme of economic deprivation is central to both accounts, and his article indicates that for many black young people, the process of growing up was almost as difficult in the twentieth century as it had been in the nineteenth. Children were still not exempt from the consequences of racial prejudice.

American Indian children, like black children, have suffered deprivation and discrimination in white society, but their relationship with the federal government has been very different from that of the blacks. One of the major developments in the history of American children in the twentieth century is the increased intervention of the federal government in the lives of children. Margaret Szasz shows how this activity was foreshadowed in the government's involvement with Indian children. Federal boarding schools were the primary tools in a policy of assimilation whereby children were taken from their families and sent to school. These institutions were under-funded, poorly staffed, and often more like prisons than schools. Their purpose was to train Indian children in the ways of Europeans and thereby break down tribal patterns and allegiances. This article makes it clear that the influence of the government on the lives of children was not uniformly benign.

Black children playing in Lafayette, La., 1938. Photograph by Russell Lee. (courtesy of the Library of Congress, LC-USF33-11862-M4)

10

The Play of Slave Children in the Plantation Communities of the Old South, 1820-60

David K. Wiggins

Most of the earliest studies done on southern plantation life portrayed slaves as people without a culture, without philosphical beliefs, and without educational instruments of their own. Historians often viewed slaves as barbarians to be civilized; as perpetual children at best, and animals at worst. As such, it was assumed that slaves held no strong values or convictions and that they were without a coherent culture or social organization of their own. To suggest that slaves were capable of molding or fashioning their own particular lifestyle was inconceivable. The most current research, however, has altered our perceptions of what the "peculiar institution" was really like. Many scholars now assert that slaves were capable of creating their own "unique cultural forms" largely free from the control of whites. However dehumanizing the plantation became for slaves, their struggle for survival never became so severe that it destroyed their creative instincts or prevented them from establishing their own personal way of life. The distinguishing elements of their culture — superstitions, religion, recreation, music, folktales, and language — allowed the slaves a degree of individual autonomy and self-respect. While slaves recognized the superior power which whites held as a group, they resisted the total assimilation of white culture.

The purpose of this study is to determine whether slaves living on southern plantations developed a sense of community among themselves or generally identified with the interests and particular customs of their master. More specifically, through an examination of the play of slave children between the years 1820 and 1860, this study attempts to determine whether slaves displayed an awareness of their uniqueness and separate identity as a group. Did members of the slave quarter fashion a society within a society or were they a culturally destitute group of individuals incapable of transcending such a controlled institution? What is immediately apparent from this analysis is that play was essential to slave children because it was one means through which they learned the values and mores of their parents' world. Thus play became a means by which cultural traits were preserved from one generation to the next. Like all young people, slave children liquidated some of their problems and relieved themselves of worries and anxieties by talking about and dramatizing the things which disturbed them. Through play, slave children were also able to realize a much needed sense of community not only with other children of the plantation but with the adult slaves as well. Most importantly, it is apparent from this research that members of the slave quarter community generally viewed themselves as a familial group, with similar life styles, similar concerns and problems, and a common need to stay together no matter what the circumstances. Despite individual suspicions and hostilities, as a group slaves recognized each other as a distinct society with a common historical experience and a common philosophical approach to the world. They were not a culturally rootless people but a vibrant group of individuals who created an energetic slave quarter community characterized by black solidarity not helpless dependency.

It should be stated at the outset that the evidence for this study is based largely on the first series of slave narratives edited by George P. Radwick. This nineteen-volume work, sixteen of which contain interviews prepared by the Federal Writers Project between 1936 and 1938, has some inherent problems in it. Since approximately two-thirds of the slaves were eighty or more years of age at the time they were interviewed, not only is there a concern about failing memories but also the question of whether longevity was the result of unusually good rather than typical treatment as slaves. Most of them were also recalling the experiences of their childhood, a period before the worst features of slavery were normally felt, and were likely, therefore, to give a more favorable picture of the institution. In addition, the biases, procedures, and methods employed by the predominately southern white interviewers can be justly criticized. On the other hand, these narratives, as muddled and contradictory as they are, represent the voices of the inarticulate masses the absence of which scholars are always bemoaning. In spite of their imperfections, they are not much different from other types of historical sources. Historians simply have to use caution and discrimination when using the interviews. And naturally they should make use of all the skepticism their trade has taught them if they expect to come up with an honest interpretation.

The narratives are certainly a most valuable piece of information on black history in America and should not be neglected. They contain evidence and answers for just about every kind of question that could be asked about life under slavery. For this particular study on the play of slave children, they are the single best source available.

Slave children held a rather precarious position in the plantation community. For six days a week, while their parents were in the fields toiling under the hot sun or attending to chores in the "big house," slave children were generally left alone to raise one another. Exempted from routine labor until sometimes as late as fourteen or fifteen years old, a certain portion of the slave children's early lives was spent in nurturing those younger than themselves and performing such chores as carrying water to the field hands, cleaning up the yards, fetching wood, tending the family garden, and feeding the livestock. The slave children's existence, however, was not all work and no play. On the contrary, when not engaged in their light tasks, they spent much of their time in the simple pleasures of eating, conversing, and playing with their companions.

Hardly anything was more enjoyable for the older slave children than roaming the fields and woods within the borders of their home plantation. Like all young people, slave children loved to explore the world around them. It helped them to discover their particular strengths and weaknesses and enabled them to cope with situations and events appropriate to their size and stamina. Acie Thomas spent much of his childhood roaming over the "broad acres" of his master's plantation with other slave children. "They waded in the streams, fished, chased rabbits and always knew where the choicest wild berries and nuts grew." "On Sundays we'd strike out for the big woods and we'd gather our dresses full of hickory, walnuts, and berries," recalled Fannie Yarbrough from Texas. "I was jes lying' here dreamin' 'bout how we use to go to the woods every spring and dig the maypop roots."

The younger children did not have the privilege of wandering about the plantation. During the day parents expected their younger offspring to restrict their play activities to within the borders of the plantation nursery, slave quarters, or "big house." Estrella Jones said the younger children on her master's Georgia plantation were allowed to play anytime "as long as they didn't wander away from the quarters." It was much the same way on Ann Hawthorne's plantation in Texas. "We done our playing around that big house," recalled Hawthorne, "but that front gate we musn't go outside dat."

The children frequently had the opportunity to visit their peer group on neighboring plantations. Parents usually did not mind if their children traveled to a nearby plantation, as long as they returned before nightfall. The slave children living on smaller plantations were especially anxious to make these excursions, since it was often the only chance they had to play with children of their own age group. "The patteroles never bothered the children any," remembered the Arkansas slave Allen Johnson. "And there wasn't any danger of them running off. It was all right for a child to go in the different quarters and play with one another during the daytime just so they got back before night."

Older slave boys, and less frequently the girls, willingly contributed to the welfare of their family by hunting and fishing with their fathers during the evening hours. Exemption from field labor at night gave fathers and their children an opportunity to augment their diet by trapping small game and catching fish in nearby streams. They realized a much needed feeling of self-worth by adding delicacies to the family table. Often precluded by their masters from contributing to their families' material welfare, slaves relished the chance to hunt and angle for food. Maybe most importantly, slave men found these two activities particularly satisfying because they allowed them the opportunity to teach their children the intricacies involved in hunting and fishing. There were not many activities in the plantation community where slave fathers and their children could share in the excitement of common pursuits. They both enjoyed the camaraderie and spirit that characterized these occasions. There was nothing quite like sitting around a blazing fire relating the tales of the phantom-like raccoon or the sixteen-foot catfish that got away. "My old daddy partly raised his chilluns on game," remembered Louise Adairs of North Carolina. "Mighty lot of fun when we could go with em."

Like that of most young people, the play of slave children consisted of both traditional games passed down from the older to younger children and those improvised on the spot. Phyllis Petite of Texas said they used to play a game called "skeeting" when the lake would freeze over in the winter time. "No, I don't mean skating," recalled Petite. "That's when you got iron skates and we didn't have them things. We just get a running start and jump on the ice and skeet as far as we could go, and then run some more." An ex-slave from Tennessee remembered playing a game they called "Smut." "We played it just like you would with cards only we would have grains of corn and call them hearts and spades, and so forth and go by the spots on the corn." Charlie Davenport played a variety of the more traditional games on his Mississippi plantation. "Us played together in de street what run de length o' de quarters," remembered Davenport. "Us tho'owed horse shoes, jumped poles, walked on stilts, an' played marbles." Chana Littlejohn played mumble peg, hop skotch, and "jumpin' de rope" when she was growing up on her small North Carolina plantation.

The most popular group activities of the slave children, especially the girls, were "ring games" or "ring dances," accompanied by a variety of songs and riddles. There were infinite variations in these games, but the general procedure was to draw a ring on the ground, ranging from fifteen to thirty feet in diameter, depending on the number of children engaged in the dancing ring. The participants would congregate within the ring and dance to different rhythmic hand clappings. Often during their ring games the children would berate the whites in song:

> My old mistress promised me,
> Before she dies she would set me free.
> Now she's dead and gone to hell
> I hope the devil will burn her well.

Or they would comment on their particular fears and anxieties:

> Run nigger, run.
> De patteroll git you!
> Run nigger, run.
> De patteroll come!
> Watch nigger, watch.
> De patteroll trick you!
> Watch nigger, watch.
> He got a big gun!

Many of the games played by children of the slave quarters had definite educational implications. Through the playing of games, slave children were often able to learn simple skills of literacy. "I learned some of the ABC's in playing ball with the white children," remembered Mattie Fannen of Arkansas. Anna Parkes, who lived on a large plantation in Georgia, remembered nothing about special games except "Ole Hundred." "Us would choose one and that one would hide his face against a tree while he counted to a hundred. Then he would hunt for all the others. They would be hiding while he was counting. We learned to count a playing Ole Hundred."

Much of the life of slave children consisted of role-playing and re-enacting those events which were most significant for them. Like all young people they wished to be grown-up and yearned to be wanted, needed, and a useful part of the grown-up world. It was natural for them to re-create that world using themselves as the leading characters. There were several distinguishing features about the imitative play of slave children. First, they did not necessarily re-enact those events found most enjoyable by the adult slaves. Second, they normally

re-enacted events they had witnessed and heard of rather than experienced. Third, they usually imitated the social events of their own
people and not those of the planter's family. Last and perhaps most
important, the evidence strongly suggests that slave children attempted to relieve particular anxieties and fears through the medium
of imitative play. By re-enacting certain events they attempted to
master specific problems which they were not able to resolve realistically.

Slave children were not necessarily unique in their imitative play,
but rather in the social events they chose to emulate. The frequency
with which they conducted simulated church activities, funerals, and
auctions subtly shows the importance that slaves attached to these
three "cultural affairs." Benny Dillard, who lived on a Georgia plantation that contained over fifty slaves, remembered "the best game
of all was to play like it was big meeting time. . . . We would have
make believe preachin' and baptism'. When we started playing like
we were baptizing them we throwed all we could catch right in the
creek, clothes and all, and ducked them." Dinah Perry of Arkansas
remembered how they made arrangements for a grand funeral. "We
marched in a procession singing one of our folks funeral hymns,"
recalled Perry. "We stopped at the grave under the big magnolia tree
by the gate, and my sister Nancy performed the ceremony." Abe Liv-
ingston of Texas remembered playing the game of "Auction" on his
"Massa's" plantation. One of the children would become the auc-
tioneer and conduct a simulated slave sale.

Two games which were played repeatedly by slave children were
different variations of "Hiding the Switch" and "No Bogeyman Tonight." In the first activity the players hunted for a switch that had
been concealed by one of the children. Whoever found it ran after
the others attempting to hit them. In the latter game one of the
children assumed the role of an evil spirit and attempted to frighten
the others. The girls found these games as popular as the boys. Julia
Banks of Texas said they used to "get switches and whip one another.
You know after you was hit several times it didn't hurt much." Rachel
Harris of Arkansas remembered playing "No Bogeyman Tonight" with
the white children. "One would catch the others as they ran from
behind big trees. Then whoever he caught would be the boogerman,
till he caught somebody else."

One historian of slavery feels these two particular games were means
through which children assisted themselves in coping with their fear
of "whippings" and "evil spirits." This is certainly a plausible explanation. Slave children who had witnessed the "floggings" of their
parents or heard the frightening stories of ghost-like "spirits" could

be expected to engage repeatedly in these games if it assisted them in lessening their fears. But this is only one of the possible interpretations. In these two games the children appeared to represent to themselves concretely those puzzling events they did not actually experience. The children may have been exploring their innermost feelings and emotions through a graphic representation. Or they may have been overtly "going over" two bewildering events in an attempt to confirm a vague memory. In other words, there was a need to physically re-enact "whippings" and "ghost stories" in order that their obscure features could be remembered more easily. Finally, slave children possibly participated in these two games simply for the excitement and sudden fear they wrought. Like most children they found a certain satisfaction in voluntarily exposing themselves to dangerous situations and inflicting what Roger Callois calls "a kind of voluptuous panic upon an otherwise lucid mind."

Slave children played a variety of different ball games. One of the distinctive features of these games was their simple organization, which was no doubt part of the reason why children of the slave quarters found them so popular. Like games played by their white counterparts, there were very few rules in their ball games. Simplicity of this type was necessary because of the slave children's personal level of social maturity and their inability to continually acquire "sporting" accoutrements. "Shinny was de thing dat I like best," reminisced Hector Godbold of South Carolina. "Just had stick wid crook in de end of it en see could I knock de ball wid dat." Tom Johnson, also of South Carolina, "played lots of games, like rolly hole. There are two holes and you try to roll a ball in one hole." Hanna Davidson of Kentucky remembered playing the game of "Anti-Over." "Six of us would stay on one side of the house and six on the other side," recalled Davidson. "Then we'd throw the ball over the roof. If you'd catch it you'd run around to the other side and hit somebody then start over."

Older slave boys often mentioned playing "baseball." The available evidence does not specify the rules that were used or the number of players that made up a team. In all probability the games they usually played were the various modifications of "rounders" and "townball" engaged in by white southerners. The most popular game of these boys throughout the South was marbles. It was a game that required very little playing gear. A match could be arranged anytime two boys came together who were anxious to demonstrate their "shooting" abilities. The playing of marbles, furthermore, appeared to be one activity in which slave boys could experience a temporary feeling of "power." The collection of marbles was one instance in which they could acquire objects of material worth; no matter their monetary value. "Us boys played marbles," recalled James Southall of Tennessee. "I got to be a professional. I could beat em all." Charles Coles of Maryland said that he "had many marbles and toys that poor children had then," and that his "favorite game was marbles."

Slave boys, and less frequently the girls, challenged members of their peer group to impromptu contests that would test their physical prowess. They delighted in seeing who could run the fastest, jump the highest, throw the farthest, swim the longest, and lift the heaviest objects. "Athletic" accomplishments were a source of great pride for slave children. The ability to perform well in physical contests usually guaranteed them the respect of their impressionable young playmates. One of the fastest ways for them to attain a degree of status and the recognized leadership of their peer group was to be successful on the playing field. "Because of my unusual strength and spirit I would let none of them beat me at any game," remembered Robert Ellett of Virginia. "I was best of the young boys on the plantation." Sam Stewart, who lived on a large plantation in North Carolina, recalled that the little boys "near my own age were playmates and companions and accepted me as their natural leader and chief. By the time I was eight years, I could shoot, ride, fish, and win with anyone."

The more sportive slave boys enjoyed placing a wager or two on their game playing. They were especially fond of shooting craps and playing cards but would place bets on just about any activity that was conducive to gaming. To elude the eyes of their virtuous parents as well as those of their concerned master, they often had to resort to the woods or some other secluded spot. Not having much to gamble with, their stakes consisted of any objects they attached special importance to. William Ballard and the other slave children used to play hide-the-switch, marbles, and several other games on their South Carolina plantation. But "later on some of de nigger boys started going to the woods to play cards and gamble." "De only game I ever played wuz marbles," remembered John Smith of North Carolina. "I played fer watermelons. We didn't hab any money so we played fer watermelons."

The play of slave girls differed in some respects from that of the boys. There were very few games the girls did not play or at least attempt to play during their childhood. The activity they most frequently played was "jump rope." A great deal of their time was spent playing with "dolls" and keeping "house." Maybe most importantly, slave girls had a particular fondness for dances, parties, and other social entertainments. They repeatedly expressed, like other members of the slave quarters, a desire to be among their own people engaged in group activities. In examining the girls' various play activities, there comes through a sense of mutual affection and kinship-like spirit among all the slaves. Phoebe Anderson of Georgia remembered that she would "go fishin down on the creek and on Saturday night we'd have parties in the woods and play ring plays and dance." Caroline Bevis of South Carolina said that when she was a little girl she "would play any over in the moonlight but enjoyed most the parties and dances on the plantation."

Slave children spent very little of their leisure time in combative activities. There are occasional references to boxing and wrestling in the slave narratives, but the children generally preferred to engage in gentler pursuits. Physical abuse of one child by another was considered unjustifiable and a veritable threat to the general well-being of the group. Like their parents, slave children apparently viewed themselves as a distinct body with common concerns, problems, and life styles. They recognized the need to remain together as a familial group no matter what the particular circumstances. The point here is not that slave children never fought each other, but rather that they understood that their mutual advantage required them to care for each other and to refrain as much as possible from foolish "skirmishes." John Brown stated that he and his friends saw no wrong in cheating, lying, and fighting "so long as we were not acting against one another." Susan Davis Rhodes, who lived as a slave in North Carolina said that "people in my day didn't know book learning but dey studied how to protect each other, and didn't believe in fightin' each other."

One of the significant features about the play of slave children is the apparent absence of any games that required the elimination of players. Even the various dodge ball and tagging games played by the children contained designed stratagems within their rule structure that prevented the removal of any participants. Despite the personal animosities and jealousies that individual slave children might have had toward one another, there seemed to be a mutual affection among the mass of children that precluded the elimination of any players in their games. One of the fears in their daily life was that members of their family — father, mother, brothers, sisters, grandparents, uncles, aunts, nieces, nephews — could be indiscriminately sold or hired out at anytime. Possible separation from their loved ones was frequently a source of great uneasiness and apprehension for those slave children who were old enough to realize their social position in the plantation community. Their "frivolous" play life was one area of their existence in which they could be assured that their companions would not be suddenly removed or excluded from participating. The lack of elimination in the slave children's games, moreover, can possibly be accounted for by some basic values generally held by members of the slave quarter community. A "survival of the fittest" or "natural selection" mentality did not normally characterize slave society. At the center of the slaves' social philosophy was a necessary belief in cooperation and community spirit. There was little room in the slaves' world for ruthless rivalry, unrestrained competition, and unprincipled domination. Personal conquest and individual success was certainly prevalent in their society but was considered much less important for survival than the belief in group solidarity and a sense of loyalty to fellow members of the slave quarter. Ma Eppes of Alabama remembered playing "Snail Away Rauley" all the time. "Us would hol' han's an' go 'roun' in a ring, gittin' faster an' faster an dem fell down was not outa de game but would have, tah ge' back in line." Moses Davis of Arkansas recalled that in playing "Ant y Over" they "would get six on one side of de house and six on de other. When somebody got hit we would just start the game over again."

Occasionally the slave children were permitted to continue their play at night. They longed for the close of day because it meant they could frolic with their parents and the other adult slaves, free from the continual surveillance of the planter and his family. The children loved to congregate outside of the cabins and listen to some "learned" old slave relate tales of Africa; gather around a blazing fire to dance and sing songs; accompany the more gamesome men on raccoon and possum hunts; travel with their family to a nearby plantation for a dance or corn-shucking; or simply stay around the slave quarters and "cut capers" with the other children. Pet Franks of Mississippi remembered playing "Hide-de switch" and "Goose and Gander" in the day time. "Den at nighttime when de moon was shinin' big an' yaller, us'd play ole molly bright. Dat was what us call de moon. Ud'd make up stories 'bout her." Jane Simpson, who lived on a small plantation in Missouri, recalled that "de white folks didn't want to let de slaves have no time for der self, so de old folks used to let us children run and play at night, while de white folks sleep and dey watch de stars to tell about what time to call us in and put us to bed, 'fore de white folks knew we was out."

Slave children also eagerly looked forward to Saturday afternoons, Sundays, and various holidays because it was an opportunity for them to participate in family and community activities or merely play with their friends and relatives. These moments were prized by all members of the slave quarter not simply as periods free from labor but as times when slaves could be with one another. These were the most ideal times for children to become familiar with the structure, the style, and the leading personalities of their community. Through their mutual experiences they learned the ways in which their community operated, how it made common decisions, organized secretive events, provided for common recreational needs, and generally organized itself to be as independent as possible from the personal whims and strictures of their overseer or master. Unable to spend extended periods of time with the children because of a heavy work schedule, slave parents took advantage of these moments to play with and talk to their children. These interactions provided special meaning to the children because they were extremely important in determining their personalities and the particular way in which they viewed the world. "One of de recreations us chilen had in dem days was candy pullings at Christmas times," reminisced Hemp Kennedy of Mississippi. "We all met at one house an' tol' ghost stories, sung plantation songs, as' danced de clog while de candy was cookin'." "Christmastime was when slaves had their own fun," said the Georgia slave Jefferson Franklin Henry. "They frolicked, danced, run races, played games, and visited around, calling it a good time."

Slave children not only played among themselves but frequently participated in the same games and played together in a relative degree of social equality with the white children of the plantation. Some planters did attempt to prevent their children from playing with the children of the slave quarters for fear that they would be "corrupted." Their attempts to circumscribe the play of their children, however, usually proved futile. The white children of the plantation earnestly sought the friendship of the slave children their own age and thoroughly enjoyed the opportunity to frolic in the quarters. In fact, through the playing of games, slave and white children would often develop friendships that lasted a lifetime (although those relationships usually only existed between the white children and one or two blacks who became body servants or occupied some special station in the plantation community.) "I belonged to ole Massa Harry ebber sin' he was married," recalled an ex-slave from Virginia. "He an' me was jes' about of an age, n' tended him all his life. I allers 'tended to him when he was a boy, am' went out hunting, shooting, and trapping wid him all over the place." "I hunted and fished with the slave children," responded Edward Pollard, the son of a Virginia slaveholder. "I have wrestled on the banks of the creek with him, and with him as my trusty lieutenant I have filibustered all over my old aunts dominion."

Much of the leisure time of slave and white children was spent in getting into mischief and helping each other out of difficult situations. Hand in hand they would go about pilfering the plantation hen house and performing no small amount of reciprocal trading. There are also numerous examples of white children helping their slave playmates avoid punishments or assisting them in a variety of subtle ways. "Me and young master had the good times," recalled Jack Cauthern of Texas. "He was nigh my age and we'd steal chickens from old Miss and go down in the orchard and barbecue 'em." Matilda Daniel said they sure did some "devilish" things on her Alabama plantation. "We hid red pepper in old Black Bob's chewin' bacca, an' you ought to seed de faces he made. Den we tuken a skunk dat us little white an' black debils katched an' turn him loose in de slave quarters."

Notwithstanding those occasional friendships, a caste system frequently operated within the "play world" of the slave and white children just as it did in the everyday affairs of the plantation community. Older slave children in particular were often forced to assume a subservient position in their game playing. Many of the white children of advanced age were anxious to assume their position as "superiors." Candis Goodwin of Virginia remembered that when the war first started they would "play Yankee an' Federates, 'course de whites was always the 'Federates. They'd take us black boys prisoners an' make b'lieve dey was gonna cut our necks off; guess dey got dat idea f'om dere fathers." Amelia Thompson Watts, who lived on a relative's Louisiana cotton plantation in the summer of 1832, described a scene that also illustrates the caste distinction between slave and white children: "One of the negro boys had found a dead chicken and we arranged for a funeral. The boys made a wagon of fig branches, and four of them as horses. We tied a bow of black ribbon around the chicken's neck and covered him with a white rag and then marched in a procession singing one of the quaint negro hymns, all the white children next to the hearses marching two by two, and the colored children following in the same order."

Many white children loved nothing better than to torment the slave children, and even adults, by simulating the role of an overseer or master of a large plantation in their imitative play. Soloman Northup, who labored on a number of southern plantations, recalled the ten- or twelve-year-old son of a despotic slaveholder who had no trouble in picking up all his father's habits. "Mounted on his pony," said Northup, "he often rides into the field with his whip, playing the overseer, greatly to his father's delight." Frederick Law Olmstead, while traveling through Texas, observed the play of a planter's son which illustrates this point: "This gentleman had thirty or forty negroes and two legitimate sons. One was an idle young man. The other was already at eight years old a swearing tobacco chewing young bully and ruffian. We heard him whipping his puppy behind the house and swearing between the blows, his father and mother being at hand. His tone was an evident imitation of his fathers mode of dealing with his slaves. 'I've got an account to settle with you; I've let you go about long enough; I'll teach you who's your master; there; go now God damn you, but I haven't got through with you yet.' "

Slave children were not always on the receiving end of such foolish mockings and harassments. Those children of the slave quarters who were clever enough to outwit the white children did not hesitate to return personal insults. Some planters even encouraged these rebukes because they didn't always appreciate seeing their children become tyrants. A slave from Tennessee recalled how they "teased" the white children: "They didn't allow us to even look at the white chillen. I 'member we used to slip and play with 'em anyway. About a mile from the house there was a lane, and we would git all the chillen together and play with them down in that lane where our white folks couldn't see us' then we would make 'em skit home! We say 'ya'll gwan now, here come the white folks; he, he, he. We would drive 'em home and tell 'em ole master would whip them if they saw us with 'em. . . . Next morning we would go and get 'em and play with 'em again. We would tell 'em we was better'n than they was, he, he, he."

This feeling of confidence, which shows through the account, was a theme throughout the slave narratives and the other black folklore. In fact, slave children normally thought of themselves not only as morally superior to white children but as superior on a physical level as well. Whereas most slave children thought of themselves as skillful "athletes," their white counterparts were generally felt to be less competent physically, unable to dance, run, jump, or throw! The white children were so inept they were hardly able to tie their own shoes or comb their own hair. "We was stronger and knowed how to play, and the white children didn't," recalled Felix Heywood of Texas. Remembering life under slavery in South Carolina, Josephine Bauchus concluded that "white folks couldn' dance no more den dey can dance dese days like de colored people can."

One of the most striking differences between the play of slave and white children was the type of equipment used in their game playing. In contrast to the planters' children who were normally able to purchase their own toys, the children of the slave quarters either made their own playthings, obtained various toys that their fathers handcrafted, or acquired "hand-me-downs" that the white children no longer found useable. Hanna Davidson of Kentucky said that "the kids nowadays can go right to the store and buy a ball to play with. We'd have to make a ball out of yarn and put a sock around it for cover." Sam McAllum of Mississippi didn't "recollect any playthings" they had "'cept a ball my young marster gimme." Letita Burwell, the daughter of a Kentucky planter, remembered they "early learned that happiness consisted in dispensing it, and found no greater pleasure than saving our old dolls, toys, beads, bits of cake, or candy for the cabin children, whose delight at receiving them richly repaid us."

The white children of the plantation engaged in many of the same activities as their slave counterparts. For example, Lanty Blackford, the son of a wealthy Virginia planter, played with his friends in a variety of activities that Brian Sutton-Smith refers to as central-person games. These are games in which one child plays against the rest of the group. Some of the more popular ones among slave and white children were different variations of "Goosie, Goosie, Gander," "Pig in the Pin," "I Spy," "Base," "Hide-and-Seek," "Blind Man's Bluff," and "Fox and Hounds." In addition to these games the white children in Blackford's neighborhood also engaged in such organized activities as boating, swimming, fishing, hunting, and wrestling. The children, furthermore, often reenacted different situations from southern life in their play. They were particularly fond of participating in mock "military drills," "court trials," and "political debates." Interestingly enough, what was apparently lacking in the white children's play world were any games of chance. Assuredly, the admonitions they received from the parents quite possibly discouraged the children from playing these games or at least discussing them openly. Still, in comparison to the slave children, they seemed to favor those games which principally required the skill and effort of the performers. The emphasis on these particular kinds of games seems to reflect the particular cultural focus of the white southerners more than anything else. The research on play has shown that games which emphasize physical prowess are usually found in those cultures which recognize that effort and individual initiative are the main determinants in achieving success. The planters of the Old South certainly embraced these values. Consequently, through the playing of those games that required a degree of physical prowess the white children of the plantation were possibly learning that the outcome of particular endeavors was a result of the amount of effort that was expended and that other factors were basically superfluous. On the other hand, slave children could be expected to find gambling and other games of chance particularly enticing. Survival to the slave was not necessarily contingent upon the skill and effort one put forth, but rather on a variety of other uncontrollable factors — not the least of which was indiscriminate luck.

The white children of the plantation not only placed a great deal of emphasis on the amount of effort expended in their games but were also concerned about the specific manner in which they were played. In many instances they seemed more interested in the mode of play rather than in the outcome of the game itself. In contrast to the slave children, the limited goals of their games were often subordinated to the means by which they were to be achieved. In other words, white children were not simply concerned about the effort expended in their games but found it necessary that they achieve their desired results in a deliberately stylized way.

It is evident that slave children, like their parents, viewed themselves as a special kind of people and took pride in expressing their peculiar style in many of their play activities. It was often a way to assure themselves of their own self-worth, the medium through which they established life-long friendships, and the manner in which their individuality was asserted and maintained. Their play life consisted almost solely of informal and oftentimes improvised games that could be arranged any time two children came together who were anxious to have some fun. Whether deliberate or not, slave children often learned from each other how to play games. Generally left alone to raise each other, slave children typically had ultimate control as to what they did or did not play. Despite occasional attempts to restrict them from playing with their own children, southern slaveholders did not normally concern themselves with the types of activities played by slave children. The majority of "proprietors" did allow their slaves a somewhat extended childhood in hopes they would attain the degree of health necessary to become "efficient" workers. However, this prolonged infancy did not include any formal program of games or exercise designed to improve the fitness of the slave children. In fact, the majority of planters generally did not pay much attention to the slave children's physical well-being until they were old enough to join the regular plantation work force. In their way of thinking, freedom from strenuous labor was all that was needed to ensure a "hearty" adult slave. Paradoxically, exemption from work and opportunities for play were probably more influential in providing the groundwork for a potentially more self-reliant and spirited adult slave.

Like most young people, slave children realized a great deal of pleasure from participation in various play activities. It was often the medium through which they learned the values and mores of the adult world. By simulating those events characteristic of the grown-up world, slave children were able to understand the complicated world about them and were capable of perceiving the patent differences that normally existed between a master and his servants. The evidence also suggests that through various play activities slave children were able to relieve themselves of the fear and anxiety that normally characterized the lives of most of the children. By participating in certain "amusements," they apparently attempted to overcome particular problems which they were not able to resolve realistically.

A theme that frequently appeared in the narratives was the feeling of black supremacy exhibited by many slave children in their various play activities. Apparently, only at a certain point in their lives did slave children come to realize fully that they were "servants" and that their white companions held a more exalted position in the plantation community. Many did not recognize the difference until they were separated from their white playmates and sent out to the fields or up to the "big house" to begin their life of labor. On some plantations the slave children learned when one of their family members was suddenly sold or hired out, or when the planter or overseer precluded their parents' authority in some way. Many slave children learned almost immediately because they might be forced to call a white baby "Young Massa" or "Young Misses." Still others immediately recognized the difference when they were forced to assume an obsequious position in their game playing or were excluded from participating altogether. Quite possibly then, prior to their realization that they occupied an inferior position in the plantation community, slave children were unaware of the usual decorum that normally existed between the races and therefore were probably more inclined not to comply with the desires of their white playmates. Of course, simply sharing in the excitement of various play activities probably did much to create temporary feelings of equality and fellowship between the children. It is when people are mutually involved in uninhibited merrymaking that intrinsic differences are most often disguised. The joy and pleasantry of the moment possibly helped erase some of the disparities that existed between the children. Furthermore, slave children could assume almost any attitude they wished considering there were very few adults around to keep watch over their every move. In any event, whatever the reasons for the slave children's feelings of superiority, they frequently thought of themselves as being more energetic dancers, better hunters, faster runners, and more imaginative in all their game playing. The white children were often portrayed simply as clumsy fools who were decidedly prosaical in their play activities.

Not only did slave children often exhibit a marked feeling of superiority but they also realized a much-needed sense of community with other slave members through various play activities. In fact, the joy they found in play seemed to be accounted for, more than anything else, by the group solidarity and fraternal spirit this activity brought forth. Their numerous play experiences were eagerly looked forward to by the slave children because they gave them opportunities to frolic and socialize with their peer group under comfortable conditions.

The fellowship attained during these occasions seems especially significant because it furnished individual slave children with a feeling of security they might not experience under any other circumstances. Moreover, the constant reinforcement, common language, and strong positive sanctions that normally characterized these events helped to succor the slave children in their struggle to discover their personal identities.

This did not mean that slave children ever felt any sense of community with the white children and their family. It is true that mutual enjoyment of various play activities did much to develop friendships among the children. But simply sharing in the excitement of popular pastimes was never influential enough to erase the intrinsic differences that existed between the children. To develop a true feeling of community requires at least a common life style, common interests and problems, or a common philosophical approach to the world. It would be historically misleading to say that participating in several of the same play activities was responsible for developing these sentiments between the children — even for a brief priod of time. This is not to argue that mutual participation in play activities did not temporarily eliminate the usual propriety between the races, only that play was incapable of developing a sense of community between two people whose views of this world were so divergent.

Finally, the singular style of the slave children's various games cuts deep into the heart of one of the basic differences between slave and white society — specifically their differing notions about the concepts of work and play. Planters seemed to think of play primarily in contrast to work, whereas the dichotomy between these two activities was not quite as discernable in slave society. Relatively speaking, southern slaveholders, like many people in today's world, frequently judged the worthiness of individuals by the amount of effort they expended in their work. They viewed labor as being both necessary for survival and as a virtue in its own right. This did not mean that the Protestant work ethic characterized the southern planters' personal value scheme. On the contrary, they realized that hard work was inevitable to achieve success, but not if it meant the indiscriminate acquisition of wealth, excessive abstinence, or an unrealistic devotion to "one's calling." The southern slaveholders certainly did enjoy "living it up." Their reputation as a fun-loving and frolicsome society is basically an accurate one. On the other hand, most planters considered play as generally trifling in the sense that it was immaterial to survival, should be engaged in by gentlemen only in the most organized and refined fashion, and ought to be exclusive in nature and devoid of any frivolous public displays.

Slaves seem to have had a much different view of work and play than their masters. They certainly did not place the same kind of emphasis or judge the personal worth of individuals by the successful completion of their regular plantation tasks. The slaves' sense of accomplishment was identified with the family unit and measured primarily by the successful maintenance of the familial order of the household. They realized the necessity of working long and difficult hours during planting and harvesting seasons, but expected to work considerably less during other seasons. They did not understand the incessant need for labor and resisted what they felt was senseless work. In other words, work was generally not the basis for evaluating one's personal integrity and character. Conversely, play was one activity where slaves could realize a certain degree of dignity and could affirm and sustain their unique existence. They could withstand bondage much more easily when allowed to participate with fellow slaves in a variety of different play activities.

Counts Shoe Shop, late nineteenth century, Junction City, Kan. (courtesy of the Pennell Collection, Kansas Collection, University of Kansas)

11

The Battle over the Child: Child Apprenticeship and the Freedmen's Bureau in North Carolina

Rebecca J. Scott

It is by now a familiar observation that while slavery as a legal system ended abruptly with the ratifiction of the Thirteenth Amendment, social patterns were not as quickly changed. In spite of defeat on the battlefield, the southern white community retained considerable power to resist social change. Even agents of the Freedmen's Bureau, whose responsibility it was to protect the rights of former slaves, had no very clear idea of how much of the old society should be repudiated and how much retained. A considerable body of historical literature has described the struggle of black people to define the meaning of their freedom in these circumstances.

Additional evidence of the pulling and tugging which went on among southern white landowners, their former slaves, and representatives of the bureau emerges from the Freedmen's Bureau records concerning child apprenticeship in North Carolina. Former slaveowners tried to use apprenticeship to re-establish much of the substance of slavery, while black families often resisted as vigorously as they were able. Agents of the bureau found themselves in the middle. They wanted, on the one hand, to see freedmen quickly employed and employers provided with labor. On the other hand, they were, to varying degrees, sensitive to the rights of black parents. Conflicting signals came from officials at the top, and local agents often ended up making their own determinations on questions that deeply affected black families.

While the surviving records of the North Carolina Freedmen's Bureau are not complete, they are numerous enough to provide a clear idea of the way in which these contending forces operated and to add another dimension to the social history of Reconstruction in that state. Moreover, the records include not only official correspondence but also the individual pleas of black parents and relatives, thus providing a rare glimpse into the freedmen's perception of the historical process they were living through.

Apprenticeship had been used even before the war as a means of controlling free black children, and soon after the Confederate surrender landowners seized upon the precedent to secure cheap labor in exchange for maintenance and to control not only the children but sometimes their parents as well. The Freedmen's Bureau quickly became involved because of its responsibility to supervise contracts.

In many cases the consequences of slavery became the pretexts for apprenticeship. Fathers separated from their families by sale returned after the war to find their children "lawfully bound" as orphans to a former master and Freedmen's Bureau officials unwilling to tamper with what they considered to be legal contracts. Mothers who had not been legally married or who had children by more than one man found these facts being used to classify their children as bastards and indenture them. Freedmen able to earn only meager wages for their labor found these same low wages being used as justification for taking their children from them. Responding to this situation, parents and other kin called upon the bureau to protect their rights, and a complex three-sided struggle ensued.

One landowner's point of view comes across clearly in a letter to the bureau from William Cole of Rockingham, North Carolina, in December 1865. "I understand you are authorized to bind out to the former owner of slaves all those under the age of twenty-one years, upon certain conditions," he wrote, explaining that about thirty of his former slaves were under twenty-one, and that he would like them all bound to him (preferably without his having to come to the bureau office in person). He added that he was compelled to support these thirty young people or turn them out to starve.

The point of view of two black parents was dramatically expressed in a letter from Thomson and Melvina Baker to a local bureau agent in 1867.

Col Bentzman Sir I have written you concerning my Children my wife formerly belong to Gordon R. Hinton and when She was liberated he drived hir off and would not let hir have hir children whereupon thay stay there some twelve month afterward and then left and Mr Hinton came to my house and I was not home and he came and went in my house and taken my children by force and threten to kill my wife and drew his knife and cut at hir and cut a handerkerf around her neck, and carried one of them home and had it bound out without consent and I would like to now if he can hold them please attend to this and let me here from you soon.

Since legal authority for the indenturing of children by the bureau was based both on its federal mandate and on North Carolina statutes, there was often an opportunity for ambiguity in application. Eliphalet Whittlesey, the assistant commissioner for the Freedmen's Bureau in North Carolina, stated his apprehensions bluntly. "The practice of binding out children is dangerous, inasmuch as it fosters the old ideas of compulsory labor and dependence." Still, since the bureau was charged with supervising apprenticeship, he had set out the general principles under which it would operate: ". . . children may be bound to service *with the consent* of their parents only. In law parents have a right to their children. The principle is an important one, though in exceptional cases, its application may work badly. Children who have no parents may be bound out (for the present) with the consent of an officer of this Bureau. The old forms of indenture are sufficient." The old forms to which he referred were those used by the county courts of North Carolina for drawing up indentures. These were of two types. One contained the word "orphan" and had been used to apprentice poor orphans, black and white, and certain categories of fatherless children. The other form specified that the child was a free boy or girl "of color" and had been used under the section of North Carolina law that authorized the courts to apprentice the children of free Negroes who "do not habitually employ their time in some honest, industrious occupation; and all free base-born children of color." Although Whittlesey repeatedly expressed his opposition to this distinction between white and black children, in practice he allowed the apprenticing of black children under rules similar to those applied to free children of color before the war. In his circular no. 4 of November 1865, he specified that the children of "parents who have no honest calling, or visible means of support" could be apprenticed. While this was purportedly to prevent the children of poor freedmen from becoming paupers and vagrants, the timing suggests that it may have been related to the effort to force freedmen to sign labor contracts. The same circular ordered that no more rations be issued to freedmen who refused employment and that "vagrant idlers" be arrested and punished.

Indentures were supposed to be made according to the standard legal regulations concerning white apprenticeships. Male apprentices were to be bound to "some tradesman, merchant, mariner or other person, approved by the court, until the age of twenty-one years." Females were to be bound "to some suitable employment" until eighteen. The master or mistress was to provide for the apprentice "diet, clothes, lodging, and accommodations fit and necessary" and at the expiration of the apprenticeship to "pay to each apprentice six dollars, and furnish him with a new suit of clothes and a new Bible." The master was required to have the child taught to read, write, and cipher, and the indenture could be canceled if this were not done. Apprentices, for their part, had to obey the master, labor faithfully, keep confidences, and leave the premises only with permission. They could be liable for damages if they left before the end of their term.

In practice few of these regulations were honored when black children were apprenticed. Many agents and masters simply ignored them. Often no money was specified to be given at the end of the term, children were bound without parental consent, no trades were specified, or children were bound beyond the legal age. Agents made their own determination of the meaning of the word "orphan," made their own judgment whether parents could support children, and set their own rules with respect to kinfolk and masters. The resulting policy was informal and inconsistent.

Soon after the war ended, agents were eager to apprentice children, if only to satisfy the clamoring masters and reduce the number of potential charges. In some instances, the master may have been providing a foster home for a dependent child. In other cases, the relationship was perhaps analogous to the old custom of sending one's children to the home of a relative to be raised and earn their keep. Some of the indentures of black children to uncles were probably in this category. In most cases, however, the apprenticeship was essentially a labor contract — to which the child was not necessarily a consenting party — characterized by strong restrictions on behavior and a deferred or nonexistent wage. One indenture from Sampson County actually was written in the form of a labor contract. A thirteen-year-old was bound to labor ten hours a day on a man's farm for the rest of the year and to be "respectful in his deportment." The master agreed to maintain the boy and "to encourage the establishment of schools for the children of freedmen." The pay per month was listed as "Board, Clothing, and Medical Attendance."

The labor of many of these children was of economic value — a fact that masters were quick to point out when they wished to discredit the motives of relatives trying to regain control of the children. Older children could do the work of field hands; younger children could work at agricultural tasks, such as thinning corn, or could be employed as house servants. Indenture gave the master years of jurisdiction over a child and could be seen as an investment, even when the child was too young to be of economic value at the time he or she was apprenticed.

The age distribution of apprentices suggests that a labor rather than a public welfare function was primary in child indenture. If the institution had been mainly for the support of destitute orphans, one would expect the distribution to be skewed toward the youngest and most helpless. If, on the other hand, it was used primarily for labor, one would expect it to be skewed toward the older and more productive children. A series of several hundred apprenticeship forms from 1865 and 1866 has survived. Unfortunately it is an unscientific sample since it comprises simply those forms which for whatever reason came to be deposited at Raleigh. The forms represent an unknown proportion of the total number of apprenticeships, and not all counties are represented, but they provide a rough idea of the ages of children apprenticed. The most common ages for apprenticeship, in both years, were ten, eleven, twelve, and thirteen. Children under five, whom one could think of as helpless, comprised only 5 percent of the 1865 group and 11 percent of the 1866 group. Approximately 80 percent of the children in 1865 and 70 percent in 1866 were over the age of seven. By and large, the apprentices were old enough to work. The few very young ones were almost always apprenticed with their older brothers and sisters, or as part of a family group.

The needs of the recently freed parents varied. They were often caught between a desire to support and control their children and the lack of means to do so. There were families for whom the cost of maintaining children was greater than the family income. Former slaves living and working on an employer's farm could be charged more for the maintenance of younger children than the entire family could earn, and in such cases parents might be forced to accept apprenticeship in order to hold the family together. Those who had entered into sharecropping agreements, however, could use the labor of their children directly to increase family income; they often fought against relinquishing authority to former masters through apprenticeship.

In a few cases mothers used the labor of their children as payment for the use of land. In November 1866, Mariah Harrington made a contract to bind her six children aged three to twelve years to H. W. Harrington until they came of age. In return he agreed to furnish her a house "and as much land to tend as she will fence in around the house." She was to retain the house and all she made on the land for a year.

One can only speculate as to how much freedom the woman had in this case. Unless each party has freedom to say no to a contract, it loses its ethical, if not its legal, basis. The following letter suggests just how little freedom of action freedwomen might have.

dear Sir if you pleas to do a Good Favor for me if you Pleas i have bin to Mr tilor about my children and he will not let me have them an he say he will Beat me to deth if i cross his Plantasion A Gain an so i dont now what to do About it an i wish if you Pleas that you wood rite Mr Joseph tilor A lettor an let him Give me my childrin Mr cory i want my childrin if you Pleas to get them for me i have bin after them an he says i shall not have them and he will not Pay me nor my childrin ether for thar last year work and now want let me have my childrin nother an i will close

hulely tilor

Parents or relatives who were initially willing to enter into some kind of arrangement for the labor and maintenance of children sometimes decided later to withdraw, only to find that apprenticeships were long-term binding contracts. John DeForest, a bureau official in South Carolina, explained in his memoirs that the problem with apprenticing black children was that relatives "soon sickened of the bargain and wanted to regain possession of the youngsters. If the father and mother were not alive to worry in the matter, it would be taken up by grand-parents, aunts, and cousins." DeForest attributed this primarily to their "natural affection" for the children, but he refused to break apprenticeship contracts and told relatives to take their cases to civil court. He later remarked smugly, "As an application for a writ of habeas corpus costs money, I never knew mother, grandmother, aunt or cousin to make it."

The desires and interests of the children appear only indirectly in the record. Many of the contested cases took on the aspect of custody battles, with each side claiming to know and represent the wishes of the child. However, some children expressed their opposition to ap-prenticeship by refusing to return to their employers after visiting their families at Christmas, or by fleeing to relatives. One twelve-year-old named Alfred left his master after two years and made his way to an uncle in South Carolina. In this case the master agreed to cancel the indenture and no effort was made to retrieve the child, but in other cases the bureau ordered the children returned to their lawful masters. Some children not only resisted apprenticeship for themselves but fought on behalf of their siblings as well. In March 1867, five brothers filed for a writ of habeas corpus to release their sisters, aged eighteen, sixteen, twelve, and eight, all orphans held as apprentices.

The record dealing with the apprentices of W. R. Holt of Davidson County illustrates the efforts of family members to regain control of their children. At Christmas 1865, Holt wrote to the superintendent at Salisbury that he had read indentures "to the parties" and that "with but few exceptions all with full explanations seem to be satisfied." Eighteen children were bound to him, all between the ages of ten and sixteen, eight girls and ten boys. He was sure that "after the first excitement is over, all will go on well."

He was wrong. First he went bankrupt. Then, in the course of the next year, at least five petitions were filed for the release of his apprentices. In January an agent for the father of one child argued that the father, then living in Arkansas, had received no notice of the indenture, was able to care for the child, and wanted the indenture canceled. In February Rosey Holt wrote the bureau that her granddaughter had been transferred to the purchaser of Holt's estate and was being neglected. Peter Holt, uncle of one of the children, charged that his nephew was not properly cared for and proposed to take the child and "learn him the blacksmith trade and send him to school." Orange Holt found a lawyer to represent him, and argued that his son, too, had been neglectd in W. R. Holt's care, that he, Orange, had been forced to care for him during an illness, and that the child had been "infected with vermin by reason of bad and insufficient clothing." Harriet Holt also hired a lawyer to present her argument that her two sons had been apprenticed to Holt against her will and that she had on her own contracted her and their services to another party. By January 1867, W. R. Holt himself, citing changed circumstances, asked to be released from his obligation for all but six of the children. In the case of Mr. Holt, the master probably overestimated his capacity to support the children indentured to him, but even had the enterprise gone well from his point of view, many of the parents and relatives were prepared to make strenuous efforts to regain their children.

In these contested cases, agents of the Freedmen's Bureau had no clear directives from their superiors and had to make case-by-case judgments based on their own attitudes and values. For example, in the summer of 1866 a freedwoman, Menice, complained to the district office in Raleigh about the treatment her petition for release of her daughter was receiving in Halifax, and the Halifax agent was called to account by his superiors. He replied that "it was my intention in this as in all similar cases to improve the conditions and prospects of the child." He then explained that the girl and thirteen others had been bound illegally to a Mr. Long, and that he had ordered them released. But, "Mr. Long represented to me that most of the children released would remain with him and he would be compelled to support them without any prospect of remuneration. Accordingly I visited the place and saw the children and re-apprenticed six to his son J. J. Long, Jr."

J. J. Long and Menice had clashed over who was to control the girl, employed in thinning corn. Long struck Menice herself for not working and was fined five dollars for the assault. The agent added, however, that he did not think Menice a proper person to raise a child, and that the man with whom she was living at the time of the indenture was not then her legal husband. While the agent considered the woman's reputation to be a sufficient reason for denying her custody of her child, he apparently did not consider the master's conviction for assault to be sufficient reason for removing the child from his care.

Even when they were provided with general statements of purpose and their guidelines from Raleigh, agents were strongly influenced by their own perceptions of the de facto situation of the child, of the validity of appeals of the master, and of the morals of the parents or relatives. If a child were likely to remain on a master's land in any case, because his or her parents worked there, agents were more likely to legalize the relationship and give the master claim to the child's labor. Parents who considered authority over their own children to be part of their freedom resisted this bitterly. When parents and masters disagreed about the conduct of the child, violence sometimes followed.

Agents were also influenced by their impression of the reputation and marital status of the claimants. Masters used these factors in their appeals to agents, referring to a parent or relative of the child as "a worthless fellow" or a "lazy negro" and claiming to have greater concern for the child's welfare than the child's kin had. The education clause in apprenticeship contracts could strengthen the employer's hand because relatives wishing to regain control of a child might be called upon to prove that they were as able as the master to educate the child.

In some cases, it was not the local agents but officials higher in the bureau who were unsympathetic to parental claims. George Hawley, a local agent, sent a letter to his superior in July 1866 recommending that the indentures of seven apprentices be canceled, "satisfactory evidence having been produced that the parents of said children will properly provide for them." The superior officer, Colonel Cilley, refused to cancel them without further information, arguing that "the same reason as here given [i.e., parental willingness to provide for their children] may be brought forward in hundreds of instances in the course of 5 years and the persons taking children wd be justified in charging the Bureau with bad faith if this reason alone was held to be sufficient cause for cancelling an indenture." In other words, parents should not automatically be able to obtain custody of children who had already been apprenticed. Hawley explained in reply that the state of the children had been misrepresented to him at the time he had made the indentures. One child "was represented to be an idle and worthless fellow, it has been proved that he is not such a person but well-disposed." Two others had a father who was represented to the agent as absent or dead, but "he has made his apperance & claims the children and is a worthy negro." Two had a mother only, and the master requested the cancellation of the indenture. One had a mother who had a husband and "the parents are in my opinion qualified to take care of the child." The last had a father who had been absent but returned "and claims the boy and is a good industrious negro." The superintendent of the eastern district reviewed the case and ruled that "it would be a bad precedent to cancel these Indentures, as they now stand, unless both parties will make written application requesting the cancelling of the Indentures." The parents were therefore dependent on the willingness of the master himself to relinquish the child.

These officials clearly did not share Whittlesey's view of the primacy of parental rights. They chose instead to uphold the principle of the enforceability of contracts, even those made on false premises.

Local agents repeatedly received contradictory advice from their superiors. Lieutenant Foote, the agent at Halifax in 1866, wrote to inquire what procedure he should follow when parents charged that their children had been bound without their consent. A Captain Almy replied that the charge of binding without parental consent was very difficult to provide "inasmuch as it is an almost absolute impossibility to determine the parentage of any colored child in this state." Almy further contended that there were "for every able-bodied child over ten years of age, several colored parties representing themselves to be the parents of the child" and as many white men who would insist that the child's parents were dead.

This letter must have puzzled Foote, whose records for the period indicate no such disputes among blacks as to the actual parentage of a child. Foote continued to raise the question, submitting two cases in which he felt injustice had been done. In one, a couple who had been living together for sixteen years petitioned for the return of their nine children, all of whom, down to the three-month-old baby, had been apprenticed to one man. In the other case, two teenage boys had been turned out by their former master at the time of the surrender and had subsequently found homes and jobs. Then the master changed his mind and had them bound to him. On the grounds that their mother was old and needed their support, Foote appealed for the apprenticeships to be canceled.

The letter was endorsed this time by Superintendent Brady, who approved the cancellations, cited the order under which such indentures could be canceled, and instructed Foote to do the same in future cases. Foote then forwarded his lists of approved indentures to Brady. There were twenty in the group, nineteen of which were for "colored orphan children." Brady wrote back to ask, "How is it that there are so many (Colored) orphan children apprenticed in Northampton County? Have their parents been swept away by Plague or by the ravages of War? Great care must be exercised that *none* except orphans, or children whose parents give their consent, be bound out as apprentices."

The mystery was solved when Lieutenant Foote explained his understanding of the word "orphan." Relying on Webster's dictionary, he defined an orphan as a fatherless *or* motherless child. Furthermore, he argued, "Nearly all these children were bastards and in many instances the father is dead and in the others no person knows whether he is dead or alive." Of the nineteen, only six were actually orphans in the sense of having neither father nor mother living.

This correspondence points up not only the confusion among bureau agents over policy but the disagreement between bureau agents and freedmen on the nature of kinship. Agents such as Foote labeled many children born in slavery as bastards and were often skeptical of the claims of a mother who was living with a man other than the child's father. Fathers who had been absent at the time an indenture was made had difficulty establishing custody. One father who in 1867 petitioned for the release of his children was told that the indentures were legal, having been made by a court which knew nothing of his whereabouts at the time. The father, who had been a runaway under slavery, pursued the case for a year, carrying his complaints to the headquarters at Raleigh. But the concept of the good faith of the bureau and the legality of court apprenticeships was upheld at the expense of the view of the primacy of parental rights.

Relatives had even greater difficulties than parents when they tried to retain or regain control of children. In one case the bureau ruled on an uncle's petition: "As the boy has no parents if his friends wish to claim him they must apply to the civil courts." This treatment of relatives as mere friends puzzled a man petitioning for the release of his half-brothers and sisters. "Surly the law does not Call for Childern to be bond out when their peopel is Abel to Keep them," wrote Ben Harris. A grandfather pleaded that his grandson's master would never educate the boy and charged that the man "was very cruel to his former slaves and believes that the Coloured people should remain in darkness." Sometimes custody was awarded to kin, but the petitioner was required to make a very strong case.

Decisions on contested indentures were further complicated by the problem of conflicting testimony. Agents could not investigate every case thoroughly and had to choose whom to believe. Some, like DeForest in South Carolina, rejected the testimony of freedmen out of hand; others were inclined to accept it. Masters, however, had the advantage of community standing, literacy, and a certain shared mode of argument on their side. The records are filled with cases of a simple, painstakingly written plea or an oral complaint by a freedman, coupled with a long, detailed, persuasive letter from a master, sometimes endorsed by other members of the community. Masters tried to take the moral high ground, claiming to have the best interests of the child at heart and impugning the motives of the freedmen. While claiming to keep the child only out of affection, they implicitly acknowledged the economic value of the child's labor by charging that the motive of the freedmen was to acquire that labor. When agents tried to investigate cases they found that members of the white community tended to share an assumption of innocence on the part of their fellow whites. One man wrote to the agent at Halifax, in response to an inquiry, "For my part I dont know as to the facts in the case I presume Mr Carrington would not presume to hold the children under false pretenses."

It could be difficult for an agent to separate economic interest from affection on the part of either a parent or a master. While parents were accused of wanting children back only in order to exploit their labor, masters swore that they held the children only out of affectionate concern for their welfare. If one believed in fundamental parental rights, the mixture of motives was not relevant: affection does not give a man claim to another person's children; desire for economic support does not invalidate a parent's right to his own children. On a more paternalistic view, it could be argued that the child's "best interests" required that he be entrusted to the person who could guarantee his maintenance and provide him with good "prospects." This view could give masters a decided edge over recently freed slaves. Agents wavered between the two views, and the result was vulnerability and uncertainty for the freed parents and children.

Agents who tried to break indentures in response to freedmen's complaints were sometimes faced with fury or active resistance on the part of the master. W. S. Swaringer wrote angrily to the bureau in response to the notice that an agent was canceling an indenture made to him. He denied charges of mistreatment, said he kept the boy only out of sympathy for him, and charged that the complainants "viz Adline and John are not only liars but Rogues they hold connection with the devil dayly get their living by stealing." In another case, a master was willing to relinquish children apprenticed to him only if the father paid him $4. A previous bureau agent had required this fee, illegally, for approval of the indenture. The current agent reported that this master had given the bureau trouble before, and Superintendent Brady authorized him to use force in such cases, noting, "Officers of the bureau are not to be bullied in this way in violation of all laws."

Once they had decided in favor of a freedman's claim, most bureau agents tried to defend his rights. But the process of decision undermined those rights. Agents made inconsistent, subjective, ad hoc decisions, influenced by the "reputation" of the parents and the "prospects" of the children. Class, cultural, and racial assumptions impinged on all of these judgments.

Contradictory signals from their superiors in the bureau hierarchy further complicated the decision-making process. These contradictions were the result of more than bureaucratic procedure. They reflected disagreement and ambivalence within the bureau on two crucial questions: first, to what extent should the bureau intervene to influence the bargaining positions of parties making a contract; and second, once a contract had been made, should the bureau uphold it under all circumstances?

The issue of indentures posed these questions repeatedly. Should the bureau uphold absolutely the parental rights of freedmen, or should agents allow the children of "unfit" parents to be indentured without parental consent? The first would strengthen the bargaining power of parents, the second weaken it. If a master could indenture a child simply by arguing that the child's parents were unfit, he needed to offer no money or concessions. If, instead, he had to persuade parents or kin to relinquish control, he might have to offer attractive terms. On whom should the burden of proof be placed — on the parents, to prove they were fit, or on the master, to prove he had a legitimate and worthy apprenticeship to offer them? Whittlesey at first defended absolute parental rights, then retreated. Most agents seem to have accepted the idea that the children of "unfit" parents could be involuntarily indentured under certain circumstances, thus opening up a complex debate on the character and morals of individual parents.

In answering the second question, whether apprenticeship contracts should be upheld regardless of the circumstances under which they had been made, how was one to regard a case in which a former slaveowner had persuaded a willing agent to apprentice to him eighteen of the children of his former slaves, even though the agent had never seen the children or spoken to their parents? Or a case in which a master had persuaded an agent to apprentice his workers' children to him because they were living on his plantation and eating his food?

Or the case of a former master who apprenticed children whose parents were absent because he had, under slavery, sold them to another state? Were all these to be regarded as legally enforceable agreements? The bureau never had a consistent policy. Cilley would argue that the bureau must uphold indentures, even those made under false pretense, on the grounds of good faith. Whittlesey was more willing to see indentures canceled if the circumstances surrounding them seemed unfair. Overall, the subjective way in which policies were made meant that the freedmen had to be very persistent and that the protection of their rights depended largely on the character of their local agent and his immediate superiors.

Faced with his situation, some freedmen chose to take their chances with the North Carolina courts, which shared jurisdiction over apprenticeship with the bureau. In January 1867, a petition on behalf of two indentured black children was presented to the North Carolina Supreme Court. *In the Matter of Harriet Ambrose and Eliza Ambrose,* the court ruled on the request of two girls, former slaves, aged thirteen and fifteen, to be released from their indentures. The court found that they were "industrious, well behaved and amply provided for in food and clothing" by their mother and stepfather, with whom they were living, and that they had been indentured without notice to a Mr. Russell.

The court ruled that when a petition for a writ of habeas corpus was filed on behalf of an apprentice, a court could look into the circumstances of the binding of the child. Furthermore, it held that the children and their next of kin had to have been present in court at the time of the binding for the indenture to be valid. The court did not rule on the question of whether these children came under the old laws concerning free children of color but said that, whatever their class, they and their relatives required notice for the binding to be legal.

The impact of this case was far-reaching. Indentures in which the next of kin had not been notified could be summarily declared null and void. Immediately after the ruling, some agents were canceling many more indentures than they were approving, and reversing their rulings in individual cases. Relatives did not necessarily have to file for a writ of habeas corpus to obtain the release of children illegally bound.

The North Carolina Supreme Court ruling disturbed some employers of apprentices. One wrote the bureau to complain that he thought agents were interpreting the ruling too narrowly. He objected to the fact that parents who returned from another area after indentures had been made could still claim that they had not been given notice.

He invoked the "faith of the Bureau" in asking that indentures not be broken to return children to "reputed fathers." Other masters continued to resist the spirit of the ruling, holding on to children who had been bound without parental consent. But under the new court ruling, parents and kin stood a better chance of getting back their children.

Some bureau agents by 1867 believed that the system of apprenticeship had been abused, and the court ruling coincided with their inclinations. In June one agent reported to his superiors that a woman to whom he had indentured six children at the beginning of 1866 was apparently a pauper, hiring out the children. He noted, "It is also reported that very few persons who have freed children apprenticed to them are complying with the conditions of indentures relative to learning them to read and write." He felt this should be sufficient grounds for canceling an indenture.

Other agents, however, resisted the trend of cancellation. In September 1867, John Edie, the sub-assistant commissioner at Salisbury, wrote to Raleigh explaining that he would not release a child to her mother because he suspected the motives of the woman's husband. He argued that the stepfather wanted the girl's labor and that the girl would be better educated by her master. He predicted that "if she be returned to her mother, I doubt not, she will be permitted to grow up in ignorance and, perhaps, vice." In spite of the Ambrose ruling, the superintendent told Edie to exercise his own judgment. The question of fitness of parents could still override the principle of parental rights.

In his decision in the Ambrose case, Associate Justice Edwin Reade (a native white) analyzed the abuses of apprenticeship. In North Carolina before the war, he observed, there had been few orphans to bind out. Slaves were not bound out, there were few free Negroes, and indigent white children were usually taken care of by friends and relations. "And besides, apprentices were never looked to as profitable, and were seldom taken except by those who felt some interest in their personal welfare." Since the war, he argued, things had changed. There were more and poorer orphans, and one-third of the population consisted of "indigent colored persons." It was therefore critical that the duties and rights of masters and apprentices, in the proceedings for binding, be defined. The requirement that the children and next of kin be present at the time of the binding was now crucial to the protection of the interests of the children.

His analysis implied that a reliance on good intentions and a policy of laissez-faire in apprenticeship were not adequate to protect the rights of black children and parents. An old and little-used institution, with few legal safeguards, had been transformed but was still granted the same legal status. Under the changed circumstances, apprenticeships became attractive to former slaveowners as an economic expedient and thus were liable to widespread abuse. For the Freedmen's Bureau agents to treat indentures as binding contracts, even when they had been made under the most dubious circumstances, was to ignore the compulsion and deprivation of rights involved. As Justice Reade observed, "In all proceedings of a judicial nature, it is necessary that the person whose rights are to be affected should, in some way, be a party to the proceedings." The establishment of this principle with regard to apprenticeships left bureau agents less room for subjective judgments. Though the court decision requiring the presence and consent of parents or next of kin could not alone put an end to abuse, it strengthened the position of freedmen relative to former masters who wished to employ child labor.

In the mass of social, political, and moral issues which make up the Reconstruction period the practice of child apprenticeship does not loom very large. Nevertheless it is an instructive episode, for here we can see emerging the pattern of former masters attempting to reestablish some of the conditions of slavery, black people speaking up for their rights and appealing to agents of the federal government for support, and representatives of that government wavering between a principled defense of black people's rights and deference to the interests of former slaveowners.

Nikkanochee, Seminole Indian boy. Painted c. 1800-1840 by Frank Wilkin. (courtesy of the Nelson-Atkins Museum of Art, Kansas City, Mo.)

12

Federal Boarding Schools and the Indian Child: 1920-60

Margaret Connell Szasz

For many Americans, particularly in the East, the term boarding school has special connotations. It implies an exclusive setting, a wealthy family, and an elite education. For the American Indian, however, boarding school has had quite another meaning. From the late nineteenth century to the present, most boarding schools for Indian children have been under the direction of the Bureau of Indian Affairs. Since 1882, when Congress funded the first federal off-reservation schools, the Indian Bureau has retained these controversial institutions as an integral part of its educational system.

In the early decades of the federal boarding schools, most Indian parents were opposed to the idea of sending their children, especially young ones, so far from home. Thus, the boarding school concept went against the strong family ties common among Indian people. The strongest support for the government's policy, however, came from the camp of the assimilationists. The passage of the Dawes Act in 1889 was the most significant legislative victory for assimilation, but the boarding school was one of its most effective weapons. In 1900 only 5,000 Indian children attended federal day schools; 17,000 others were sent away for their education.

By the 1920s the policy of assimilation had resulted in disastrous conditions for the Indian people. Destruction of the Indian land base, a result of the Dawes Act, was compounded by disease, starvation, and a short life expectancy rate. Indian Bureau boarding schools had become notorious. Pressures for reform were so strong that Secretary of the Interior Hubert Work ordered a government investigation of federal Indian policy. The results of this study were published in 1928 under the title *The Problem of Indian Administration,* more commonly known as the Meriam Report. In the area of Indian education, the Meriam Report drew harsh conclusions. "The first and foremost need in Indian education is a change in point of view," it observed. Indian education should be "less concerned with a conventional school system and more with the understanding of human beings."

The Meriam Report made official what reformers had been publicizing throughout the decade. When the conditions in the Indian Bureau boarding schools were revealed, the nation was shocked. The system contained so many wrongs, reformers hardly knew which to attack first. Basic to all criticism, however, was the lack of federal monies. Dependent for support on a parsimonious Congress, the Bureau of the Budget, and the Indian Bureau itself, federal boarding schools frequently did not receive sufficient funds even to feed and clothe the children, let alone hire professionally trained teachers and staff. Most schools were unable to provide a balanced diet. Bread, potatoes, molasses, and black coffee sufficed at Rice Boarding School in Arizona. At another, a doctor reported the absence of fresh milk, butter, eggs, vegetables, and fruit. Among the clinical and hospital cases he found a number of children "with conditions very much like scurvy." Health was further weakened by overcrowded dormitories. School administrators often deleted names from official attendance lists so that a school reporting 275 children might have as many as 350. These conditions led to widespread illness, including both tuberculosis and trachoma, a disease of the eye that can lead to blindness.

Student labor kept the schools running. Almost every type of vocational training also doubled as a means of operating the institutions themselves. At Haskell Institute in Lawrence, Kansas, each hour of vocational training was matched by three hours of routine industrial work on campus. A pre-World War I student at the Santa Fe school recalled recently that "student training wasn't just student art, like now; there was work, you learned work." Girls learned to sew, cook, launder, and keep house, but in so doing they did most of the mending, sewing, cooking, and cleaning for the school. Boys learned farming methods, blacksmithing, plumbing, carpentry, stone masonry, and many other skills, but in the process they also raised crops for the school, cared for the livestock, made shoes for themselves, repaired the plumbing, kept the boilers going, constructed new buildings, and repaired old ones. "It is true the student labor is probably less efficient than paid help would be," wrote Haskell's superintendent in 1924, but in the process of maintaining the school "they acquire not only skill but habits of industry and thrift." Here then was a practical compromise, born of necessity and vital to the boarding school system through its first half-century of existence.

With such a schedule it is not surprising that the problems of discipline frequently became major. The physical conditions of routine, hard labor, coupled with crowded facilities and inadequate food, might alone have caused unrest. Of equal weight, however, was the contrast between the institutional milieu and the homes from which the children had been taken. The greatest hardship for the students was probably that of being torn from an extended circle of close-knit relatives, but the physical features of the school itself — regulation clothing and shoes, strange food and surroundings, and the daily harassment of contending with a foreign language — added further discordant notes to the general fear of being so far from home.

Most boarding school administrators saw student unrest as a potential threat and adopted a military system of discipline. Early morning drill was a common sight on campuses, and from there students were marched to breakfast, to class, and to other events of the day. "We used to have a soldier's uniform, those blue uniforms," a former student recalled. At the famous Carlisle school, roll call was taken by company, while at Haskell Institute directors sponsored competition among companies. Administrators praised their military systems, but they continued to maintain school jails. The "lock-up" system was common, but other forms of punishment were applied according to the whim of each superintendent. At Albuquerque, anyone who missed roll call was forced to run between a line of students who struck the offender with belts. One boarding school visitor reported seeing children whipped with a hemp rope and, on another occasion, with a water hose. In these early decades discipline and military rules formed the structure of daily existence.

The school day was divided into specific blocks of time, for the goal was to teach each pupil to use his time wisely in preparation for "useful citizenship." The message of the boarding school was "Forget your former ways," but sometimes the message failed. Teachers discovered that it was often difficult to penetrate the outer reserve of their students. A sympathetic observer who visited Carson Indian School in Stewart, Nevada, in 1925 told of two brothers whose father had brought them a gun for rabbit hunting. After they had made the mistake of firing the gun near the school, they were taken to the disciplinarian who took away the weapon with no explanation. The boys responded to the decision without emotion, but the next morning both they and the gun were gone. Their home, the visitor added, was 100 miles from the school.

Runaways symbolized the negative qualities of the boarding school, and despite persistent efforts to return these students, others followed their example. In their defense one former student explained, "They are home-loving kids; they want to go back home." Nonetheless, students who fled were often caught and punished on return. "The superintendent has found it expedient and desirable to use corporal punishment in a few cases, especially in connection with immature girls who habitually run away from the school," wrote Haskell Institute directors in 1924. In Oklahoma directors of Chilocco Indian School had a standing agreement with nearby police departments. If the police captured runaway children, they received a fee ranging from $1.50 to $5. Whenever possible, this fee was removed from funds that belonged to the children but were held for them by the school. One irate parent complained that almost all of her daughter's $35 in savings had been used to pay for the girl's recapture. In reply, an assistant commissioner suggested that desertion was the student's "own fault," and therefore the student, not the government, should bear the expense for her return.

These were some of the conditions in the boarding schools when the Meriam Report appeared in 1928. Before 1930 the only significant change the government made was to increase the food allocation to bring the daily school diet up to the standard minimum requirement. In 1930, however, the Indian Bureau appointed Will Carson Ryan, the first professional educator to serve as director of Indian education. In 1933 John Collier, the leader of the 1920s reformers, was appointed commissioner of Indian Affairs. Under Collier's guidance and with the aid of emergency New Deal funding, federal Indian policy was subjected to the first serious reform in fifty years. In his initial years in office, Collier introduced changes in Indian policy through the Indian Reorganization Act and other measures, but a number of difficulties hampered his progress and by World War II Collier's Indian New Deal had lost its strength. Between 1930 and the war, Education Director Ryan and his successor, Willard Walcott Beatty, had only a dozen years in which to perform sudden miracles with Indian Bureau schooling.

In the early thirties the Depression served as a pervasive influence on the boarding schools. Many Indian families lost their crops; savings and jobs virtually disappeared. Food was scarce and clothing was hard to come by. Under these circumstances, boarding schools were under pressure to increase their enrollments. In 1934, for example, the Cheyenne River boarding school was filled beyond its capacity during the entire year.

Improved conditions within the boarding schools heightened their appeal. They had always provided some food and clothing; by 1931-32 most schools served a balanced diet. In addition, the Indian Service had hired a corps of doctors to provide preventive medicine and emergency care. The children's weight was checked regularly and those who were underweight were fed between meals. Fulfilling these needs gave a new and more positive image to federal boarding schools.

It was ironic, therefore, that Indian Bureau educators chose this precise moment to close several schools. Heeding the advice of the Meriam Report, Ryan and Beatty sought to cut back on the total number of boarding schools and to decrease the enrollment of pre-adolescent students. The closure policy continued in spite of the Depression and was given a boost during World War II when limited budgets closed additional schools. In 1928, when the Meriam Report appeared, there were seventy-seven boarding schools with an enrollment of 21,000. By 1941 only forty-nine boarding schools remained with an enrollment of 14,000. Thus, between the introduction of the Meriam Report and the war, the number of children attending boarding schools declined by a third. A significant percentage of these students transferred to Indian Bureau day schools, which tripled in enrollment; the remainder went to public schools.

Closure was achieved through several means. Some schools, such as Genoa, Nebraska; Rapid City, South Dakota; and Tomah, Wisconsin, were closed outright. Despite vehement opposition by congressmen who represented the district concerned and local businessmen who feared the economic impact following closure, the Indian Service held firm. Other boarding schools became day schools, but there was still another group that remained in an indefinite status.

The life of Salem Indian School in Oregon hung in the balance for much of the decade. In June 1933, Commissioner Collier ordered it to close; in September this order was rescinded and Salem opened as a two-year vocational school with a reduced enrollment of 300 students. The subject of an intensive investigation during the 1933-34 school year, the school's future was still in doubt at the end of 1934. One educator was so discouraged with the school she concluded that unless it was strengthened, "it would be best to have the agony over with and have it closed." Although Salem, or Chemawa, as it was beginning to be called, managed to stay open through the thirties, when the war began, the old problem returned. "I would suggest now is the time to close this school permanently," wrote the superintendent of education in December 1941. Perhaps the plant could "be offered to the War Department for defense training or for military purposes," he added. Chemawa did conduct classes for the National Defense Training program, but it was not closed; it maintained its identity despite policy shuffling within the Indian Bureau.

A number of boarding schools survived the Collier administration by adapting their programs to the general thrust of the Indian New

Deal. Between the 1880s and the 1930s, the schools had theoretically prepared students for life in urban, white America. When the students left school, however, they generally returned to their reservations, "fresh from contact with white customs as taught them in the boarding schools." No longer able to speak their own language, they were also differentiated by their clothes, shoes, and hair style, and, most important, they had lost the values that separated their people from the others. The result was that former boarding school students did not belong anywhere, neither in the city nor on the reservation.

In the early 1930s Indian Bureau educators argued that there was little logic in training students for nonexistent urban jobs. On the Western Shoshone Reservation in Nevada, nine out of ten boys who went away to boarding school returned home. At Cheyenne River, boarding school directors wrote, "We are confronted by the fact that a majority of these students do return to the reservation."

As educators pieced together these responses, it became clear that boarding schools should be preparing students for reservation life. "What they need is training for rural living," wrote Alida Bowler of her students at Carson, and this was the goal adopted by New Deal educators. While their predecessors were convinced that Indian education meant a transformation of the young Indians, many New Deal education leaders were sold on the values of reservation life.

In neither period, from 1880 to 1930 or from 1930 to 1945, did Indian Service educators suggest that Indian parents or Indian leaders take a significant part in the decision-making. Bureau educators of the thirties, however, did return to the original treaty promises by attempting to reinvigorate agriculture. Many Indian treaties included provisions for farmers, blacksmiths, wheelwrights, and others who would encourage reservation farming. Not until the late nineteenth century had farming yielded to the notion of industrial training. The Indian New Deal educators acknowledged that the agricultural idea was probably the better one.

Most boarding schools of the thirties stressed preparation for reservation life. In the Great Basin, home of Carson Indian School, training was geared to the multiple demands of small ranching: dairy cows, beef cattle, swine, poultry, farming, gardening, farm carpentry, painting, and wiring. At Cheyenne River students raised beef cattle on tribal lands. At Chilocco girls were trained in practical home economics: "how to cook nice, plain foods, and how to can food properly." Chilocco directed its program toward land-based Indians and, like a growing number of schools, encouraged students to develop individual farming projects. Even Haskell Institute, traditionally the business training center for the network of Indian schools, felt the pressure of rural vocational education. Some Haskell women instructors insisted that all their students would be "ladies of leisure" upon graduation, but the superintendent lamented to Beatty that the girls were badly in need of some "down-to-earth training." The girls must return home, he explained to Beatty. "In fact, there is no other place for them to go."

Since these students would probably return to their own cultures, the educators of the thirties attempted to obviate potential alienation. To this end they introduced courses in Indian history and Indian art. Chemawa instituted an even more dramatic change. Concentrating on tribal identity, it divided all of its students into home rooms according to reservation. Each of these twenty-one home rooms was governed by a student-elected tribal council and tackled problems similar to those they might encounter on their reservations. At other schools students prepared for tribal responsibilities through study of the Indian Reorganization Act.

The students responded favorably to this new approach. Indian history classes were filled and the art work completed at the Santa Fe Indian School was praised throughout the nation. Traditional strictures against Indian religions were relaxed and where students lived near their homes, they were allowed to return for religious holidays. After urging by Collier and others, most schools moved away from a military routine and the atmosphere "was a little bit more free," as one student of the mid-thirties remembered.

Despite these changes, the boarding schools remained basically Anglo-oriented. L. E. Correll, Chilocco's superintendent from 1926 to 1952, exemplified the administrative carry-over of Anglo values. Firmly convinced that education was a process of individual character building, he gave his students large doses of the Puritan ethic. A typical memo from Correll suggested, "[M]any girls are forgetting to be business-like about their education or intelligent about their affairs. There is a great waste of time, yours and someone elses. . . . [T]he tendency to get into shiftless habits will certainly bring failure upon you." Even in those schools without a Correll, students were separated from teachers and staff by a cultural dichotomy. Despite courses in Indian history and art, Anglo-American culture prevailed during the Indian New Deal.

World War II brought an abrupt halt to these programs of the thirties. Wartime demands meant less funding for Indian Bureau education; at the same time the war itself served as a dynamic influence on the Indian people. An estimated 24,000 Indians served in the armed forces and some 40,000 others were employed in war-related jobs. In the postwar years, many of these were drawn to urban centers. Cities offered jobs and the comforts of affluence that had not yet penetrated the rural reservations. But cities also meant loneliness, job instability, and access to alcohol. An Acoma Indian described it,

i seem walking in sleep
down streets down streets grey with cement
and glaring glass and oily wind
armed with a pint of wine.

But in the postwar stage of Indian urbanization, these drawbacks were not recognized, and most bureau educators were eager to implement the change. Plans for teaching Indian pupils how to adapt to an urban world were in the discussion stage as the war drew to a close. In the summer of 1944, a special teacher-training course on "Education for Life Outside the Reservation" was planned. Indian veterans were the first recipients of the new approach. In 1944 boarding schools instituted vocational training for veterans. Eventually, these included Haskell, Chilocco, Albuquerque, Flandreau, and others. While agriculture was offered to the veterans, other courses in welding, printing, machine trades, and building trades suggested an urban orientation.

The most dynamic effort of this postwar shift was the Navajo Special Program. Initiated in 1946, this project sought to overcome some of the deficiencies in Navajo education. Indian New Deal educators had tackled Navajo schooling in the thirties, but the war years had eroded their efforts and in 1946, there were at least 10,000 young Navajos who had received little or no schooling. At the same time, overpopulation of the Navajos' land led to the growing conviction that some of the tribe would have to work off of the reservation. These overwhelming problems led the Navajo tribe to take its case to Washington, D.C. There, tribal interest was supported by bureau educators and led to one of the most unusual programs ever developed within the bureau school system. The goal of the Navajo Special Program was to equip overage Navajo youth with a vocational skill, plus sufficient English, to guarantee an off-reservation job.

At first, it was not difficult to find space for this program, as a number of off-reservation boarding schools had declined in enrollment during the war. Chilocco had spaces for 100 additional students in 1946, and Chemawa's enrollment had dropped to a dangerous low. The Navajo Special Program brought new life to these boarding schools. In the fall of 1946 the first Navajo students boarded the train for Sherman Institute in California. Most of them did not speak English; few had been to school. In about five years they would possess vocational skills and a grasp of the English language and would be employable in uran areas. By 1961 about 4,300 Navajo youth had graduated from this schooling.

The Navajo Special Program was unique, but its successes depended on several features not available to regular boarding school programs. First, it was a short-range project with definite goals. Second, it received adequate funds, a feature never enjoyed by the regular programs. Finally, its directors and teachers were among the best in the Indian Service. The contrast between the Navajo program and the regular boarding school system soon became apparent. During its fifteen-year life span, the favored treatment it received led to resentment among regular staff and teachers. Its record-breaking successes in job placement and English-speaking skills were envied by those struggling under the traditionally inadequate system.

It also fostered a growing resentment from other tribes. Chemawa was a case in point. Between 1948 and 1957 the Indian Bureau made a radical change in Chemawa's student population. When the Navajo Special program began, the maximum Navajo enrollment was 200, balanced against 400 northwest students. Soon friction developed between the two groups, and by 1957 northwest Indians were protesting that they no longer had a school for their young people — all northwest Chemawa students had been sent elsewhere. Similar conditions prevailed at Stewart (formerly known as Carson), where all of the Great Basin students were phased out in order to accommodate the Navajos. Thus, in less than a decade these schools lost their regional character. Others, like Chilocco, juggled dual programs of both Navajo and regular pupils.

Another issue was involved in the changing status of these boarding schools. In the late forties and fifties, Indian Bureau personnel labeled most of Chemawa's northwest students "welfare cases" and urged that they be placed under state agency care. Stewart reported that at least two-thirds of its Nevada pupils were "orphans, pre-delinquents, or the products of broken homes." Chilocco was classified in the same category. Its personnel were accused of failing to recognize that most boarding school pupils "have serious enough deficiencies that they cannot, as yet achieve successfully in normal, public school situations."

By 1969, when the Kennedy Report was published, it was widely recognized that the unstable nature of these students had become the most challenging problem of Indian Bureau boarding schools. The Kennedy Report pointed out that up to 75 percent of the Chilocco students were there because of "severe social or emotional problems." Stewart was described as "a school exclusively with problem children." The Kennedy Report failed to mention, however, that Indian Bureau educators had been trying to cope with this dilemma for over thirty years. Their requests to Congress for social workers, psychiatrists, and other additions to regular staff went unfulfilled year after year. During World War II and the postwar decades Indian children reflected the increasing instability of a partially urbanized people, and the problems they brought with them to boarding schools only contributed to greater unrest in the schools themselves.

By the 1960s many tribes were calling for increased Indian control over Indian Bureau boarding schools. The virtual autonomy granted to the Navajo Special Program was declining and, in spite of increased Alaska Native enrollment, some schools, such as Chemawa, responded to Indian pressure and once again began to serve local Indian educational needs. Indian school boards also gained a small measure of control, as witnessed in the 1969 uproar over the proposed contracting of Chilocco to a private firm. In some areas Indian tribes achieved sole responsibility for boarding schools. One of the earliest of these was the pioneering and controversial Rough Rock Demonstration School, opened in 1966. Since then the number of tribal-controlled schools contracted to the federal government has gradually increased. One of the most recent examples is the Pierre Indian Learning Center in South Dakota, formerly Pierre Indian School, now under the control of the Pierre Indian Board of Education.

Between the 1920s and the 1960s Indian students in bureau boarding schools were subjected to a bewildering variety of educational theories. Perhaps further solutions to the unique problems of these students will depend on the growing assistance of their own people, who are now beginning to determine the directions of their children's education.

Children on the streets of New York City, c. 1946-49. Marion Palfi, photographer. (courtesy of the Spencer Museum of Art, University of Kansas, gift of the artist)

13

Childhood in an Urban Black Ghetto: Two Life Histories

Melvin D. Williams

Belmar is a black neighborhood in Pittsburgh, Pennsylvania, whose middle-income residents (black and white) were invaded in the 1950s by low-income blacks displaced from the Hill District of Pittsburgh by a redevelopment project designed to expand the central business district (downtown area). And while statistics have documented these population movements, they fail to capture the trials, tribulations, and disorientations of some of the people displaced. This essay sketches the formative years in the Hill District of two brothers who now live in Belmar. The life histories reported here were collected during three years of anthropological observation. This included residing in the neighborhood, visiting the homes of the neighbors, intensive interviews with a select group of these persons, some survey research, and participation in a local citizen's organization. The life histories were collected to provide an internal glimpse of processes that are often accounted for in a quick stroke of the sociological pen.

Ray is now forty-six years old and has lived in Pittsburgh's black ghettos all his life. He has four children and is a maintenance worker at one of the large buildings downtown. His father came to Pittsburgh from Georgia after the death of Ray's grandfather. The older children of the family (Ray's aunts and uncles) arranged for their entire family (mother, three girls, and three boys) to travel to Pittsburgh. Ray's father often recounted his family's hardships in coming to Pittsburgh when there was neither welfare nor social security. The family often slept in one room with the children sleeping in shifts because beds were in short supply. When one of them was fortunate enough to obtain employment, he or she would support the entire family providing welfare and social security. This process continued until each member "got on his feet."

Ray's mother and her family of orientation were from North Carolina. She went to Pittsburgh after her mother's death to live with her oldest sister, who earlier had left home, married, and settled there. She was the third sister to go to Pittsburgh; the others were married homemakers while Ray's mother still attended school. Becoming bored with school and the limited provisions of her oldest sister, she soon found a job in a laundry.

While she was working, attending church, and dating, Ray's mother met his father. Ray's father had held various menial jobs; he was unemployed when he met his wife, however. Still, he was frugal with his money, and his oldest sister, who was employed, provided his meals, shelter, and "spending change." Ray's mother once described him as "a good dresser who could foot you to death." Persuading her that he had money, a job, and "came from a good family," he joined her church and cajoled her into marriage.

Only after marriage did she discover their plight — no job, no money, and no home. Her sister had warned her not to get married, suspecting that the future husband was a "ne'er do well." She insisted that if her sister got married against her will she could no longer live with her. Nevertheless, the young couple started upon their rugged path of life together. The husband's sister continued to help, and he worked periodically. But the nearly constant lack of security for herself and the children was a psychological trauma that Ray's mother would never forget. She was frequently ill and worried most of the time.

Ray's mother explained her "bad nerves" as a result of incidents such as moving into houses before leasing them and moving out before being discovered by the landlord. Many times Ray's paternal aunt became the family doctor when no other physician would come to the house. She also fed them when the cupboards at Ray's house were bare. In fact, for many years his father ate his meals at her house to keep from using the meager resources at his own home.

Ray's oldest maternal aunt divorced her husband and moved to another city; another older sister of his mother moved to Pittsburgh and married a man with a secure job. This sister never had any children of her own and helped Ray's mother. She continued to help Ray and his siblings even after most of them reached adulthood.

Ray's oldest brother had died at the age of four, so Ray was reared as the eldest for most of his life. His mother believed that poor obstetrical care in the delivery room had injured the brother so that he never fully recovered. His congenital injury was complicated by the lack of adequate health care due to the family's low income.

Ray begins his own story with the statement, "I was born in the Hill. My parents lived in a two-room basement apartment." He continues, informing us that his father had a bad heart due to a childhood case of rheumatic fever, and that the heart condition kept Ray's father unemployed for many years. His family moved several times during Ray's early childhood, and Ray recalls his father's many survival techniques during those bleak days. When most of the neighbors' electricity was shut off for nonpayment of bills, his father secured power for the family "by climbing the tellie pole and putting a jumper on the electric wire." In this way they had a refrigerator when such luxuries in the neighborhood were rare. Occasionally the children received large expensive toys such as a new fire engine which could seat two children up front and one in the rear. These purchases were made on credit. Once, when confronted with one account in arrears which was not likely to be paid, his father denied the purchase. When asked to sign the paper, he wrote an "X" for his signature; the creditors dismissed him in anguish. These "survival" tactics continued through Ray's childhood, and he recalls, "How proud we kids were when we went out riding in one of the very few cars around here." Such tactics often required that valuable property, such as automobiles, be legally owned by relatives. It also required that the father learn a trade (paperhanging) so he could work on those rare occasions when he felt well enough. Frequently all members of the family were gainfully employed, the children with their newspaper and shoeshine routes.

Ray recalls spending much of his childhood with his neighborhood peers. He learned early from them that one was ranked according to size and aggressiveness. The larger boys would twist his arms behind his back and force him to call them "daddy" to amuse the groups and display their rank. Even at this tender age (approximately eight years old), these ghetto boys had learned to value the elusive "daddy" that several of them lived without. The older girls would often beat him for the same reasons of displaying rank. One had to be bold and aggressive, albeit somewhat accommodative to avoid too much bruising. Aloofness and individuality were not tolerated. In fact, Ray explained that his younger brother was accepted by the group before Ray because he conformed and cooperated more than Ray.

When Ray was seven years old, the neighborhood girls had already introduced him to sexual petting, and he learned to enjoy the pleasure of these tactile experiences before he was able to have intercourse. He had his first girlfriend at the age of seven and walked her home from school and visited her after school. The girl's mother would often allow him to enter the house to avoid the nuisance of their communicating from opposite sides of the first-floor window. Another girlfriend of Ray's would keep him and his male companion waiting for hours outside just to catch a glimpse of her at her second-floor window or in the corridor. Her parents were not so tolerant, but it was worth every waiting moment just for the rare pleasure of seeing her. "It was just fun to be near her house," Ray remembered.

Ray received no allowance nor did he have any conception of what it meant. He earned most of his spending money by running errands, selling scrap metal and rags, and establishing a network of adults in the neighborhood who provided him with money for various reasons. This network became so well organized that many of the homes he visited (scheduling visits so as not to be a "pest") were a source of money with or without any related chores (because of the good will he had established with the residents). Many of these sources were homes of relatives or friends of his parents with whom he made a special effort to become acquainted. In general, at a very early age Ray was spending much of his time in the neighborhood streets — hustling, playing, and courting. He explained that if he or his brothers remained in the house during mild weather, his mother suspected that "something was wrong."

These were days when Ray did not know what a library or a museum was. He would not learn about them until years later during the school field trips. He was never taken downtown, and his parents subscribed to no newspapers or magazines. There was no television, and children were not permitted to use the radio. These were his formative years for developing alternate values.

Throughout Ray's recollections weaves a thread of violence — among his peers, from his teachers, and in the streets. One of his early experiences with violence in the streets was when he was about five years old and witnessed a woman being beaten near his house. According to Ray, "She kept crying and he kept hitting her and hollering at her. She looked white and seemed so pretty and helpless. I was high yellow or shit-color and I knew how many times I got beat just for that so I felt sorry for her. She was out of place in that neighborhood just like I was out of place everywhere." In addition, certain neighborhood parents "went for bad" welcoming any excuse for an altercation to display their prowess for aggression. Disputes among their children were frequent sources of these excuses.

One of the family's heroes during these early years of Ray's life was his maternal uncle. "He was a good-looking man, a gambler and a braggart. The women liked him and gave him money while the men liked to hear him talk. It didn't matter that he was separated from his wife and two children, without a job, frequently in jail, and had had several children out of wedlock. Still he would maintain: 'They ain't no kids of mine.' "

When Ray was eight years old his family moved again. He enjoys recalling the small details of this house where he spent many years. He remembered the several months of labor that his father, his brothers, and he put into a five-room brick house before it was fit for human habitation. Even with these efforts it was still a modest house with two bedrooms on the second floor and a frame kitchen set off from the house. Without a basement under it or a room over it, the kitchen was the coldest room during the winter. The only heat came from the range. Often the water was left running to keep it from freezing and bursting the pipes. Initially, the house was heated by a large coal burner in the dining room and a living room fireplace that also burned coal. Later the fireplace was abandoned for a small gas space heater, while the coal burner was moved to the basement with a large opening in the dining room floor directly above it. The arrangement allowed better use of the precious space and made the only bath, located in the basement, more tolerable.

The house sat on the side of a precipitous hill that overlooked the Allegheny River, Bigelow Boulevard, and the Pennsylvania Railroad Station. Ray discovered many riches here in this poor, predominantly black neighborhood. The geographical location was a treasure for boyhood play and imagination. Thirty feet away, at the end of the hillside, he could clearly see the boats guiding their freight up and down the river. He could watch the trains moving in and out of the station. He could watch the vehicles racing up and down the boulevard. Ray saw his first seaplanes in action along the river; a river terminal was used for excursion flights. He could fly his kites up and over the hillside, free from the usual obstacles of the urban streets. Ray spent many hours playing in the streams that ran over the hillside. Part of the hillside was covered with trees and brush, so he and his peers had their own urban forest. They would roam or camp there for hours, often with food, only a hundred yards from home.

Ray remembers with great pleasure the "bull rope" swings that the larger boys would mount. On another portion of this hillside, these swings extended from the upper reaches of a telephone pole. The boys would swing in Tarzan fashion from one side of the hill, around the pole, out over the precipice, to the other side of the hill. The ride was dangerous but thrilling. The younger boys had few opportunities to swing while the larger boys were on the rope, but it was a pleasure for them just to watch the excitement. Then, at the end of the day, the big boys would abandon the swing, and Ray and his peers could ride until dark. When there was no school they would arise early in the morning and race to the swing to occupy it for several hours before the older boys arrived.

Ray seems especially appreciative of living in this small ecological niche. From large cardboard boxes he and the boys would make sleds to ride the loosely packed dirt down the steep hillsides. They had rock wars with the boys who lived much higher on the hillside, boys with whom they did not interact in other ways. They sat upon favorite stoops and porches and through interaction established cohesive peer groups that endured until they moved away or became adults. These stoops were usually located on a corner so that they could see neighborhood interaction in four directions. They observed, talked, told stories, sang, joked, and humiliated one another. They teased the girls, the neighborhood drunk, and the local imbecile. The drunk had been gassed in the First World War, and he walked on his heels. They called him "staglee," and he answered to the name. They would call to him, "Why do you walk on your heels?": and he would answer, "To save my sole." He would often threaten them when they were disrespectful, and they enjoyed the threat of danger. The imbecile was about nineteen years old, and his energy never seemed to wane; he chased the boys for hours. Their fear of him made the play more exciting.

During the winter they made tracks for running and sliding on the sidewalk, battled with the snow, and sledded down their steep street. When the weather was warmer they played football and baseball in the streets. Their form of baseball was one in which they bounced the ball off a wall instead of using a bat. They went swimming in the recreation center pool and often took the time to play in the center's ball field or the schoolyards as well.

During these years school was an extension of the street activities. One was forced to abide by certain rules which had little meaning. For example, one was encouraged to be "bad" by peer group pressure. Often this merely meant that one behaved in school as disruptively as one did outside of school. Thus teachers put the "agitator" in a corner or under the desk. Sometimes they would beat his knuckles with a ruler, or lead him by his ear lobe to the principal's office where he spent the rest of the school day waiting for a paddle displaying, all the while, his bravado to his peers.

My teachers were white and they seemed so clean that they made me feel dirty.... And when I was bad that's when their true color would show.... Starting even in the first grade you could sense that when their own children were bad they didn't treat them like they treated you when you were bad.... They could look at you like you were an animal and if they had to touch you it was with the tips of their fingers or a mean kind of grab.... They never really touched you like they did the one or two white kids in the class.... They never got close to you, hugged you, or put their arms around you so you could feel a part of the school.... They talked at me, taught at me; they were teaching in the room and I could catch it or not.... The school belonged to them and I could stay in the building as long as I watched myself, stayed in my place. Once in that building, you were out of the ghetto and you better act like it. The school was not part of the ghetto which was part of me.

In the ghetto Ray not only had to contend with the ethos of teachers and their mainstream institutional control and restrictions, he also had to fight or avoid altercations only to suffer physical injuries and humiliation. The pecking order in his school was determined not by grade averages but by aggression, as was status in the neighborhood. Aggression as a major source of excitement and entertainment was almost impossible to avoid. Even when there were no fights, the threat still hung over one like the fabled sword of Damocles on its slender thread: "I'm gon' beat your butt after school"; or, "I better not see you outside"; or, "You gon' get your butt kicked." Then there were the bullies who, upon passing a smaller guy in the hall, would grab him by the collar and demand money or sweets or just humiliate him. According to Ray, "There was one guy, Winston, who was into body-building and weights and he was a 'punch-you' addict. . . . He was always punching the little guys in the arm or shoulder to show you his strength."

Learning in school was incidental and peripheral to the main business of life. That business was to interact, to tease, to court the girls, and to fight. In the sixth and seventh grade the girls would be attacked with romantic play episodes if the teacher left the classroom. This behavior, combined with frenzied attacks among the boys themselves, continued until the teacher returned. The favorite game in the gym classes was the violent use of basketballs to hit and put "out" one another. The teacher enjoyed this as much as the boys.

Violence in school merged with violence in the home. Ray described how a man shot a woman, "five times right there near me." The man was reacting to a common-law disagreement. At age nine, Ray witnessed a neighborhood woman severely "cutting" another woman with a knife after an argument. The woman victim in the knifing incident had been arguing with a teenage girl. At the height of the argument the girl's mother ran out with a knife, and both she and her daughter attacked the victim. The mother was famous in the neighborhood for her knife-wielding exploits and was rumored to have even killed someone.

On one occasion the knife-wielding woman rushed into Ray's house to vehemently protest the aggression of Ray's younger brother against her grandson. Ray explained that his mother was almost in a state of shock as he sat nearby and watched the incident. His mother was taken by surprise as she stood at the ironing board ironing her weekly wash. The woman, her famous knife in hand, yelled and screamed at Ray's mother who hardly knew what was happening. Her voice was so loud that Ray's father rushed downstairs and surprised the woman, who thought he was away. He ordered her out of his house with such rage that the woman never bothered to speak to him — she quickly left. His father was upset that his mother had not used the iron to defend herself. He dressed immediately and went to the local office of the justice of the peace to file charges.

Ray recalls the freedom he had as an adolescent and especially as a teenager. He and his brother (one year and two months younger) came and went almost as they pleased with very little restriction from their parents. Their parents were only concerned that the boys not cause them trouble. There was little if any pressure to get "good grades" in school, to work, to come home for dinner, to go to bed, or any of the other parental coercions typical in mainstream lifestyles. So Ray's summer-evening activities lasted until morning, long after his peers had been called home and the group had dwindled to a quiet twosome. Then Ray and his brother would return home for sleep.

Nevertheless, his parents reminded him that education was important for "good jobs" and professions. But academic excellence was one's own choice, and college was merely a word with little substance in his household. In addition, a few schoolteachers and Ray's newspaper "boss" often reminded him of the value of education. Yet such ideas were remote when reinforcement was lacking in the context of his life style.

As Ray and his peers became teenagers, their attention turned more and more to heterosexual relationships. Their games and their play often focused upon exclusive time with females. He remembered his unrestricted experiments with sex in the summer evenings. Neighborhood families in which both parents worked provided convenient shelters for adolescent and teenage sexual experiments. Homes in which parents were seldom present, day or night, became "dens of iniquity." Ray's brother had an unpleasant experience when his girlfriend was impregnated at such a house at the age of eleven. He was thirteen; an older boy was responsible, but he felt obligated to accept the fatherhood. The baby died.

Ray and his friends played several variations of hide and seek, but for most the real game was hide and "pet." Although sexual intercourse seldom occurred, many of them were exposed to the "real thing" on some occasion. All of Ray's sexual education took place in these play encounters. He knew some of the girls who were impregnated during these times and remembered their maternal experiences. He recalled the youthful marriages precipitated by such experiences. Often the males would resist marriage in spite of their paternal status, but the status itself usually had a profound impact upon their future interests. School became even more confining, and one was anxious to fulfill one's role as a man. The adult world of menial work, money, street life, and heterosexual companionship beckoned them. Thus the cycle continued — poverty, undereducation, and institutional deprivation. Value stretch was adaptive and simultaneously restrictive. This institutionalized poverty is similar to that that Wolfe surveyed among Latin American peasants. And this description is consistent with Padfield's call for participants themselves to describe the content of the so-called culture of poverty.

Ray himself impregnated a casual friend when he was only sixteen years old. She was fifteen. Their parents encouraged marriage, as they were long-term friends. The girl's mother insisted. Ray was reluctant. The girl's parents prosecuted him, and the judge gave him a choice — marriage or incarceration. He married her, but he felt he had been "had." She had first met Ray when she took a job at the local hospital where he worked as a part-time animal caretaker. There the relationship was consummated. He claimed she was the aggresor and he the victim, but he could not sell the judge his story. They were married for little more than a year before they were divorced. Both married later, but the male child of his first marriage created many heartaches for Ray's kin.

Ray's family had moved to Belmar before he married for the first time, and he and his wife lived with his parents. Ray claims that his wife was a good homemaker and a good wife, but that she required his presence at home when he was not working. Both of them had quit school, and Ray was given a full-time job where he had been working part-time. Ray believes the marriage would have endured if his wife had not been so conscientious about the manner in which a household operates — the husband staying at home with his family.

Ray recalls grocery shopping for his mother as a teenager; he did not mind the two-mile walk to the grocer, because he would always secretly add cookies to the shopping list. Of course he had to consume them before he arrived home. Often misjudging his appetite, he was forced to give portions of his sweets to children he encountered on his return. He was often fearful when he heard the disputes that his mother had with the storekeeper on "check day." She would refuse to pay for items she had not ordered. Fortunately for Ray, his scheme was never discovered.

This account reveals a despondent impression of socialization within a poor ghetto. Perhaps Ray expressed it best when he commented, "If I had died when I was young, the world wouldn't owe me nothing."

Ray is reacting to a lost world. Yet notwithstanding the economic deprivation, the adjustive features of these poor life styles have captured his emotions here.

Fred

A brief account of the teenage experiences of Ray's brother, Fred, provides a glimpse of the variations in socialization experiences even within the same family. Ray and Fred are two different personalities. Fred's ability to relate well with adults and the adult world, contrasted with Ray's early vulnerability to the responsibilities of family life, account for some of their differences in interpreting similar experiences.

Fred is fourteen months younger than Ray, but he was always considered the more mature of the two. Because of this it seems to him that he had never been a child. Somehow, as long as he could remember, he had participated and functioned well in the adult world. He recalls that at the age of eleven it was his responsibility to travel the several miles from the Hill to the North Side via public transportation (the incline and the streetcar) to collect his mother's portion of his father's pay, so she would be able to go shopping before his father returned home on payday. Fred was sent downtown almost weekly to pay utility bills and insurance premiums for his parents and his mother's sister. It was also his responsibility to retrieve his aunt's check from the mailbox every week, cash it, and pay her respective debts. When Fred's parents would leave the city or the state on kinship "call to duty," they would leave Fred in charge of the siblings. He recalled that as early as eleven he would help his father drive the car on the Pennsylvania Turnpike while sitting on a pillow to see the road. At the time these duties seemed ordinary to Fred because he was able and expected to perform. As he recalls these periods, however, he is impressed with how much time was spent fulfilling adult responsibilities.

During this same period Fred began to sell mail-order products from door to door in his neighborhood. He started with cloverine salve; after several successful orders he began to sell other items. He subsequently sold a variety of black periodicals and earned profit and prizes. He never forgot his first prize — a monopoly game. Gradually he learned that he was endowed with a unique ability to sell. In fact, the quantity of a product seemed to be no problem; only his desire to sell mattered. Fred believed that "if I wanted to sell it and I tried, I could sell it."

Fred's periodic enterprises brought him into persistent contact with life in the street. He spent many hours in the old Fullerton and Wylie nightlife area. He traveled Webster, Wylie, Center, Herron, and Bedford avenues week after week. He frequented the barbershops, beauty shops, bars, speakeasies, gambling "joints," pool rooms, private clubs, restaurants, shoeshine parlors, jitney stations, hat-cleaning shops, fish markets, and private homes. Because of these activities, he spent more time mingling with adults than with his peers. He enjoyed his sales activities, and he continued to be very successful. Again and again he proved to himself that he could sell as many periodicals as he wished. Fred accumulated a considerable amount of money as a result of these activities, but he had little time to spend it. There were many late evenings when he had sold several hundred periodicals but refused to quit and return home until he had sold the last item. The weight of the periodicals had been replaced by the bulk of coin and his entire body was tired from walking and carrying the merchandise, but he pushed on until the end. Week after week this process continued to be a personal challenge that brought him the admiration of his parents, his paper "boss," and other adults, as well as the envy of competitive paperboys.

These activities allowed Fred to mingle with a variety of people in the Hill. He sold to the educated, the uneducated, the intoxicated, hustlers, gamblers, barmaids, bartenders, pimps, prostitutes, secretaries (in insurance companies and other offices), jitney drivers, barbers, beauticians, and theater attendants. He was rebuffed by the belligerent, the aggressive, the exasperated, and the defeated. Many a beleaguered and thus bellicose tavern owner or bartender tried unsuccessfully to keep him out of the bar and away from the patrons. Other proprietors and customers, whether they condemned or praised him, knew him and accepted him as a regular part of the scene. Some proprietors and bartenders accepted defeat after being continually outwitted by his tenacity. Some even became friends and customers after witnessing a boy who would use a series of strategic maneuvers to reach potential customers. These maneuvers would usually entail his getting in the door and to the rear of the bar before being discovered. Then even if he were discovered, most of the patrons would already have been exposed to his wares; few proprietors were aggressive enough to stop a patron from making a purchase if he so desired. On some occasions, though, an exasperated bartender would insist that the patron follow Fred outside to make the purchase.

These regular appearances on the "avenue" and in customers' homes created close ties between Fred and some of his patrons. Some women almost adopted him and would always reveal in the sound of their shouts that this was their "boy." One woman customer had to be "straightened out" by Fred's aunt because she had romantic designs upon him, notwithstanding the fact that he was fourteen years old and she was forty. Thus, Fred was a regular part of the people parade that marched from tavern to tavern, corner to corner, street to street, and encounter to encounter, wondering most of the time, "Will I find my love (or goals) today." He was one of the players in a human drama, most of whom had long been abandoned in the economic scheme of things. They played out their lives together in the "spit," sex, liquor, drugs, violence, and games of chance; even "foreigners" (whites seeking entertainment) would come and pay to see these acts but deny them any value when they returned home. Fred was often fascinated by the pomp, ritual, and ceremony of his customers on their public stages — the "high yellow" with their "good hair" and their private club; the "high society" and their favorite grill; the Friday night "big spenders" who were "broke" on Sunday; the flesh merchants; and the dream peddlers. The nucleus of this drama was Fullerton and Wylie streets which were eliminated by the economic scheme in urban redevelopment. After all, it was only a wasteland, a slum, an area of blight too close to the nucleus of the city's economic center — downtown Pittsburgh. So Fred's world was destroyed along with his house; he took his savings and made a down payment on a house in Belmar for his parents and his siblings. He was an unwitting part of an economic process that created urban deserts, forced him to invest in them, coerced him to live in them, blamed him for their existence, and then destroyed them when it became profitable to do so.

Further, as mentioned previously, Fred had extensive periodical sales routes in residential areas as well as along the "avenue." His job took him into the homes and social networks of his many residential customers where he learned how they lived. Because many of them required credit even for such inexpensive items as newspapers, he also learned about their problems. Over a four-year period he became a familiar face; many customers became fond of him and demonstrated their fondness with Christmas bonuses. Many credit customers' payments were collected at their local bars, gambling haunts, or barbershop "hangouts." To other customers he loaned money for cigarettes, the numbers (lottery), milk, or beer to be collected with their newspaper payments. Thus, Fred was more than a paperboy; he was absorbed into the poor black incorporation process, and as he recalled experiences, one could believe that he "liked it."

However, Fred stresses that his experience was not an isolated one. There were many boys like himself who participated in such lifestyles. Shoeshine boys with their homemade boxes traveled the same "avenue" routes and competed for the limited money there. Other newspaper boys often raced him to a particular bar to hawk the same wares. Other boys combed the area to beg or "roll" the drunks or to rob other young peddlers. Fred marveled that in all his years of roaming dark streets, alleys, corridors, and tenements, he was never robbed or molested. He consistently carried home large amounts of coins and dollar bills without incident. For him the dangers of the ghetto were never realized, and he insists that most of its victims are in part responsible for their own plight.

Finally, Fred describes his plight in Belmar.

When we moved out here there was a lot of phony people. They didn't have nothing and most of them were nobodies but they thought that Belmar was high class so they didn't want to associate with us [genuines]. Their avenues didn't have the roots [generations of black social existence and structure] like those on the Hill. These avenues were just trying to get started so the phonies didn't have their own places like they did in the Hill and they would run into the nitty-gritty brother [genuine]. This kept the avenue from being the place it was in the Hill and soon the phonies stopped coming out or moved and without their money the avenue started to die. You just didn't have that good mix of Blacks that keep things jumping. So I moved to Belmar but I left my heart and soul in the Hill.

The life history is a recognized technique in anthropological research. In urban anthropology it is one approach to viewing the complexity of city life as it impacts upon the experiences of a resident. This approach opens the ghetto walls as well as the hearts and souls created behind them. It gives us an important personal perspective of the pain and the pleasure of being black in an urban black ghetto. It provides us with some important clues of a human complexity that often strain the more limited methods of the social sciences.

Selected Readings

Adams, David Wallace. "Education in Hues: Red and Black at Hampton Institute, 1878-1893." *South Atlantic Quarterly* 76 (Spring 1977): 159-76.
———. "Schooling the Hopi: The Federal Indian Policy Writ Small, 1887-1917." *Pacific Historical Review* 48 (Aug. 1979): 335-56.

Axtell, James. *The Indian Peoples of Eastern America: A Documentary History of the Sexes.* New York: Oxford University Press, 1981.

Blassingame, John W. *The Slave Community: Plantation Life in the Antebellum South.* Rev. ed. New York: Oxford University Press, 1979.

Coles, Robert. *Children of Crisis, Vol. I: A Study of Courage and Fear.* Boston: Little, Brown, 1964.
———. *Children of Crisis, Vol. 4: Eskimos, Chicanos, Indians.* Boston: Little, Brown, 1977.

David, Jay, ed. *Growing Up Black.* New York: William Morrow, 1968.

Davis, Allison, and John Dollard. *Children of Bondage: The Personality Development of Negro Youth in the Urban South.* Washington, D.C.: American Council on Education, 1940.

Eastman, Charles A. *Indian Boyhood.* n.p.: Fenwyn Press Books 1902, rept. 1980.

Elkins, Stanley. *Slavery: A Problem in American Institutional and Intellectual Life.* New York: University of Chicago Press, 1959.

Finkelstein, Barbara. "Reading, Writing and the Acquisition of Identity in the United States." In *Regulated Children/Liberated Children: Education in Psychohistorical Perspective.* Ed. Barbara Finkelstein. New York: Psychohistory Press, 1979, pp. 114-39.

Frazier, E. Franklin. *Negro Youth at the Crossways: Their Personality Development in the Middle States.* Washington, D.C.: American Council on Education, 1940.

Freeman, Patricia A. "Kiowa Apache Concepts and Attitudes Toward the Child." *Papers in Anthropology* 12 (Spring 1971): 90-160.

Genovese, Eugene D. *Roll, Jordon, Roll: The World the Slaves Made.* New York: Pantheon, 1974.

Gutman, Herbert G. *The Black Family in Slavery and Freedom.* New York: Pantheon, 1976.

Kiple, Kenneth F., and Virginia H. Kiple. "Slave Child Mortality: Some Nutritional Answers to the Perennial Puzzle." *Journal of Social History* 10 (Mar. 1977): 284-309.

Kremer, Gary, and Linda Gibbens. "The Missouri Home for Negro Girls: The 1930s." *American Studies* 24 (Fall 1983): 77-93.

Johnson, Charles. *Growing Up in the Black Belt: Negro Youth in the Rural South.* Washington, D.C.: American Council on Education, 1940.

La Flesche, Francis. *The Middle Five: Indian Schoolboys of the Omaha Tribe.* Lincoln: University of Nebraska Press, 1900, rept. 1978.

Moranian, Suzanne E. "Ethnocide in the Schoolhouse: Missionary Efforts to Educate Indian Youth in Pre-Reservation Wisconsin." *Wisconsin Magazine of History* 44 (1981): 242-60.

Pettitt, George A. *Primitive Education in North America.* University of California Publications in American Archaeology and Ethnology, vol. 43, Berkeley, 1946.

Rose, Lee. "Childhood in Bondage." In *Slavery and Freedom.* Ed. William Freehling. New York: Oxford University Press, 1982, pp. 37-48.

Schlegel, Alice. "The Adolescent Socialization of the Hopi Girl." *Ethnology* 12 (Oct. 1973): 449-62.

Szasz, Margaret Connell. *Education and the American Indian, 1928-1973.* Second ed. Albuquerque: University of New Mexico Press, 1977.

————. "Native American Children." In *American Childhood: A Research Guide and Historical Handbook.* Ed. Joseph Hawes and N. Ray Hiner. Westport, Conn.: Greenwood Press, 1985.

————. " 'Poor Richard' Meets the Native American: Schooling for Young Indian Women in Eighteenth-Century Connecticut." *Pacific Historical Review* 49 (May 1980): 215-35.

Trennert, Robert A. "Educating Indian Girls at Non-Reservation Boarding Schools, 1878-1920." *Western Historical Quarterly* 13 (July 1982): 271-90.

————. "Peaceably if They Will, Forcibly if They Must: The Phoenix Indian School, 1890-1901." *Journal of Arizona History* 20 (Autumn 1979): 297-322.

Warner, Lloyd, Buford Junker, and Walter Adams. *Color and Human Nature: Negro Personality Development in a Northern City.* Washington, D.C.: American Council on Education, 1940.

Webber, Thomas L. *Deep Like the Rivers: Education in the Slave Quarter Communities, 1831-1865.* New York: W. W. Norton, 1978.

Williams, Melvin D. *On the Street Where I Lived.* New York: Holt, Rinehart and Winston, 1981.

PART IV

Children in the Twentieth Century: Trends and Issues

Introduction

According to Peter Uhlenberg, the decline of mortality in the twentieth century has been "greater than the total mortality decline that occurred during the 250 years preceding 1900." Professor Uhlenberg examines the influence of this striking demographic phenomenon on children and the character of family life in America. He says that (1) the increasing survival of infants has strengthened the emotional bonds between parents and children; (2) decreasing numbers of deaths between the ages of twenty and fifty have reduced the proportion of children who experience orphanhood and increased the proportion who have living grandparents; (3) decreasing infant mortality has encouraged family planning and a reduction of fertility.

Another important issue affecting the lives of children in the twentieth century has been the extent to which the federal government through its policies and programs has contributed to or encouraged the separation of children from parents. In her article, Barbara Finkelstein identifies three basic types of strategies concerning families that have been employed by the government: (1) child saving strategies, which distinguish between the interests of children and those of their families, separate children from parents, and channel money into services and institutions that serve as family substitutes; (2) family tutoring strategies that identify the interests of children and family together and normally are designed to keep children with their parents; (3) family saving strategies in which the government has special obligations to specific groups of parents, such as veterans and their families.

Of course, even those children who live with their parents do not normally spend all their time at home with their family. In a unique essay, John Clark, an American social historian, provides a sociocultural analysis of the subculture developed by the children in the streets of New York City where he grew up in the late 1930s and 1940s. Created by children, inhabited by children, and to some degree controlled by children, these subcultures were powerful mechanisms of social control and an essential locus of identity for children growing up in the potentially bewildering and destructive complexity of the modern city. Within the bounds of their block, Professor Clark and his childhood friends were able to come to terms with some of the basic features of human existence and learn many of the social skills and attitudes necessary for survival in their environment.

It seems likely, though, that most urban parents were not entirely at ease with the street culture and its potential influence on their children. Especially during the twentieth century, American parents have consulted "experts" for advice on child rearing. Dr. Benjamin Spock's famous *Baby and Child Care,* which appeared first in 1946, had a predecessor in *Infant Care* published annually by the U.S. Children's Bureau after 1914. Nancy Weiss compares the first *Infant Care* with Spock's book and also compares the reactions of readers of both books by looking at the letters they wrote to the Children's Bureau or to Dr. Spock. Weiss concludes that in many respects the earlier book was superior because it reflected a world view closer to the realities of mother's lives. An added bonus in this article is its review of the major trends in child-rearing advice in the twentieth century, as it points to some of the important factors in determining adult attitudes toward children in the twentieth century.

The Breen Family in mourning, late nineteenth century, Junction City, Kan. (courtesy of the Pennell Collection, Kansas Collection, University of Kansas)

14

Death and the Family

Peter Uhlenberg

The impact of mortality change upon family structure, although sometimes mentioned, has been seriously neglected in studies of family
history. Many of the most significant changes in the American family — the changing status of children, the increasing independence of
the nuclear family, the virtual disappearance of orphanages and foundling homes, the rise in societal support of the elderly, the decline in
fertility, the rise in divorce — cannot be adequately understood without a clear recognition of the profound changes that have occurred
in death rates. And the decline in mortality in this century has been
dramatic. At the beginning of this century about 140 infants out of
every 1,000 born died in the first year of life; now only 14 out of 1,000
die. In this same period the average life span has increased from less
than 50 to 73. The mortality decline in this century is greater than
the total mortality decline that occurred during the 250 years preceding
1900.

In searching for the meaning of aggregate statistics on death for
individuals and families, we must consider the effects of a death upon
the survivors. Habenstein suggests that "each death initiates significant responses from those survivors who in some way have personally
or vicariously related to the deceased. Inevitably, the collectivities in
which the dead person held membership also react." The family is
often the most important group in which an individual has membership
and in which close relationships exist, so it is here that we should
expect death to have its greatest impact. The loss of a parent, a child,
a sibling, or a spouse disrupts established family patterns and requires
readjustment. As the experience of losing intimate family members
moves from a pervasive aspect of life to a rare event, adjustments in
family structure become imperative.

If the mortality decline since 1900 has been so large and if this
decline has major repercussions for the family, why has it been ne-

glected in studies of family change? One important reason is the difficulty involved in trying to measure accurately the effects of a mortality change. Suppose, for example, that we want to describe the effect of mortality upon the family position of children at various historical times. If we attempt to specify the situation in its full complexity, we must deal with the age of mothers and fathers at the birth of their children, the birth position of children, and the age-sex configuration of siblings. Furthermore, we must recognize that cohorts of individuals live out their lives in a dynamic environment in which the force of mortality is constantly changing. Even if we could construct a conceptually complex model to elaborate the detailed mortality experiences of individuals, we would not have the necessary statistics to make use of it. Nor can a retrospective survey provide the data we would need, since only survivors to the present could be interviewed.

The purpose of this essay is to suggest an alternative approach by constructing relatively simple measures of how different mortality levels affect important aspects of the family. Rather than attempting to summarize the total impact of mortality upon a cohort, the present study develops hypothetical situations to provide insights into the dynamic role of death in family life. The emphasis is upon ways in which mortality impinges upon family structure, and how observed changes in mortality over this century have encouraged change in the American family.

For a perspective on historical change in mortality, I will focus upon three dates in the twentieth century: approximately 1900, 1940, and 1980 (actually, 1976). At each date, the role of mortality will be considered from the perspective of individuals at four different locations in the life course. The stages of life are childhood, young adulthood, middle age, and old age. The calculations use period life tables for each date, which means that the measures do not reflect the actual experience of any cohort. Rather, the picture presented reveals the implications of mortality conditions at specific points in time. In other words, the question asked is how would mortality at the 1900 (or 1940 or 1980) level impinge upon the family experience of individuals?

Childhood

Mortality change has affcted the family experience of children in three ways. First, an increasing likelihood that a newborn will survive through childhood may influence the nature of parent-child relations. Second, declining mortality in the middle years of life affects the chances of orphanhood for children. Third, changing adult mortality also alters the prospects for having grandparents alive during childhood.

Parent-child relations

There is widespread agreement that mortality levels in a society constrain attitudes and feelings that parents have toward their infant children. As Ariès writes, under conditions of very high infant and childhood mortality "people could not allow themselves to become too attached to something that was regarded as a probable loss." As infant mortality has declined, childhood has become a more clearly differentiated stage of life, and families have increasingly focused upon children and emphasized the nurturance of children. Comparing the modern and historical American family, Skolnick concludes, "What seems to have changed is the psychological quality of the intimate environments of family life. . . . Within the home the family has become more intense emotionally." Surely other factors in addition to changed mortality encouraged the deepening of emotional bonds between family members. But a look at the extent of changing survival prospects for infants since 1900 points clearly to the critical role that this change played in the increased intimacy of the parent-child relationship.

Several calculations to demonstrate the magnitude of the drop in child deaths since 1900 are presented in Table 1. First, the probability that an individual baby would survive his or her childhood increased from .79 in 1900 to .98 in 1976. The second calculation answers the question, what is the probability that a couple bearing three children would have at least one child die before reaching age fifteen? The answer is that under 1900 mortality conditions half of the parents would experience the loss of a child; under 1976 conditions only 6 percent would. But the rate of birth as well as death fell over this century. As a result, the probability of an average parent experiencing the death of a child changed even more. Women bearing children around 1900 had, on average, 4.2 children, while projections suggest

Table 1. Measures of Death to Children in Families: 1900; 1940; 1976.

Year	Probability of Surviving from 0 to 15	Probability of 1 or More Dying out of 3	Average Number of Children per Mother[a]	Probability of 1 or More Dying out of Average Number of Births
1900	.79	.50	4.2	.62
1940	.94	.17	2.8	.16
1976	.98	.06	2.1	.04

[a] For 1900 and 1940 this is the average completed family size for women who were aged 25-29 at these dates. For 1976 the figure is the expected completed family size for women aged 25-29 in 1976.

that women currently bearing children will average about 2.1. Thus the third calculation in Table 1 shows that the probability of a child dying for parents with an average number of children for that period dropped from .62 in 1900 to only .04 in 1976. As the parental experience of having a child die changed from routine to exceptional, the stimulus to invest greater emotion and resources has grown.

Orphanhood

The dependency of children upon adults for care and socialization necessitates fully developed social arrangements to deal with orphans in societies with high rates of mortality. Adoption within an extended kinship system and placement of children in orphanages were two mechanisms used to deal with the social problem of orphans in nineteenth-century America. But during the twentieth century orphanhood changed from a common occurrence to a rare event. Consequently, social institutions designed to deal with this problem have virtually disappeared. From the perspective of successive cohorts of children, the change has profoundly altered their experiences in families.

Table 2 contains data which show the effect of varying mortality levels upon the probability of orphanhood. Since probability of death is related to age, some assumption about the age of men and women at the occurrence of parenthood is required. Over this century the median age of women at the birth of their children has ranged from 27.2 to 25.4, and fathers have, on average, been about three years older than mothers. Therefore, the choice of a mother aged twenty-seven and a father aged thirty for the calculations in Table 2 is a reasonable approximation to the typical experience over this time interval. From the table we can read the probability of orphanhood for those born under these circumstances.

If mortality levels characteristic of 1900 persisted over time and the probability of death for the father and mother was independent, about 24 percent of the children born would lose at least one parent

Table 2. Probabilities of Parents and Siblings Dying Before a Child Reaches Age 15: 1900; 1940; 1976.[a]

Year	Probability of 1 or More Parent Dying	Probability of 1 or More of 2 Siblings Dying	Probability of Death to Member of Nuclear Family
1900	.24	.36	.51
1940	.10	.12	.21
1976	.05	.04	.09

[a] See text for specific family context of the child.

before reaching age fifteen; one out of 62 would have both parents die. Under mortality conditions existing in 1976, only 5 percent of all children would see a parent die, while one in 1,800 would lose both parents. So declining mortality has operated to increase greatly the family stability of children.

Of course, increasing divorce has had the counter influence of increasing family disruption for children. At current levels of divorce, about 36 percent of all children will experience a disrupted family. But the social significance of disruption due to death differs from disruption due to divorce. Current discussions of the effects of family disruption upon children should consider the very high rate of family instability that has been the historical experience of children prior to the modern era of low mortality. Further, those interested in designing social policy for the family would benefit from studying the historical ways of dealing with orphans.

In addition to the reduced probability of losing a parent during childhood, there has also been a great reduction in the probability of a sibling dying. One good example indicates the magnitude of this change. Consider the situation of a first-born child to a mother aged twenty-seven and a father aged thirty, where the parents have two additional children at two-year intervals. That is, the first-born child has siblings born when he or she is two and four. What is the probability that this child will experience the death of a sibling before reaching age fifteen? Under 1900 mortality conditions the probability is .36, while under 1976 conditions, it is only .04. Combined with the possibility of a parent or sibling dying during childhood, the chances of a child losing someone in the nuclear family before he or she reaches age fifteen drops from .51 to .09. Since the average number of siblings for a child born later in this century is much lower than for someone born earlier, the actual experience of encountering the death of an intimate family member has declined even more dramatically than these calculations suggest. Compared to the past, children now are almost entirely shielded from the death of close relatives, except that of elderly grandparents.

Grandparents' survival

Not only did the mortality decline improve the likelihood that all members of the nuclear family would survive one's childhood, but also it increased the average number of living grandparents. Consider the probability of a child having grandparents alive if he or she is born to a father aged thirty and mother aged twenty-seven and if both parents were similarly born when their fathers and mothers were thirty and twenty-seven respectively. Under 1900 mortality conditions, one-fourth of the children would have all grandparents alive at birth; by 1976 it increased to almost two-thirds (Table 3). The probability of three or more grandparents being alive when the child was age fifteen increased from .17 to .55. Thus, mortality change has greatly increased the potential for family interaction across more than two generations. The actual role of grandparents in the lives of children cannot be determined from these simple demographic data. But the increased presence of grandparents suggests that statements about their declining importance in the lives of children are probably exaggerated or wrong.

Young Adult

The mortality decline since 1900 has greatly altered the prospects that a marriage between young adults will be broken by death before old age. If a man and woman marry when they are aged twenty-five and twenty-two, the probability that either of them will die within forty years after their marriage dropped from .67 in 1900 to .36 in 1976. This decline in early widowhood more than offsets the rise in divorce (Table 4), so that the stability of marriages during the child-rearing years has actually increased over this century. When the declining age at completion of childbearing is also considered, the higher probability of both husband and wife surviving to the empty nest stage of life is even more marked.

With current low mortality the prospective view of married life is quite different from what it was in the past. A man and a woman marrying at the average marriage age can anticipate jointly surviving a median of forty-five years, i.e., until the husband is seventy years old. The prospect of living with one person over such a long time period, especially when one anticipates significant but unknown social

Table 3. Distribution of Children by Number of Living Grandparents when Child Is Aged 0 and 15 under Conditions of 1900, 1940, and 1976.[a]

Year	Number of Grandparents Alive at Age 0				Number of Grandparents Alive at Age 15			
	0-1	2	3	4	0-1	2	3	4
1900	.08	.26	.42	.25	.48	.35	.15	.02
1940	.02	.13	.40	.46	.29	.39	.26	.06
1976	.00	.05	.31	.63	.12	.33	.39	.16

[a] See text for details.

Table 4. Probability of Marital Disruption Due to Death or Divorce within the First 40 Years: 1900; 1940; 1976.

Year	Broken by Death[a]	Broken by Death or Divorce[a]
1900	.67	.71
1940	.50	.63
1976	.36	.60

[a] Assuming husband is 25 and wife is 22 at time of marriage.

change, may influence one's view of marriage. In particular, it may cause higher uncertainty about whether or not the marriage can survive until broken by death. If a couple enters into marriage accepting the option of divorce as a possibility, the chances of actually ending the marriage with a divorce are probably increased. Further, the period of time in which a divorce can occur has been lengthened. Thus it seems likely that the decreasing likelihood of marital disruption due to death has contributed to the increased rate of divorce in recent years.

Another, and more frequently noted, effect of lowered death rates upon the family behavior of young adults concerns fertility decisions. As shown in Table 1, the experience of having an infant or child die has moved from a common to a very uncommon event for American parents. The great variability that existed in 1900 between the number of children ever born and the number that eventually reached adulthood has disappeared. It is now possible for parents to anticipate the survival of all their children through childhood. Thus, the planning of family size has become feasible, and the need to have additional children to protect against possible loss no longer exists. A couple bearing two children can now be almost 95 percent confident that both will reach age twenty. Consequently, an interesting effect of lowered mortality is the downward pressure it exerts upon fertility.

Middle Age

Discussions of the family role of the middle-aged have generally emphasized the changes involved as children leave home and as relationships with adult children are developed. Two ways of viewing the changes that occur when parents no longer have dependent children are noted by Winch. On the positive side: "With the fulfillment of the parental role and the consequent reduction of responsibilities comes the promise of a more relaxed mode of life and the ultimate leisure of retirement." While on the negative side: "The 'empty nest' psychology implies that since the parents' job is completed, they are no longer needed. They may look forward to declining strength, declining productivity, declining health, and, usually, in retirement to diminished income." Both of these views picture the post-parental phase as a period of greatly reduced family responsibility. Clearly the average length of this segment of life has grown as the probability of surviving into old age has increased. But interestingly, the fall in mortality is also altering the nature of the empty nest stage of life. Brody has nicely captured this change when she writes, "The 'empty nests' of some of the grandparent generation are being refilled with members of the great-grandparent generation."

An increasing number of persons entering the "young-old" stage of life have parents who are still living and who are in need of substantial assistance. Older people are not generally abandoned by their children. Rather, adult children are now, as in the past, the primary caregivers to the elderly in American society. The big change has not been in norms regarding the responsibility of children to their elderly parents, but in the likelihood of a middle-aged person faced with the actual situation of having parents still alive. A quantitative assessment of the increased presence of parents for the middle-aged is given in Table 5.

The number of parents and parents-in-law still alive for a husband aged fifty-five and a wife aged fifty-two under mortality conditions prevailing at selected historical periods is shown. The calculations assumed that both husband and wife were born when their fathers were aged thirty and their mothers were aged twenty-seven (which is close to the average age at parenthood over this century). As in the previous calculations, period life tables are used to capture mortality conditions at specific time periods, so the data do not reflect the experiences of actual cohorts. A shift from 1900 mortality conditions to those of 1976 implies an increase in the proportion of middle-aged

Table 5. Distribution of Middle-aged Couples by Number of Their Parents Still Alive under Conditions in 1900, 1940, and 1976.

| Year | Number of Parents Alive: | | | |
	0	1	2+	Total
1900	.52	.38	.10	1.00
1940	.37	.43	.20	1.00
1976	.14	.39	.47	1.00

couples who have living parents from 48 to 86 percent. With 1976 mortality conditions, half of all middle-aged couples would have two or more elderly parents alive.

Old Age

As discussed earlier, marital instability prior to old age has declined over this century. At the same time, the remarriage rate for those with disrupted marriages has increased. Consequently, a much larger proportion of men and women are married and living with a spouse when they arrive at old age, and a slightly higher proportion of the total older population is now married (51 percent in 1900 vs. 52 percent in 1970). But while these data indicate an increased involvement of older persons in nuclear families, it is also true that average number of years that women spend in widowhood has greatly increased. The increased period of widowhood is a result of the much greater improvement in life expectancy for women than for men. The lengthening old-age period of life is increasingly divided into two parts for women: an earlier phase in which they are married and a later phase in which they are widows.

Selected values of life expectancy from life tables for men and women are presented in Table 6. From these values it can be seen that under the given mortality conditions, the average number of years that a typical wife can expect to outlive her husband has increased from 3.8 in 1900 to 9.7 currently. Primarily as a consequence of the increasing survival advantage of females over males, the ratio of widows to widowers over age sixty-five has grown from 2.2:1 in 1900 to 5.6:1 in 1976. With such a large imbalance, remarriage is clearly an option for very few of the older widows. Therefore, mortality change has created a major increase in the significance of the final stage of life for women, a period of widowhood in which few men are around. What the family experience of the rapidly growing number of older women, whose children themselves are approaching old age, will be

Table 6. Average Years of Life Remaining at Selected Ages for Men and Women in the U.S.: 1900; 1940; 1976.

	Life Table Values					
Year	(1) $\overset{\circ}{e}_{22}(F)$	(2) $\overset{\circ}{e}_{25}(M)$	(3) (1)-(2)	(4) $\overset{\circ}{e}_{62}(F)$	(5) $\overset{\circ}{e}_{65}(M)$	(6) (4)-(5)
1900	42.3	38.5	3.8	14.0	11.5	2.5
1940	49.5	43.3	6.2	15.6	12.1	3.5
1976	56.8	47.1	9.7	20.4	13.7	6.7

is not entirely clear. In 1976, however, about 70 percent of the widows over age sixty-five were living either alone or in institutions. Thus, a large majority of older women are now living their last years of life outside of a family context. Of course, this does not mean that they necessarily lack significant kinship links, but it does indicate that their daily life is not enmeshed in a family.

Conclusion

Declining mortality during the twentieth century has had a major impact upon the American family. The role of mortality as an independent variable producing change has been noted in the following areas:

1. Increasing survival prospects for infants have encouraged stronger emotional bonds between parents and children.

2. Decreasing deaths of adults aged twenty to fifty have reduced the proportion of children who experience orphanhood.

3. Decreasing mortality has eliminated the experience of a member of the nuclear family dying for most children.

4. Increasing survival rates have increased the number of living grandparents for children.

5. Decreasing mortality has increased the number of years that marriages survive without being disrupted by death. This change has probably contributed to the increase in divorce.

6. Decreasing infant and child deaths have allowed more careful planning of family size and have encouraged a reduction in fertility.

7. Increasing survival rates have lengthened the "empty nest" stage of the family.

8. Decreasing mortality has increased the number of elderly persons dependent upon their middle-aged children.

9. Increasing survival advantages for women relative to men have lengthened the period of widowhood at the end of the life course.

Schoolchildren at Farm Security Administration farm worker's camp in Caldwell, Idaho, 1941. Photograph by Russell Lee. (courtesy of Library of Congress, LC-USF34-39130)

15

Uncle Sam and the Children: A History of Government Involvement in Child Rearing

Barbara Finkelstein

This essay concerns the relationship of the federal government of the United States to American children and youth. Although it has not been as directly involved in the lives of children as state and local governments, Uncle Sam has nonetheless been at work since 1819 regulating the condition of the rising generation. My own interest in the subject arises from a dual concern: that government policy all too often contributes to the severing of relationships between parents and children, even when it is intended to protect and support family life; and that parents, wittingly or not, are passing the nurture of their children to agencies outside the household, a category within which I include the passive babysitting of television.

The devastating effect of separation between parents and children is expressed by a variety of labels which are affixed to the young. Those who wind up in the juvenile courts are labeled as throwaways. Others, who enter empty houses after school, have been called latchkey children. Still others, beaten, neglected, and abused are labeled battered children. Children whose parents can barely survive — captives of the economic rut into which they were born as migrant workers, sharecroppers, mountaineers, or recipients of public assistance — are called children of poverty. Those children of the affluent middle classes who leave their families and enter into the total institutional life of hierarchical religious groups are called the children of affluent permissiveness. The labels — themselves expressions of humanitarian concern by diverse child advocates — all reflect the terrible human cost of separation between parents and children in this society.

Of course, the separation of children and parents is not unvaryingly understood to be devastating. Most Americans believe that the emergence of schools and colleges has organized beneficial separations enabling young people to develop new relationships, skills, visions, and perceptions and otherwise acquire the independence which they need to grow up. There is as well a long tradition of admiration for the Huck Finns of our mythology, making their independent way through a parentless world. And there are contemporary education critics who believe that children and youth are ill served by long years of schooling and dependency and ought, instead, to enter the labor force at earlier ages. Finally, there are those like Bruno Bettleheim and Urie Bronfenbrenner who find much to praise in systems of child rearing where dominion over children is lodged in group nurseries and where separation between parents and children is publicly sanctioned, supported, and institutionalized. Indeed, Bettleheim has characterized the children of Israeli Kibbutzim as "Children of the Dream." My own view is that children are badly served when there are no adults "irrationally commited" to their welfare, no matter whether they are reared collectively or within individual family units. My fear is that government has either compelled or encouraged the separation of parents and children willy-nilly, without consciousness of its effects. It is the phenomenon of separation that I wish to focus on in this essay, looking at congressional legislation as an expression of social arrangements and preferences, exploring the meaning of separation as it has been incorporated historically and as it inheres today in legislation affecting young children.

From 1819, the year when Congress first appropriated money to support teachers for Indians, to 1983, the year when the House Select Committee on Children, Youth and Families emerged in Congress, congressional action on issues related to children and youth has been focused in times of economic and social crisis. No bills attempt directly to focus on the relationship between parents and children. Indeed, concern for children has been a by-product rather than an object of federal legislative decision. Children's bills, if we can call them that, have been part of appropriations designed to conduct wars against Indians (from 1816 to 1895), wars between the states, wars with foreign nations, and even wars against poverty. Children's bills have been part of appropriations going out to create new deals, square deals, new frontiers, great societies, and new beginnings.

Even though political and economic expediency have dictated the timing of congressional effort, the bills are nonetheless meaningful to the relationships between young children and their parents. Embedded in federal legislation throughout our history as a nation lurks a conviction that the guardians of children have an obligation to provide an atmosphere of moral vigilance. When, in the wisdom of the Congress, families have not provided proper settings, Congress has set in motion what we can call *child saving legislative strategies*. Distinguishing the interests of children from those of their families, child saving legislation worked to separate children from parents. It channeled public expenditures into services designed to replace families with morally and politically sanctioned substitutes. Recipients of this kind of legislative effort have, as we shall see, changed over time. Native Americans were the first, followed by the urban immigrant poor, blacks, and by those more recently labeled as disadvantaged.

When parents are regarded as victims of economic and social injustice, rather than of moral degeneracy, Congress has set in motion what can be called *family tutoring legislative strategies*. Identifying the interests of children with the interest of their parents, Congress has provided services to families in the form of parent education programs and nursery schools which parents may or may not choose to use. Examples of such legislation can be found in congressional action after the Civil War, during the New Deal, and in the 1960s as part of the War on Poverty.

When parents have been regarded as special obligations of the federal government, as veterans have been, Congress has identified the interests of children with the economic well-being of their families and channeled income directly into families — underwriting unemployment insurance, providing pensions to widows, and supporting children, no questions asked. Some legislation passed during the New Deal, after World War I and World War II, exemplifies what can be called *family saving legislative strategies*.

The first legislation passed was of the child saving variety. In 1819, with the passage of the so-called Civilizing Act, Congress appropriated $10,000 to hire teachers of "good moral character to Instruct Indian Children in agriculture and the 3 R's." Part of an effort to separate Indians from valuable land, and from white society, the "Civilizing Act" was ultimately designed to turn Native Americans into New England farmers, and their children into literate Protestants. The secretary of war made this intention explicit in 1818. "In the present state of our country, one of two things seem to be necessary. Either that those sons of the forest should be moralized or exterminated. Humanity would rejoice at the former, but shrink from the latter. Put into the hands of their children, the primer and the hoe, and they will naturally, in time, take hold of the plow and as their minds enlighten and expand, the Bible will be their Book and they will grow up in habits of industry and morality."

Indian efforts to resist both removal and Christianization, and to nurture children Indian-style, inspired the Congress to step up child saving efforts. From 1850 to 1895, when the policy was explicitly reversed, Congress not only appropriated money to build, design, and populate reservations, but also to build boarding schools intended in the parlance of Congressional debate "to dissolve all tribal relations"; in the parlance of Protestant theology, to remove children from the demoralizing influence of families; in the parlance of modern sociology, to transform the social network of Indian parents and replace the home with the school acting in loco parentis. Government agents did not stop short of kidnapping Indian children, of confining them in boarding schools, of indenturing them during vacations as domestic servants, of prohibiting any use of their native languages, and after 1887 of threatening to cut off food and clothing supplies from parents who refused to hand children over voluntarily. Congressional support for child saving work took two forms: enabling laws and appropriations to support educational personnel.

Between 1819 and 1865, American Indians were the sole recipients of congressional social largess. Attempts by Dorothea Dix to secure grants from the federal government to build asylums for the indigent insane were thwarted by President Pierce in 1856 with this declaration: "I cannot find any authority in the constitution for making the Federal Government the great almoner of public charity." As late as 1860, only the threat of Indian massacre seemed to pry open the congressional pocketbook for social services.

Rising out of the ashes of the Civil War came two emergency relief measures designed by Congress to rescue newly freed slaves and their families from the jurisdiction of the rebel states and to provide emergency relief to the veterans, orphans, and widows of the Union Army. Congress responded to these groups in two different ways, articulating two different strategies. For the families of Union soldiers who had been killed or disabled, Congress provided money directly in the form of pensions to widows, disabled veterans, and orphans. In 1865 Lincoln created national military and naval hospitals. By 1890 Congress had passed the Pension Act, treating veterans and their families as special obligations of the federal government. For the first time, Congress articulated a family saving strategy, identifying the interest of children with the economic well-being of families and substitute families, placing a financial floor under those who cared for young children — mothers, fathers, and heads of orphanages.

For newly freed slaves in the South, on the other hand, Congress created a Federal Bureau of Refugees, Freedmen and Abandoned land, transferring jurisdiction over former slaves from the various rebel states to the Freedmen's Bureau. Proceeding on the assumption that the institution of slavery as well as the Civil War had devastated black family life and obstructed black attempts to acquire literacy, agents of the Freedmen's Bureau engaged in activities designed to provide children of freedmen with a highly controlled and structured educational environment in which parents as well as teachers would compensate for past adversities and exercise dominion over the children.

Preventing attempts by former slave owners to enter into apprenticeship arrangements with black children, dispatching teachers to teach the fundamentals of literacy to parents and children alike, and supporting the development of industrial training colleges, the Freedmen's Bureau sought to re-create a facsimile of home and school environments characteristic of white yeomen farmers in New England and the Midwest. In the process, it elaborated a federal legislative strategy I would call a family tutoring strategy, where the interests of children and parents were tied together and where services were made available in the form of parent education programs and support for schools — but without direct grants of money.

By 1900 three patterns of legislative involvement, child saving, family tutoring, and family saving, had emerged. Though family problems have changed since 1900, these three patterns of congressional support have persisted. Indeed, *no new forms* of legislative support or regulation have been forthcoming in the twentieth century.

Throughout the nineteenth century, as Congress was defining a relationship to some of the children of the nation, growing numbers of families were experiencing as well as creating what we can call geographical separations from one another, transforming the ambiance of nurture within households. On family farms throughout the country, parents, in increasingly larger numbers over time, were securing literacy for their children by sending them to school outside the household during slack seasons, when the labor of children was not needed on the farm.

In factory towns and in the cities, the location of workplaces created distance between members of a family as fathers, mothers, and children worked either separately or together in factories, in shops, or in schools located outside the household. For members of middling and wealthy families, where mothers and children did not have to work, the opportunities for work drew fathers out of the household, leaving mothers responsible for the supervision and nurture of children with help from domestic servants if they could afford them. For children in well-to-do urban families, mothers shared responsibility with teachers for nurture, protection, vigilance, and education in a variety of arrangements. For the immigrant poor who settled in cities, and whose survival depended on the labor of all members of the household, separation between parents and children during portions of the day had inevitable and devastating consequences. Not only were the children exploited mercilessly by factory owners who demanded long hours for a pittance of reward, but children who were not at work nor in school were often unsupervised, unnurtured, and abandoned as their parents tried to cope with the urban marketplace and with the psychological difficulties of living in a new land. Cruelty, neglect, and abandonment of children were painfully visible in the cities.

Humanitarian reformers created three basic strategies to deal with the devastating effects of unhealthy separation and to institutionalize what they regarded as healthy separations. Engaging in child saving efforts, bevies of humanitarian reformers sought to remove children from families whom they considered to be unfit and to place them instead in asylums, located preferably outside the cities. The commitment to so-called outdoor relief was analogous to the child saving efforts of the federal government, emphasizing the separation of children from the demoralizing effects of their parents.

Reformers also preferred the school instead of the factory as a major place of work for children. Like federal government involvement with the freedmen after the Civil War, reformers on the local level also supported policies reflecting a belief in the moralizing effects of literacy. They advocated school attendance laws and laws regulating child labor, engaging as the federal government had done in family tutoring strategies, advocating home and school as the ideal agencies of child rearing.

In the last quarter of the nineteenth century, social service workers emphasized the need for foster home rather than asylum care and reasserted the right of children to be nurtured within a family. To that end, they supported direct money grants to mothers in an attempt to protect the family environment, thus engaging in family saving as the federal government had done with war orphans and widows.

Child saving, family tutoring, and family saving efforts thus were carried on within the states and localities throughout the nineteenth century by diverse groups of female volunteers and male philanthropists. The consolidation and organization of groups of social workers and philanthropic organizations such as the General Federation of Women's Clubs, the American Association of University Women, and the National Congress of Mothers (to become the national P.T.A.) brought the need for social service support to the attention of the federal government. Urging the federal government to engage in further activity in behalf of children, they convinced Teddy Roosevelt — himself something of a social worker — to call the first White House Conference on Children in 1909: "The state has dealt generously with her trouble-some children; but what is she doing for those who make no trouble but are simply unfortunate? Some are orphans or half-orphans, some are abandoned by heartless parents, some are victims of cruelty and neglect. They are not delinquents; they are accused of no faults; they are simply destitute and neglected."

Roosevelt prepared the way for William Howard Taft, who in 1912 established the Children's Bureau to care for what Lillian Wald called the nation's child crop. Locating the Children's Bureau in the Department of Labor, the enabling legislation gave the bureau broad authority to "investigate and report . . . all matters pertaining to the welfare of children and child-life among all classes of our people."

From its founding in 1912 as a kind of federal child-protective presence, to its absorption in 1968 into the Office of Children and Youth, The Children's Bureau functioned as a lobby within the federal government. Child protection was its goal and emphasis, legal advocacy and information dissemination were its instruments. The construction of multiple involvements between Uncle Sam and the nation's children were its fruits. Children's Bureau employees engaged the federal government in partnerships with states and localities, discovering the grant-in-aid as a principal means by which to channel federal financial resources to local social service agencies. They collected information from across the nation, creating data bases from which to dramatize and improve the state of maternal and child health and the conditions of child labor. Through an aggressive publication effort, they acted as a channel of diffusion for scientific norms of child rearing as they were being formulated by physicians, social workers, psychologists, and educators. They provided a center for parent education, receiving thousands of letters seeking advice about child rearing.

Whether they did research, provided advice to parents, argued in Congress, drafted bills, advised presidents, or otherwise advanced the political prospects of children, the women who ran the Children's Bureau, from Julia Lathrop to Grace Abbott to Martha Eliot, consistently identified and responded to the problems of separation besetting American families. Fundamentally committed to the notion that the well-being of children was tied to the ability of families to nurture, protect, and guide, the Children's Bureau consistently linked together the interests of children and their parents. Using the argument that economic security and family stability proceeded simultaneously, agents of the Children's Bureau labored on behalf of a minimum wage for parents, pensions for widows, and aid for needy mothers. They worked for the construction of regulated public settings and in behalf of preventive health measures for mothers and children.

In effect, agents of the Children's Bureau helped to extend and refine the character of federal involvement in the lives of the young by emphasizing two of the three strategies of government involvement then in effect: family tutoring and family support. Eschewing child saving, they lobbied in behalf of the federal programs that linked the fate of children with that of their mothers.

By 1921 their efforts, in the words of Grace Abbott, "to secure an appreciation among women of what constitutes good prenatal and obstetrical care and to make resources available on demand" had succeeded. The Sheppard-Towner Act, passed in 1921, appropriated $7 million to support the development of community departments of maternity and infant hygiene. Extending the responsibility of the federal government beyond research, advice, and dissemination, the Sheppard-Towner Act established the use of federal grants to aid in the development and maintenance of state and local social programs. For a brief decade the Sheppard-Towner Act, together with publications providing advice to mothers on the care of children, formed a newly elaborated version of the family tutoring strategy of congressional involvement.

It took a major economic depression to move the Congress to pass legislation broadly extending the largess of the federal government and stepping up its regulatory activities. Responding to massive and visible economic dislocation, prodded by the Committee on Economic Security to address the plight of the nation's workingmen and -women, encouraged by the Federal Emergency Relief Administration which President Franklin Roosevelt created to provide an emergency fund for various categories of the needy, Congress passed the Social Security Act in 1935.

In two of its several titles, the Social Security Act embodied and extended all three of the legislative strategies previously set down by the Congress, applying them across a broader range of families and defining what was to become characteristic of relationships between Uncle Sam and the children of America until the present time.

Title IV, Aid to Dependent Children, had its social origins in the Mother's Aid Movement in the various states. There, children in fatherless families were treated as special sorts of dependents. Their mothers received direct money grants enabling them to stay at home and look after their children. As written in 1935, Title IV provided grants to support the efforts of states and localities to keep fatherless families together, thus elaborating the family saving strategy.

Title V, making provisions for grants to states for maternal and child welfare, exemplified both family tutoring and child saving strategies, allowing the Children's Bureau to engage in three kinds of work. First, the bureau was empowered to set up advisory groups; second, it trained personnel; third, it provided consulting services to states and local agencies, bringing together federal machinery to plan programs assisting states and localities in the development of services. Title V encouraged the development of services to mothers and children. Defining some victims of separation — those labeled as neglected, abused, and abandoned — as candidates for social services rather than financial aid, the legislation underwrote efforts at family tutoring and child saving rather than family saving. In effect, Title V, Section 3, in its provision for child welfare, institutionalized the separation of children from their parents by creating a service rather than an income policy for the devastated poor in the cities, and by defining a machinery to identify children whom government agencies believed would benefit by seperation from parents.

In 1938 attempts by the Children's Bureau and other social service agencies to bring child labor under the control of the federal government finally succeeded with the passage of the Fair Labor Standards Act. Intended to protect the economic security of adults by completely removing children from the industrial marketplace and dramatizing a diminishing economic role for chidlren within families, as well as a separation of adults and children, the act provided implicit support for the emergence of the school as an alternative place of work for children under sixteen. By disentangling children from the workplace, the legislation furthered separation between parents and children.

Despite the emergence of a powerful child advocate presence in the federal government, and after 1938 of major advances in the amounts of money made available for children and families, federal policy has remained essentially unchanged. The twentieth century has seen no new strategies of legislative involvement. The three — child saving, family tutoring, family support — continue to dominate.

What is more, congressional legislative action has focused and accelerated the separation of parents and children since 1940. While developing no new initiatives, Congress has, in fact, provided incentives encouraging parents to work outside the home, and disincentives for them to oversee, or even manage, their children. In addition, Congress has provided no support for child-care facilities in workplaces, even though more and more parents have had to seek paid employment outside the home. Nor has Congress followed the French, Swedish, or Canadian examples of providing child-care allowances. Apparently unwilling to support child care in the family, Congress has been assuming incorrectly that if there is enough money coming into a household, then children will be all right. While Congress identifies family stability with economic security, a correct identification I believe, it has failed somehow to recognize as well that parents cannot work outside the home and simultaneously raise children in it. Congressional involvements for the past half-century have transformed family support strategies into child saving ones — effectively institutionalizing separation between parent and child.

The family saving strategy defined in Title IV-a of the Social Security Act has been transformed by subsequent amendments so as to curtail the number of families receiving financial support. Efforts to contain the growth of the Aid to Dependent Children program are expressed as restrictions on entitlement. Residency requirements effectively exclude migrant workers, as well as the families of the rural poor who have immigrated to the cities in search of job opportunities. Punitive rules limiting eligibility to families without males drive fathers away from the home, thus undermining the two-parent household.

In 1962 the range of services provided to families receiving assistance under A.D.C. was broadened to include day-care facilities for children and work incentives for parents, emphasizing a shift from income maintenance to service delivery and an emphasis on involvement of parents in the labor market and of children in child-care facilities. The shift from a strategy of family saving to one of child saving was forwarded by specific legislative action when, in 1974, A.D.C. and child welfare provisions of the original Social Security Act were combined into a new title: Title XX of the Social Security Act.

Title XX is the single largest federal social service program providing funds to states to suppport a wide variety of social services including child care. Its original provisions were of two sorts: money for the support of child-care services and regulations setting standards, among which was a strict caretaker/child ratio set by child development specialists. Aiming in part to put an economic floor under families receiving funds under A.D.C., Title XX made child-care services available only to parents (usually mothers) who entered work retraining programs. Designed to prepare parents to enter the labor force, Title XX implicitly worked to separate parents and children. Because receipt of public assistance was rationalized and conditioned by the willingness of mothers to place their children out in order to survive or improve their economic condition, separation was an implicit, but nonetheless fully elaborated, policy. There is tragic irony in a bill purporting to support families that simultaneously orchestrates the means of separation and forecloses choice for parents or children.

Also reflecting an attempt to institutionalize high-quality child care as well as encourage parents to work, Title XX placed the federal government in the business of regulating children's environments and of setting standards for their care. Attempts to protect children by federal regulation have proved uncertain as the administrations under Nixon, Carter, and Reagan have qualified if not effectively eliminated the regulatory power of Title XX. Thus, the work of child saving is proceeding apace in the administration of Title XX.

The strategy of family tutoring also continues to motivate congressional actions toward children. Headstart legislation, originating in the summer of 1965 as part of the Great Society program, was designed to encourage the growth of community action agencies and to provide for the establishment of summer programs for young children. Expanding steadily until 1982, when its level of support was effectively frozen, Headstart now represents a main channel through which the federal government provides education for children under five years of age.

Like the work of members of the Freedmen's Bureau and of the Children's Bureau, the work of those engaged in Headstart presumes an identity of interest between parents and children. Providing services in the form of child-care centers for poor and handicapped children from the ages of three to five, it sanctions a benevolent sort of separation that has been tested for years in middle-class communities throughout the nation.

Parent education programs have continued to be made available, thus expanding the involvement of the federal government in attempts to tutor families. Parent and Child Development centers (PCDs) serving parents of children under three; Homestart programs, a sort of visiting education program for eligible families with children ages three to six; and courses in good parenting for teenagers, originating in the 1970s, have all extended and elaborated traditional involvements of the federal government in children's lives.

Family saving strategies, designed to channel income to families for the purpose of keeping parents and children together, are no longer discernible. Nixon's family assistance scheme failed to pass. Negative income tax measures have not been adopted. Indeed, money grants in the form of tax incentives benefit parents who choose to work rather than to stay home. Children are economical for parents primarily when the parents go to work.

All three forms of congressional involvement with young children have been fraught with meaning for American families. Uncle Sam has been deeply involved in the lives of children over the past 175 years. Congress has moved in times of crisis, but it has not moved systematically, consistently, rationally, or even justly at all times. Not only has the federal government created family policy for almost two hundred years, but it has done it badly, if one uses coherence, generosity, compassion, and principled action as standards of judgment.

It has regulated vigorously in systematic attempts to separate parents and children in the name of child saving. It has induced parents to work without regulating the conditions of child care in public agencies. It has substituted parent education for substantive political reform. Its goals have been confused, if not contradictory; its levels of funding have been low. Worse, perhaps, its policies have more often than not forced parents to choose between the well-being of their children and the family's survival in a competitive economic system.

While the federal government has no business meddling with the emotional relationships between children and parents — indeed the results have been horrendous when it has tried — it has and will continue to create family policy. To date, government policies have placed little value on the child rearers of the nation and expressed no public love and concern for children. It is possible to support parents and children. Congress could provide money for the guardians of its children. It could spare no expense in the construction of child-care services. It could reward parents who care for their young, encourage flexible working arrangements, and provide tax incentives to private agencies offering quality child care. An array of alternatives is as yet unexplored. To do less than explore them systematically is to cheat the children of the nation.

Boys playing in the streets of New York City, May 18, 1937. Records of the Works Projects Administration (69-N-16171-D). (courtesy of the National Archives)

16

The Stoop Is the World

John G. Clark

The city has always been a potent instrument of culture and preeminently the center of culture for the surrounding countryside. The city has also been the center of power for the establishment. Within the city itself there are numerous subcultures and subcenters of power, some in opposition to the establishment, some exercising powers delegated by the establishment for the achievement of its own purposes, and some subcenters which function within a context of their own making. Most of these subcultural units are the creation of adults, and when they do act primarily upon children, it is with the express purpose of imposing upon the child the ways of the adult. There was, however, in the New York City of the 1930s and 1940s, a subculture which was the creation of children and which had on the children composing it an impact no less enduring than the school, the church, and perhaps even the family. This was the stoop.

It is a wonder to me that sociologists, now that they have discovered the city and become less enraptured with the countryside, have failed to subject the stoop to analysis. Of course — to mention one possible reason — such types as sociologists would have been treated with little tenderness on the stoops that I have known. But a more basic reason is the unfortunate propensity of sociology to descend from the general to the particular. They discovered the city, then they came upon the neighborhood, and finally wandered into the block. But they have yet to penetrate the secret of the block — the stoop.

Most stoops are communal institutions. A stoop goes with a particular apartment building housing anywhere from thirty to sixty families. These families are, in spite of their economic position as renters, the proprietors of their stoop. They act as possessively over this piece of poured cement as the Jeffersonian yeoman farmer over his quarter section. This feeling of ownership is particularly intense among the kids in the apartment. There is no need to "post" a stoop;

everyone on the block knows that you frequent any stoop but your own by invitation only. This has become so ritualized as to demand that various games make the rounds of all the stoops, that meetings of the teenage athletic and social club — or the gang — move from stoop to stoop, and that courting occurs on the boy's stoop where he will feel more at ease and be less subject to harassment. This is the twist that the city gives to country-style courting on the girl's front porch.

The stoop is the special possession of the young and the old. Not the very young or the halt and the lame, but the adolescent and the middle-aged and almost old. What the personal involvement of the latter in the stoop amounts to is conjectural. Few were children on that stoop, although many were parents of the stoop's breed and there are memories enough involved in that. To borrow a concept from the historian of the frontier, Frederick Jackson Turner, the stoop is a "safety valve." It is escape from the suffocation of an insect-ridden, under-windowed, greasy-smelling, and porous-walled apartment. It is the gathering place for crones and cronies. It is the last step before the sidewalk and all of its uncertainties. It is the home port — the Golden Gate of sidewalk mariners. How many times has Mrs. Gustavo or Mrs. Delaney sighed with relief when, heavily burdened with the day's groceries, she finally plants her foot on the first step while balancing four sacks of groceries on one knee, wiping her brow with a free arm, and gazing with something like disbelief at the distance she has just covered. She must have felt something like kinship to Columbus in those moments. And for the fledgling entrepreneur who moved quickly enough, there was a dime to be earned — providing he belonged to her stoop.

The stoop has increasing significance for the young from the time of toddling until the child went off to high school and its conflicting pulls. The stoop was a dominant factor in the life of a block child during adolescence. For a good long time it was perhaps the central environmental fact outside of the three to five room apartment upstairs.

There were, of course, more temporarily exciting places which the block child quickly discovered. There were the fire escapes, but they were made for climbing or to supply a ladder for purposes of sidewalk basketball. There were the stairwells inside the apartment houses. They were convenient places to use when a trip upstairs to the toilet was positively out of the question. There were the roofs. But they were meant to be crossed when playing guns or ring-go-leevio, or to provide sanctuary from the neighborhood cop or the cruelties of the bigger kids. Cellars were abundant — the Lost Caves of the block child. But they held terrors that made them useful for little but the testing of one's courage — the super's big red dog that came out for air on the end of a heavy chain three times a day and otherwise roamed the cellar; the colored porter entertaining his girl on a stack of newspapers destined to serve the war effort; and the huge rats and even bigger alley cats that leapt out at you from behind primeval mountains of junk. None of these places could substitute for the stoop. It was to the stoop that one returned after venturing into those murky and forbidden places.

From the time a block child left the stroller, he was navigationally oriented to the stoop. The child was forever commanded not to leave the stoop and was always replying that he was only going to Manus's stoop — if Manus would have him. And that was the essence of the stoop. For Manus was the proud and aggressive champion of his stoop. It was his territory.

There is much in the life of stoop children in their stoop world that squares beautifully with the animal world Robert Ardrey writes of persuasively in *The Territorial Imperative.* Whether the correlation is biological or cultural is beside the point and whether this limited example of territoriality is part of nature's scheme to guarantee the existence of the group is beyond my comprehension. The fact is that Manus fought like hell if a strong kid threatened the stoop or if someone he was on-the-outs with at a particular moment sought admittance without permission. And Manus was well-nigh invincible when fighting against reasonable odds to maintain the integrity of his stoop. In addition, there was a very visible line dividing the hinterland of one stoop from that of another, and a fight generally went less well for Manus when he crossed over that line into foreign territory. Then he became the invader and his antagonist the defender, and the tide of battle turned. In the fury of successful battle, while in hot pursuit of the invaders, the child rarely noticed that he had crossed the line. I have in that way experienced the German end of many a Stalingrad.

The stoop as well as the field and the forest had its rules for the treatment of the maverick and stranger. In stoop society the maverick was usually someone considered queer in some way. Obviously this was before the stoop kids knew what a "queer" really was. The odd kid may have been excessively fat or skinny or the kid who consistently screwed up in the various games. The strangers may have been friends and relatives visiting the stoop. They were the most vulnerable and met with disaster on all stoops. As for the odd ones, they were at the lowest point, even below the girls, in the pecking order of the stoop. They had no status. They contributed nothing to the stoop and derived no benefits from the stoop. But no one could touch them while on home territory except their co-residents — which was certainly no big deal for those unfortunates. When they did venture out they were battered from one stoop to another, but there was no crossing of territorial boundaries to pursue the prey. These poor souls remained prey to be sure but the names of the predators changed. It was a perfect sharing of the good time until the bloody, beaten, and screaming child made it to the less than secure sanctuary of his own stoop. By that time there was little enough left of him and his stoop masters generally allowed him access to the front door with little more than an innocuous shove or derisive remark.

The stoop was more than a field of battle. It was a society and, as in any society, there were the chiefs and the Indians and functional specialization. Age had certain prerogatives. Each step on the stoop corresponded to a certain grade in school and one advanced in sitting privileges along with the advance in school. Top step for sixth graders with the choice seats on the railings for junior and senior high. There were stoop leaders for each age group and a generalized stoop leadership chosen from those demonstrating superior physical and intellectual abilities. The captain of the stoop stickball team was not necessarily the leader when the stoop determined upon a foraging expedition in Woolworth's. The stoop leaders vied with their counterparts from other stoops for block leadership and beyond the block was the enemy. Leadership was derived from the grass roots, and the stoop provided in-service training at all ages. If a block society had been faced with the same set of problems as the plane load of English boys in *Lord of the Flies,* survival would have been accomplished with much less damage to individuals and culture.

The stoops were owned and used in common by the children of multi-family living-units. Access to its myriad facilities required acceptance of certain residual, inviolable responsibilities. The stoop was the location of the child's first experiences in social living — in sharing, in cooperation. He had learned all that he really needed to know before junior high. He became more sophisticated and knowing in the ways of the group through his life as a part of the stoop society than he could ever achieve in grades one through six in P.S. 152. Schools thrived and maintained a semblance of order by pandering to the herd instinct. The stoop child fought this with obviously disastrous effects in terms of conduct marks and ratings as to cooperativeness, sociability, and other similarly absurd behavioral categories. It was on the stoop that the child developed his unique qualities and a capacity to live with and frequently defer to his peers and superiors. Life in the stoop group taught that the strength and success of the whole depended upon the perfected talents and individual abilities of the parts. Stoops were pitted against each other in athletic and other forms of competition. The neighborhood rating of the block was determined by the success of each stoop in providing an outlet for talent while providing group cover for individual weakness. This was true whether or not the particular skills were, from an adult or perhaps police point of view, basically antisocial. They were social from the more crucial viewpoint of the stoop and the block. The lad from an efficiently organized block faced few difficulties when journeying unattended through other blocks in the neighborhood.

If an alien walked the entire length of the block, his total impression after the experience would be one of anarchy and chaos. The block at any time of the day swarms with children. The racket is frightful. Gritty little kids of all sizes and shapes, and ages (after 3 p.m.), mill around in apparent confusion. The sidewalk itself is an endless gaming table. There might be seven or eight potsee games going on — one in front of each stoop. The boys have chalked up the sidewalk for numerous skully games, played with bottlecaps filled with melted crayons purloined from school. Sets of four engage in furious boxball matches or, using the brick fronts of the buildings, a game of King with the loser "asses-up." At either end of the block where the billboards hang, boys stand fifteen to twenty feet away and aim a Spauldeen at the low pointed end of the sign. Hit the point just right and the Spauldeen is lined out over the boys' head. Catch it on a fly and you're out, but for each bounce you get a base. The stoops were used for stoopball, the curbs for curbball, the walls for off-the-wall; the streets were used for stickball, association (a version of touch football played with a rightly rolled-up Sunday *Daily News* serving as the pigskin), or rollerskate hockey — the most brutal game of them all.

Practically every square inch of the sidewalk and street was put to use and all at once. The block was impossible to navigate without getting belted by some flying body or object — the type of object depending upon the season of the year. But the alien intruder, believing that he had just witnessed the law of the jungle in operation, was way off base. Everything was highly organized right down to the most individual of all the games, the contest between the boy and the point of the billboard. He was running a league, keeping score and the standings of the clubs. He was also using the billboard at a scheduled time, for other boys were running other leagues and billboards were in short supply. You learn turn-taking and, if you are at all reluctant to give up the board, your Spauldeen winds up in the sewer or on some roof.

Everything had its season. Spring was the signal for marbles. But marble games had to be adapted to the absence of earth. Generally, the crowd broke down into two groups: proprietors and customers. The proprietors were the owners of a business establishment consisting of a lidless cigar box and a plentiful capital in marbles. The cigar box had three or four notches cut in one side. The notches were of varying sizes, a marble just fitting through the smallest. Above each notch was a number, the largest number over the smallest notch. A boy stood in the street facing the cigar box which was flush against the curb. Taking painful aim, he rolled his marble toward the box. If his aim was true and the marble went into a notch, he received his own shooter back plus the number of marbles the notch was worth. Each entrepreneur employed a sweeper responsible for keeping the frontage free of obstructions. There were joint-stock organizations with the company running perhaps three or four games of varying types. If the company was cleaned out, each partner was liable for only that percentage of the corporate debt corresponding to his original investment in marbles. None of these boys had ever heard of — or probably ever would — limited liability. None belonged to Junior Achievement. It just seemed the most reasonable arragement. There was lending at interest. Old establishments went broke and new establishments took their places. Disputes were referred to a board of arbiters consisting of all those proprietors and clients present at the time. There were no fights. This, I suppose, was the ultimate proof of success.

Everything had its time. When a boy was Barmitzvah-ed he stopped playing skully and took to the street for stickball or punchball. These street games had precedence over all others. This was one of the prerogatives of age and skill. Stoopball and curbball games came to a halt when the stickball game began, for latitudinal games did not mix with longitudinal. At that point the smaller fry, with no questions asked, retreated to the sidewalk and the adults retreated to their apartments.

Stickball is a classic sport. It is played with a sawed-off broomstick and a Spauldeen ball. Sometimes there is pitching on one bounce, with English, and sometimes you toss the ball up and hit it. Sometimes you run three bases and sometimes you run to the next manhole cover — about where second base would be — and back to home — another manhole cover. There were few three-manhole hitters. I only knew one and he is now a nuclear chemist at Berkeley — an absolute decline in status. Stickball is a demanding, competitive sport. The ball comes at the fielder at great speed in a variety of shapes. You need a bale of loosely packed cotton for a glove to hold on to a liner or squibbler. The ball, if hit in fair territory, must be played off car fenders, windows, walls, hydrants, occupied baby buggies, and Mrs. Gustavo. The toughest play is the shot to straightaway center. Running at full speed, never taking your eye off the ball, you have little chance to see the seltzer truck approaching from the opposite end of the block. Fortunately, the seltzer man always stopped. Why, I don't know, for his wares were at a premium (there is nothing in this world like a fight with compressed seltzer and as a result the truck never left the block without a few missing bottles).

Each stoop had its own stickball team. The boys worked their way up through the minors: from stoopball to curbball to stickball. Not everyone made it but all tried. It was stoop versus stoop with the best from each stoop composing the block team which competed with similarly chosen squads from other blocks. To be chosen for the block team was the crowning achievement of a boy's career. Everything subsequent tended to be somewhat anticlimactic. Of course there were high school teams of one kind and another. But school was an annoying interruption of the day's activities. The day did not really begin until you were back on the block. It was there that the desire for status was fulfilled or thwarted. The status achieved in high school remained in the school building between 3 p.m. and 8 p.m. and all day Saturday and Sunday. The rank achieved on the block was with the boy twenty-four hours a day. It was ineffaceable.

As I said, before yielding to dreams of ancient heroics and heroes on the stickball field, the stoop carried obligations. One was the instruction of the young in the skills necessary to stoop and block power. There were always some of the more promising young included in most activities. In fact, as I recall those days, the young were positively deferred to. They generally were first-up or had first throw. They were never exploited in such traditional games as hide-and-go-seek, kick-the-can, or three steps to Germany. They were defended if chased home by the tough kids from Sherman Avenue. They were dealt swift but impartial justice if they got out of hand. The punishment was a matter of stoop discipline, ideally by an older brother, but at the least by the closest neighbor kid. The parents accepted it and rarely complained unless there was some question as to actual guilt. As a result most kids were well trained and well behaved in the ways of the stoop.

Girls received equal and respectful treatment before puberty. After that they became somewhat more equal. The girls had a social structure paralleling that of the boys: separate but equal with occasional integration that increased as both sexes matured. Naturally enough there was minor harassment practiced by both sides, but by and large the girls played their games in their own times and seasons and under the same rules as the boys. When the girls became young women there was a pairing off between the sexes and surprisingly little discord over the choices. Mostly block boys went with block girls, at least until the last year or so of high school. Then the older group began to break up and maybe start going with a girl from Staten Island or a boy from the Bronx. This was not a sad time and there was no recrimination, for the stoop had served its purpose. In the wings were innumerable minor leaguers waiting to take over.

The stoop offered training in government as well as premarital life. There was an active hierarchy of leadership within each age group whose function was to organize the various activities; schedule the events, supply the equipment, provide the space, negotiate disputes; and in general establish justice, ensure stoop and block tranquility, provide for the common defense, promote the general welfare, and secure the blessings of liberty. It was all there in the stoop. The stoop group had never heard of James Madison and most would go to their graves trying to connect him with the 1940 Dodgers. And so what! He had nothing to teach the stoop. Nor did those unimaginably tedious classes in civics that came one after the other from J.H.S. 52 through George Washington, Xavier, or Peter Stuyvesant high schools. The stoop was far more successful in achieving the designs of the constitutional generation than their creation ever will be. Washington, Hamilton, Adams, and Jefferson all wished ardently for a government by the natural elite — composed of such men as themselves. But they were unable to guarantee this beyond their own lives. On the block, however, the government was federal in nature, democratically administered by a natural elite chosen by common consent. No elections, no mediocrity, but complete egalitarianism. One for all, all for one. The stoop was heir to the traditions of the Roman forum and the New England town meeting. As in the British cabinet, dissent was allowed until the decision was made. At that point, discussion ended and unity prevailed. What better training could a boy receive. Once again it must be recognized that this unity could serve antisocial purposes, as the neighborhood Woolworth's manager could attest to.

So the stoop was a school. There was always the not-so-remote chance that you would have to fight someone. The stoop guaranteed that you would know how. There were boxing lessons provided by the best boxers in the next age group. In the beginning all you learned was to tuck your nose and ears into your elbows and bob and weave and hide your tears as best you could. There was the world of sex. This was picked up as you went along. The new biology teaches it differently but the stoop kids learned it just as accurately on the roof or under the stairwell. Only the terminology was really different. The stoop demanded cooperation and respect between its members. You made your own way on the stoop and status could be changed with improvement. It was a mobile society and the ladder to success was wide enough to permit movement in both directions. The stoop fostered determination, competitiveness, individualism, and sociability. It did all the things that Professor Turner attributed to the frontier. Professor Turner probably never saw a stoop, and never hoped to see one, but given his imaginativeness and capacity to generalize it is regrettable that he did not grow up in the New York City of the late 1930s and early 1940s.

There is nothing remarkable about the physical appearance of a stoop. It is not structurally noteworthy and rarely makes its way onto the pages of a text in art and architecture. By an outsider, the stoop is seen only as an architectural appendage of the building behind it. But for the stoop group, the building was an appendage of the stoop. The small apartment where you ate and slept was significant of course because of the family. It was also significant because it gained you entry to the stoop.

Whatever the joys of the apartment, however much love and care were lavished on the child by the parents, regardless of the daily thrills of radio's Jack Armstrong or the Lone Ranger, three rooms and a bath could be terribly restraining. And so it was out the door, zooming down four flights of stairs three at a time, with a quick glance under the stairwell, and perhaps a kick at the door of the irascible Mrs. Pissato or sticking your gum on the door knob of no one in particular, and out the plate glass door onto the stoop. Picture Balboa at his moment of achievement. With the green jungle behind him and the infinity of the Pacific below him, he wonders what to do next. Thus, the perplexity facing the stoop child when he hits the stoop at 7 a.m. Saturday morning. There was a teeming world below him. With a Rebel yell and a mighty leap over the last six steps, he was off the LST and on the beach at Iwo or Anzio.

During the course of a single day the stoop, while apparently undergoing no visible alteration, was constantly in metamorphosis. It might start out as the bow of an LST and wind up as the watch tower of a castle under attack by an unknown but evil enemy armed with trashcan cover shields and orange crate broadswords. It was defended to the death by Prince Valiant and his companions. Between early morning and early evening it was a hundred other places and attacked and defended by a hundred different armies. It was the quarterdeck of a frigate or the bridge of a battleship, a stagecoach, a fort somewhere out west beyond the Hudson, the scene of a great bank robbery, a dry gulf (we meant gulch but had no way of knowing our error).

The stoop crowd passed through a thousand years of history in a single day, reenacting the monumental battles of mankind, admittedly with no respect for chronology or accuracy. The victor at any given battle might or might not be the historical conqueror. The weapons used were formidable and wielded with passion and dexterity. The broadsword easily shattered against the corrugated iron of a trashcan cover in which case you were run through with ease. But the sword was just as easily splintered against an exposed limb, denoting victory. If the battle called for firearms, the stoop boys had their own ordinance in ingeniously contrived pieces of wood shaped with great care which fired squares of linoleum by means of a heavy rubber band nailed to one end, brought up tightly over the other and released with the thumb. They were accurate. A well constructed rifle could send a one inch square of linoleum over the roof of a six story apartment house. Since any plane whizzing through the air has a tendency to veer, the trajectories had to be calculated nicely. There were many Sargent Yorks on the block. The kids were also mechanized. Three or four of the linoleum rifles were mounted on top of scooters, made from orange crates, 2 x 4's, and roller-skate wheels. Thus equipped, Nu block frequently launched attacks against Academy Street or Sherman Avenue. It was not unusual to field fifty to sixty scooters for a given assault. There was never any question about who was hit.

All of these games had to do with war. But at this particular time fathers, brothers, cousins, uncles, Sonny from upstairs, all of these men and millions like them were waging a war that the stoop kids believed to be — without knowing why — of the utmost importance and which the increasing number of gold stars on the thousand-windowed block effectively accentuated. So, in a way, the stoop kids participated in the world's violence. They acted it out in a hundred ways on as many different days. They were barraged with patriotic appeals. They sat through "Wake Island," "Back to Bataan," "Corregidor," and all the other war movies. On two of the billboards were pictures of slant-eyed, evil-looking Japanese soldiers. In the schools, more than normally, history became solely a recitation of great American victories against overwhelming odds. Few would ever learn of the equal responsibility of the United States for the Mexican War or that the Spanish-American War was something less than splendid. But in spite of the brainwashing, this was not a violent bunch of kids. Whatever substance there is to the concept of American fair play, it was a rule of the game on the stoop. The vanquished were treated with dignity and respect, the wounded well attended by both sides, and the defeated went through the motions of surrender with a symbolism sufficient to the demands of the victor. There were no Nurembergs, for the stoop kids realized — better than their elders — that today's victory can be followed by tomorrow's defeat.

On this block of concrete stoops each jutting out onto the sidewalk like a great club-foot and crawling with life, there was a special stoop hidden from view. One reached it by walking through a passageway no more than 4½ feet wide into an alley about 15 feet wide. On the immediate right were stairs into the cellar and over this was an iron stoop with railings and only two steps. At one time it must have been a bright orange, about the color that is interminably splashed on the Golden Gate, but as I knew it, the stoop was rusty and rickety. I came and went over this stoop at least 70,000 times over a period of eighteen years. The apartment appended to the stoop contained three rooms, a bath and a long hallway that was meant to be public but quickly became private, serving as storage room, workshop, laboratory, study, meeting place, sleeping place, and exit onto the stoop. In that apartment of 400 square feet dwelled a family of four, sharing it with occasional dogs, cats, fish, and roaches. There was also all the parental affection, discipline, and instruction that a boy could need.

But it was still down the hall and out the door to the stoop — but with a difference. Being on the stoop had more or less significance according to the order of the day. Once on the stoop all that could be seen was a whitewashed wall about eight feet away or the Pritchard's bathroom window directly above the passageway and directly under five other bathroom windows. The state of the weather was not always immediately apparent nor the state of the block. This information was at the daylight end of the passageway.

I had the unrivaled advantage of a choice between two worlds. As an honorary member of all the stoops on the block, I lit where I pleased for the day and was graciously accommodated. As the owner of a stoop, a world of my own invention was available, to be shared with whomsoever I pleased or to be inviolably private. The privacy was occasionally challenged and not won without a struggle. But not only were the invaders on alien ground, fighting against the territorial instinct, but they had to get at me through the passageway. It was a veritable Thermopylae. Now, at the other end of the apartment house was a similar alley connected across the back with mine. How simple to send one force in that alley to attack in the rear. But it never happened. It was a frontal assault or nothing; an assault against a determined boy through a heavily barricaded passageway. Armed with a high-powered linoleum rifle, I was all but invulnerable. All but — for occasionally the rubberband broke, forcing a hasty and humiliating retreat into the hallway. But these piratical incursions were infrequent for this stoop was too useful to risk alienating its owner. And I was one of the gang and not to be treated lightly.

This stoop was neutral territory and served as the general meeting place of the block. The passageway or alleyway was a good place to sit out a rain or get in out of the bitter wind or play some cards or just take a break and do nothing. Unlike the stoop, it was open to all. It was only with my consent or in spite of my dissent that the stoop was used. But one way or another I figured in the decision. It was never used by my peers or superiors when I was absent. This was as much unwritten law as the prohibition of attack from the rear. While the stoop group may have envied my good fortune, they recognized the private character of that one stoop. My use of it, on the other hand, was minimized by the ability of all the stoops to retaliate by denying me entry into the games of the block. So it was necessary, even while I was driven headlong into the hallway, to initiate the process of reconciliation. Frequently I was too obtuse or embittered to accept this gracefully, and I harassed the barbarians with sniper fire from tiny portholes cut through the window screen or by a sudden sally with a dishpan of hot water. It was always my refusal to accept the extended hand that postponed the moment of peace. Peace always came and always with arms and banners retained. It was a peace without victory and, again, beyond the accomplishment of our elders.

For a time in the life cycle of the block child his horizons were more limited than those of the Ancients. The stoop was the most secure place on the outside. The stoop was the world or the center thereof. Without knowing it, the stoop group functioned in a Ptolemaic universe. All of the world that needed seeing could be viewed from the stoop. It was a self-contained and self-sufficient world — a unity. None of the stoop group believed of course that the world could be shut out or that one should venture no further than Post Avenue and Dyckman Street. They did get shunted off to school. There was the excitement of 181st Street or Fordhal Road and Grand Concourse. They could easily slip under the turnstiles of the subway and ride to hell and back — say Flushing Meadows or 242nd Street. There existed the remote possibility of a trip to New Jersey or even Connecticut with the CYO (Catholic Youth Organization) or PAL (Police Athletic League). And, as the years passed, more and more of the stoop group did these things. They went, whether to Kansas or Korea or both, as graduates of the stoop school.

The products of that unique school are far more explicable as human beings because of their lives on the stoop than they are as members of the institutions and organizations imposed on and provided for them by adult society. Schools, secular and religious, Boy Scouts, the Lone Star Battalion, the local youth center, the YMCA — none of these well intentioned organizations really made a damn bit of difference. Their ultimate purpose was to get the kids off the stoop and the street, but the kids cooled it by taking the stoop with them. It was a triumph of folkways.

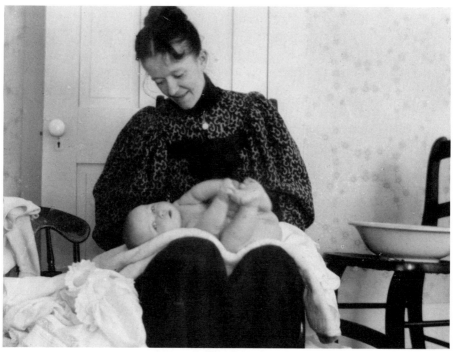

Mother bathing child, late nineteenth-century Wisconsin. (courtesy of the Van Shaick Collection, State Historical Society of Wisconsin)

17

Mother, the Invention of Necessity: Dr. Benjamin Spock's *Baby and Child Care*

Nancy Pottishman Weiss

Describing a family at Sunday dinner, a young man told of his father standing at the head of the table carving the chicken. His mother sat next to him and was the first person served; then the father served himself. The storyteller explained, "I was the youngest of five children, and by the time I was served, all the white meat was gone. It looked so delicious, but I never got to taste it. I swore to myself that when I grew up I would eat all the white meat I could. So I'm grown up and a father — and my children get first choice!" This father's lament conveys the swiftness with which child-rearing patterns have changed in the space of three generations. It points as well to a significant facet of child-rearing advice, whatever its particular wisdom — the advice structures the life of the parent as well as the child.

Scholars have assessed rules for rearing the young, but have neglected to ask questions about what these rules meant for adults. Although this article begins with a story about a father, it focuses on the daily existence of a mother. In one serious sense child-rearing manuals might be renamed mother-rearing tracts. Behind every rule concerning desirable child behavior a message to mothers was couched, advising them on how to act and recommending the right, proper, and moral way to conduct their own lives.

Women have left us direct evidence of their reactions to this counsel. They wrote letters to manual authors which unveiled their home life, asked for the clarification of rules, and sometimes scolded them for impractical ideas. This correspondence, paired with the manuals, offers us some important insights into women's lives and provides us a means to understand how mothers interpreted child-rearing lessons. This article will compare Dr. Spock's *Baby and Child Care* with *Infant Care* of 1914 in light of women's responses to them. Some striking themes in Spock — the increased emotional demands on the mother, the depoliticization of a once political domesticity, the shift from reliance on a network of women to dependence on a patriarchy of doctors, the nagging sense of worry and guilt that underlie self-confidence — surface more clearly through comparisons with the earlier manual.

Despite certain similar assumptions about family and home governing child-care literature throughout the century, such as the ideal of the homeostatic, self-sustaining mother-child dyad and the view of the home as a professional enterprise requiring job training, managerial know-how, and scientific expertise, the actual rules of child rearing and their meaning for women have changed dramatically since 1914. Scholars tend to view later manuals as improvements over earlier advice. In this framework, Spock's book represents an advance in salutary counsel for care of the young. However, one can question the idea that child-care dictums were more salubrious later, or that permissive advice is necessarily socially functional, by examining this literature from the perspective of the child rearer. Dysfunction for the caregiver, not social fit, may be associated with the permissive mode which, in turn, may correlate strongly with a high level of maternal anxiety.

Both *Infant Care* and *Baby and Child Care* attracted a large audience, for the books contained information women could obtain nowhere else. Mothers of all backgrounds wanted help and asked for it. Thousands of letters written to the Children's Bureau from 1914 to 1928 point to a need for instructions on care of the young. This correspondence also conveys a nostalgia for a sense of shared enterprise once furnished by female networks. The manuals in this sense serve not only as expert tutors or informed curricula, but also as substitutes for friends and relations. Women used the manuals for purposes other than those intended by the authors: the manuals might have served emotional ends that family or tradition once furnished, and they even filled religious needs, broadly construed as something to believe in. Women frequently referred to *Infant Care* and *Baby and Child Care,* only half-jokingly, as their "Bible," or the "Gospel," or the "often-blessed book" that "has been my staff." The historical significance of Dr. Spock's manual can be more richly defined by relating it to the earlier best-seller of the genre, *Infant Care.*

As one of her first official acts, Children's Bureau Chief Julia Lathrop commissioned Mary Mills West, a professional writer, widow, and mother of five children, to write a child care pamphlet. *Infant Care* was the second in a series on child care which Mrs. West's *Prenatal*

Care initiated in 1913. Women responded favorably to the literature and the first edition was immediately depleted. Originally free of charge, it was geared to the "average mother of the country" and written in a style "simple enough to be understood by uneducated women and yet not so simple as to seem condescending to the educated," according to Dr. Alice Hamilton, Lathrop's associate. It was, Hamilton claimed, "really an excellent piece of work." Readers concurred, for the demands for *Infant Care* continually exceeded the supply.

Any estimate of the circulation of *Infant Care* (or the readership of Dr. Spock's later manual) must necessarily go beyond raw sales figures to take into account the nature of child-rearing advice. Women told other women about techniques that worked, lent copies of manuals to each other, and even learned about child care from their own American-educated children. A mother from Bellingham, Washington, requested a second copy of *Infant Care*. "Unless I learn it by heart," she stated, "it will do me little good, for, as was the case with the first monograph, I am so constantly lending it, that I never have it on hand for quick reference. . . . it could hardly be placed in any more appreciative hands." And in a reversal of traditional mother-daughter patterns, young girls brought the latest child care advice home to their mothers. Learning techniques of baby tending in "Little Mothers' Leagues" at school, they announced, "Don't give the baby herring; Don't give the baby beer to drink; Don't let the baby eat dirty things from the floor that she threw down at first; also pickle." More rules followed. "Don't try to awaken its intelligence and make it laugh"; and the final words for the harried mother, "Don't leave the baby sit on the stove [presumably while heating bath water]. Don't mind your house — mind your children." Here was contemporary child management translated by children to make sense in their own homes.

Letters from mothers reached the bureau in increasing numbers each year, often totaling as many as 125,000. Commonly beginning, "Dear Friend," this correspondence requested advice on rearing children but also revealed lives in vivid detail, including unwanted pregnancies, worry over ailing infants, brutal prairie living conditions, poverty, troubled husbands, and a medical profession largely indifferent to their needs. The replies by Julia Lathrop, Mary West, Dr. Grace Meigs, Dr. Anna Rude, or Dr. Dorothy Mendenhall (the latter three from the bureau's Division of Child Hygiene) are the kind that might be anticipated from a friend, but are particularly startling emanating from a Washington bureaucracy.

Mothers' correspondence covered many subjects and included not only semi-literate letters or letters dictated by women to young children who apparently translated and did the actual writing, but also letters evidencing a high degree of education. "Please," writes a childish hand, "can you send me your book 'Infant Care' in Greek. We can read American, but mothers cannot. We will be very pleased if you send us a Greek book so they can read it their own selfes [sic]." Older children often appear as conduits of child-care information in these letters. Other women wrote formal letters on bond asking, "Would you kindly tell me where I can obtain instructions and help in trying to teach my little girl to carry a tune." Bureau mail prompted by *Infant Care* also included letters from milk companies, advertising firms, physicians, agricultural institutes, boards of education, visiting nurse associations, university extensions, congressmen, publishers, medical schools, unmarried girls, and older women who wrote for information for their daughters.

The bureau letters are interesting documents for several reasons. First, they demonstrate that the pamphlet *Infant Care* circulated among the poor. Secondly, they show that working-class women felt sufficiently interested in the advice to ask for more information. In addition to replying by mail, the Bureau frequently sent emissaries to their letter-writing public. Acting as a cluster of individuals rather than as a federal agency, bureau members provided their correspondents with help in the way of layettes, medical care for lying-in, and donations of money.

Both the quantity and range of mail received by the bureau point to a broad spectrum of women who found advice in *Infant Care* meaningful. Turning to the text of the manual, we see two reasons we might briefly call socioemotional and sociopolitical to explain why the pamphlet appealed to women from differing backgrounds. The socioemotional component relates to the concern for maternal well-being in the context of the mother-child dyad. By more permissive contemporary standards the advice tendered in *Infant Care* of 1914 and the revision of 1921 is typically viewed as strict and harsh to infants. Dr. Spock assesses the earlier wisdom in his own book: "During the first half of this century in this country, babies were usually kept on very strict, regular schedules. . . . Doctors did not know for sure the cause of the serious intestinal infections that afflicted tens of thousands of babies yearly. It was believed that these infections were caused not only by the contamination of milk . . . but also by irregularity in feeding. Doctors and nurses feared irregular feeding so strongly that they came to disapprove of it psychologically, too. . . . In the general enthusiasm for strictness, mothers were usually advised to ignore their baby except at feeding time." And Dr. Spock ends his accounting of earlier practices by stating, "You don't know how lucky you are to be able to be natural and flexible."

Infant Care touted strict scheduling, stopping an infant's crying without cause by ignoring the wails, advocated early toilet training, and advised against rocking, tickling, or playing with infants. However, these rules were more than the dictates of the new pediatrics, for women interpreted the admonitions as protective of mother as well as child. *Infant Care* interpolated the asepsis and scheduing derived from the new pediatrics into a system that benefited the caregiver and emphasized consideration for the mother's role. "The care of a baby is readily reduced to a system," *Infant Care* read, "unless he is sick. Such a system is not only one of the greatest factors in keeping the baby well and in training him in a way which will be of value to him all through life, but it also reduces the work of the mother to the minimum and provides for her certain assured periods of rest and recreation." This "system" was an eminently useful technique for easing a mother's life, a necessity Mrs. West emphatically repeated. Playpen use was not justified in the manual for its educational value or even charter-strengthening virtues. Instead, Mrs. West boldly stated, "An older child should be taught to sit on the floor or in his pen or crib during part of his waking hours, or he will be very likely to make too great demands upon his mother's strength." And with the voice of experience, she comments, "No one who has not tried it realizes how much nervous energy can be consumed in 'minding' a baby who can creep or walk about, and who must be continually watched and diverted, and the mother who is taking the baby through this period of his life will need to conserve all her strength, and not waste it in useless activity." Mrs. West developed her perspectives from the large body of information she amassed from women writing to the bureau as well as from her own experience. Letters like the following shaped *Infant Care*'s hints on scheduling the baby. A *"busy* mother of three dear babies — aged 3 years, 20 months and 3 months," wrote the bureau that she was on the horns of a dilemma. "I have wanted babies for years," she confides, "and now, when I'm so tired and with unfin- ished work everywhere I turn, I could scream at their constant prattle." Recognizing that infancy is a fleeting state she continues,

I love them until it hurts and know that, when they are out of their babyhood, I can never forgive myself for not making more of these precious years.
Is there not some way that I can do all these scientific and hygienic duties for babies, keep our house up in proper fashion and still have time to rock and play with my babies? What of all my housework and baby-care could best be left undone. I do not ask time for myself but it would be nice to have a

short period during the evening in which to read as I feel that I am growing narrow with no thoughts other than my household.

Thanking you for all the past helps your department has rendered to me.

As a kind of motherhood engineer, Mrs. West surveyed the logistics of this woman's day and offered her two pages of practical advice, including one dishwashing a day, feeding and nap schedules for the children, and a bedtime promptly at six o'clock. With the rationale behind an earnestly kept schedule she writes: "If you have not tried putting away your children at six o'clock, you have no idea what a relief it will be to you. It can be done; I have done it myself with three boys, and no mother who knows the satisfaction of having the care of her children cease before her own evening meal, and the quiet comfort of a still hosuehold in the evening, would fail to immediately begin the training necessary to make it possible." And with delicacy she closes her letter: "I hesitated to offer these suggestions, because I know how impossible they might seem to you and to me, if I understood your situation more clearly. I hope you will write me more details of your problem, and let me be of any service in my power." To the middle-class woman between the Scylla of a "comfortable, attractive, sweet-smelling home" and the "the 'ten-hour day' in housework," and the Charybdis of eternal vigilance over her children, Mrs. West offered a vast sympathy and some practical short-cuts. For women with a need to improvise ice boxes to chill milk, feed seven or more people routinely, and sew diapers from scratch as well as wash them by hand, Mrs. West also had some helpful hints. The socioemotional element of *Infant Care* shaded into the sociopolitical sphere.

In addition to addressing the "average woman," *Infant Care* was meant to be a do-it-yourself manual for women lacking medical help or the attention of public nursing facilities. The bureau's infant and maternal mortality studies had concluded that lack of medical care was a contributing element in the deaths of women and children, and therefore readily available medical knowledge was imperative. Other factors contributed to the high maternal death rate. Daily life for women, particularly in rural areas, was often arduous and confinement for childbirth brought no respite. As one woman of the Northwest matter-of-factly remarked, "The men expect work done up just as well at that time as at any other." *Infant Care* was a landmark attempt to demystify medicine and to reach women of diverse social groups. Women recognized the booklet as directly helpful and gratefully claimed the pamphlet "saved my baby's life." Another wrote, "Without your books I would have been like a ship on a strange sea without a compass." One woman stated, "I feel hoped up by reading the kind words you rote [sic]."

Appreciative letters were interspersed with queries on how to tailor the advice to meet the demands of difficult lives. One Wisconsin woman wondered how she could reconcile bureau wisdom with the realities of her day. "Now if any of your advice covers what an ordinary farm wife can carry out I would like to have it. Most of the advice I have read says — Fruite in plenty a bath every morning-gentle exercise . . . music-pleasant surrounding now I have a perfectuly fine husband and a loveing home but here is my day — get up at 5 a.m. hustle breakfast for 5, wash dishes help milk feed pigs clean up bakeing-scrubbing washing- (where is the gentle ex?) . . . where could I have the time for a bath every morn?" Another letter from Idaho reads:

What I am to do I dont know I am living 25 miles away from any Doctor we have 4 small children my Husband is only makeing 1.35 a day and everything is so high it takes all he makes to keep our baby in clothes and food. . . . I would like for you to answer if you can how am I going to get 35 dollar to have a doctor for he will not come for less and not unless we have the cash, talk about better babys when a mother must be like some cow are mare when a baby comes if she lives all wright and if not Just the same . . . so please answer me if you can and . . . send me a copie of Bulletin and if I live thought it then I will try to flower is as close as I can [*sic*].

And finally a woman from Georgia writes angrily, "And poor people love their babies as well as the rich, but *how* can they pay a Dr. such a price and live at all. . . ."

The bureau responded to these letters like a motherhood broker, putting the writers in contact with specific welfare agencies, public health officials, and physicians known personally by bureau members. The modus vivendi of the agency was shaped by the experience of the first two chiefs, Julia Lathrop and Grace Abbott, both recently emerged from a social settlement background stressing self-help and voluntarism.

Progressive reformers in the Children's Bureau and other organizations were vitally concerned with issues of childhood and concurred with Ellen Key — this was to be "the century of the child." But the dream of the century of the child was a bifurcated vision. One version was private and inwardly oriented and led to a preoccupation with children in the home and a growing stress on the application of science to child rearing. Along with this private vision of childhood, reformers of various persuasions held a public, group-centered variation leading to reforms in the schools, the establishment of juvenile courts, the development of playgrounds and other public recreational facilities, and the institution of protective child labor laws. During the Progressive Era, in contrast to the post-World War II period, these two ways of perceiving childhood were closely interwoven, for even the private sphere had public elements. In the early twentieth century, the food consumed by the family, the purity of the water, and the cleanliness of the streets were grist for the political mill. As Rheta Dorr, journalist of the period, phrased the intermingling of the public and private in women's lives: "Woman's place is in the home. Home is the community. The city full of people is the Family. The public school is the real Nursery. And badly do the Home and the Family and the Nursery need their mother." What is pertinent to this argument is that even the most private and domestic act, child rearing, was both a metaphor for social action and a justification for political intervention. This rhetoric often extended beyond middle-class reform circles and influenced the thinking of ordinary women of the time. By the late 1920s, however, both the larger political scene of government and the smaller one of the home had changed — and so had child-care advice to mothers.

With the advent of behaviorism in the 1920s and its hegemony in child-rearing literature through the 1930s, the care of children began to lose the political effect and concern for maternal well-being that marked Progresive texts. John B. Watson, psychology's *enfant terrible,* wrote popular articles on child rearing for *Collier's* and *Harper's.* His behavioristic psychology, and particularly ideas from *Psychological Care of Infant and Child* (1928), were swiftly incorporated into child-rearing advice of the late twenties and thirties.

"Dedicated to the first mother who brings up a happy child," *Psychological Care of Infant and Child* was as much a diatribe against motherhood as it was currently practiced as a manual forwarding the new applied psychology. The book proves that how things are said is as significant for historical understanding as what is said. The actual advice of Watson's book does not differ radically from *Infant Care,* on a case-by-case comparison; it is the tone in which it is written and the rationale for the procedures that change. In Watson, toilet training is early, habits are critical, crying infants are allowed to cry, scheduling must be maintained at all costs, and indulgence is frowned on, all of which can be found in early *Infant Care.* What changes is the attitude towards the caregiver: the mother in Watson is an impediment to the scientific upbringing of the young and, even worse, a potential threat. Watson made no mention of how useful the advice might be for the mother observing it. Indeed, he is mainly concerned that women restrain their own satisfaction in child care. Reminding the reader of the gravity of her behavior, he enjoins her not to give in to her own self-interest. "When you are tempted to pet your child," he warns, "remember that mother love is a dangerous instrument. An instrument which may inflict a never healing wound, a wound which may make infancy unhappy, adolescence a nightmare, an instrument which may wreck your adult son or daughter's vocational future and their chances for marital happiness." With so much at stake, maternal convenience was hardly a subject worthy of attention. Dr. Spock's manual, although strikingly distant from the techniques or bristling language of Watson, pushes these arguments much further, and through its friendly, informal expression more effectively leads women in their widespread retreat to the private, depoliticized sphere of the new child care.

At first glance, Spock's manual and Watson's tract appear to have little in common. In fact, Spock seems to be reacting directly to the tutelage of the psychologist's book, revamping his directions for feeding, sleeping, toileting, and handling the child. Spock's mentors are Dewey and Freud, not Pavlov. But viewed more closely, the two manuals have more in common than meets the eye. Spock's injunctions also posit a watchful mother, competent to cope with all circumstances that may arise and capable of offering the encouragement, praise, and enrichment the child is presumed to need to gain his or her full potential. The caregiver in Spock is a monitor of her child's development as well as a self-scanner, obliged to have "a natural, easy confidence," "encouraged to be firm" at times, but always readily available for a baby-mother interchange.

Although their child-care techniques differ, Spock and Watson share a central belief: the life of the child can be harmed by improper mother love. In Watson, the mother is a top sergeant who precisely times her interventions in the child's day in order to build good habits. In Spock, the mother is a prime observer who must monitor both the baby and its environment for cues on when to act. In *Infant Care* the life of the child could literally be jeopardized if attentive care were not given to proper feeding and nursing of infant ills. But once accomplished the mother might rest easy, for worry over her child's emotional state was not yet in her lexicon of concerns. This was not entirely an oversight on the part of the bureau, but a deliberate omission of reference to a literature bureau authors thought was still in its infancy. According to Dr. Mendenhall, co-author of the first revision of *Infant Care,* "The literature of child psychology is so muddled and contains so much twaddle, that the average American mother should be warned against it. . . ."

The earlier advice from the third pamphlet in the care of the child series authored by Mrs. West indicated how differently than in either Watson or Spock the issues mothers might consider in their off hours were defined. "Have I taken pains to see that the milk that comes to my house has been handled in a clean way. . . . If I was obliged to serve skim milk for the sake of cleanness or economy, did I supply a little extra fat in some other way. . . . Was the bread soggy? If so, was it because the loaves were too large, or because they were not cooked long enough?" And finally, mothers should consider the object of all these comestibles: "Was the child made to eat slowly and chew his food properly?" Watson turned these physical concerns into considerations of character building and habit training. By the time of Spock, the *manner* of feeding and character building takes center stage. Mothers are not only cautioned about feeding children, they are admonished to "enjoy him," "don't be afraid of him," and to remember that "feeding is learning." Checking the bread and milk the child eats and seeing that he or she chews it well are concrete labors mothers can complete. The permissive tasks of enjoying a child at the table and considering the learning element in feeding are by their nature less susceptible to being finished. These are tasks of Sisyphean proportions that linger on.

The early manuals of the bureau were concerned with the mother's well-being as well as the child's and advocated a rough equity in the division of labor called for in the child-rearing process. Baby work paralleled mother work, for if the woman was obliged to learn the best techniques of training, cleaning, and provisioning her child, the infant was required to avoid excessive crying, becoming spoiled and fussy, and acting, according to Mrs. West, as "a household tyrant whose continual demands made a slave of the mother." Spoiling the baby for Spock is also a serious matter, but construed as something for which the mother is largely responsible and for which she must use willpower and "a little hardening of the heart" to overcome. Though she must curb herself, it is the baby she must think of.

A division of labor implies a shared enterprise. With Spock, infancy is endowed with a moral neutrality and an emotional tabula rasa even greater than in Watson's environmentalism. This shearing of moral obligations from the child's role accompanies an expansion of maternal moral responsibility in the child-rearing arena and the decline of the only kind of child labor the bureau supported: the child's help in establishing a synchrony of interests in the dyadic relationship. In Spock, an emotional workday is superimposed on the mother's physical workday, in part devoted to monitoring her own behavior so as to provide the proper environment for her offspring's " 'self-realization' through 'self-discovery' and 'self-motivated behavior.' " All child work is defined as mother work, for it is she who must preside over the teaching of bathroom protocol, restraint of aggression, and adjustment to peer norms, lessons which lack an explicit correlation with the maternal well-being stressed in the earlier literature. In toileting the child, for example, the energy spared from washing diapers (or sewing them) is reinvested in psychological procedures. Dr. Spock instructs a mother "to watch her child — to see what stage of readiness he is in." Here watching, considering whether or not to intervene, and determining the magnitude of insistence to use in guiding the child's potty behavior replaces and — one can argue — expands other maternal labors. Furthermore, the mother is furnished with a self-scoring achievement test to correlate the result — whether or not the child is trained, and once trained does not lapse back into old habits — with maternal competence, or as Dr. Spock phrases it, "whether the mother has been encouraging or a bit too bossy in her efforts."

Although opposed to the manipulation of the baby's superego, Spock's advice tended to create a modern parental conscience to guarantee proper watchfulness. Mothers had the potential for more lapsed responsibilities, but fathers were not exempt from feeling uneasy either. "Every time I yell at my kids, I have the feeling I'm being reported to some secret psychiatric police force," one father confessed.

If permissive literature could provoke worry among people over their abilities to make childhood fun, and eating and toileting true learning experiences, it nonetheless drew positive responses from readers and professionals in the field. Those who did react with disquietude resorted to an old cure to ease their concerns: the more they worried, the more information they sought and the more they read. They looked for help in the unprecedented overflow of articles and books on how to raise happy, healthy children — information which supplemented, and in many ways paralleled, the advice in *Baby and Child Care.* Eda LeShan, a psychologist, recently characterized the way in which many child-rearing manuals actually prompt a lack of confidence. In a review of thirty books on child care, she commented, "If I were a young parent today I might cut my throat. . . . raising a child today seems to have become about as pleasurable as trying to build a house without blueprints, and with faulty materials. The specter of its coming out crooked or falling apart is ever present."

Dr. Spock has been disturbed by some of the reactions to advice in *Baby and Child Care* and particularly by the zeal of women heeding his words. His book belongs to a category of genre household terms like kleenex and frigidaire, which young mothers routinely use. Confronting an infant crying without apparent cause, mothers run for their Spocks. Some women make certain they don't have far to run, for they squirrel away copies in bedrooms and bathrooms, as well as in the living room and kitchen, and in the glove compartment of the family car. Dr. Spock himself is chary of his apotheosis as a St.

Christopher of motherhood, for he meant to build confidence in natural maternal inclinations, not anxiety nor the elevation of his advice to a creed. Yet, though he has tried to be a "confidence man," in Michael Zuckerman's descriptive phrase, shoring up the fading belief in a young mother's capacities to handle the baffling problems of infants and toddlers, his book has overtones of the second meaning of the term, that of a trickster. The permissive mode, designed to build self-confidence, in fact undercuts it by allusions to the physician's veto power, reminders of the pitfalls of improper child care, and orchestrations of daily events in a mother's life. In the words of one reviewer, "By not identifying these common problems of resentment and loneliness, while being so conscientious about identifying others, the books may contribute to the anxiety of women who read them."

The letters prompted by *Baby and Child Care* indicate a change in audience response. A high degree of literacy marks the letters, indicating more formal schooling among correspondents than analogous mail to *Infant Care*. Mothers who write frequently praise Dr. Spock's advice, calling his book "dog-eared," or "literally used to death," and they require fresh copies for succeeding children. One mother wore out her copy "on the seat-of-their-troubles," a use which Dr. Spock would hardly approve. Strikingly reverent in tone, the mail contains a number of requests for the details on such problems as rearing twins, cajoling children into eating vegetables, coping with conflicting ideas among family members on discipline, propping babies on their side to sleep, and dealing with school-age bedwetters. Children also write to Spock, no longer as go-betweens for their mothers as in the mail to the Children's Bureau, but on their own recognizance, asking why Dr. Spock chose prediatrics as a profession, complimenting him on his book's usefulness in coping with an adopted baby sister, and seeking advice on how to handle a sibling's touchy attitude toward privacy.

Only a few of Spock's correspondents describe serious problems, such as sexual child abuse by a father. But problematic letters receive the uniform suggestion to "get some counseling from a family social agency." Counseling centers are viewed as capable of handling a great variety of difficulties ranging from a four-year-old who fails to speak in sentences, to a five-year-old who wets her pants and whose father is an "overpowering influence" precipitating "violent quarrels while the children are looking on," to a mother who has trouble getting her children to eat nourishing food. It is also to the experts in general but no expert in particular, that Dr. Spock sends the mother suffering a post-partum depression whose husband writes, "I'm asking for your help. I will pay you for your help. Please, please Dr. we need good sound advice and we need it bad."

Even a mother's expertise is insufficient to solve smaller but still troublesome problems. In the final analysis, mothers must rely on outside experts. In letters to Dr. Spock, the ultimate irony is reached, for even women with master's degrees in nutrition have children who refuse to eat fruit and vegetables. One woman confesses: "When I feed my kids the meals I do, I feel — well — apostate. How do I go about getting them to eat new foods without creating an aura of emotion about it? Or had I better not try? I have a very vivid memory of being made to eat food I didn't like. How come my parents got away with it and I can't?" And the woman ventures a guess why. "I know that a lot of my problem is personal, rooted in my own emotionalism and lack of control." Timidly she posits a theory that perhaps things were better in the old days. "Why all the hurry to give them vegetables, cereal, meat? How did babies live before strainers? How do they live in a more primitive state? Honestly, I'm not a reactionary, deploring anything new. Just wondering."

The advice to this woman is meant to be reassuring — that she needs emotional support and guidance and she might turn to a social agency for it. But what Spock fails to acknowledge to his readers is that the social agency is being asked to deflect the magnified emotions engendered by either massive inputs of one adult on a small child in relative isolation or the reverse, massive inputs of a small child on the solitary adult caregiver. For anything that is amiss is amplified to an unbearable decibel level. Still, it is this delicate balance that is considered the norm in the permissive literature and conveyed in casual language meant to assuage worry.

Medical specialization triumphed in the postwar era, bringing with it a host of medical advances and also further encouraging the public's dependence on the medical profession. Doctors even felt the need for advice from other doctors. Dr. Spock's mail includes letters from a pathologist, an internist, and a dentist. One internist took his reticent three-year-old to a psychologist who "has suggested more attention from his father." "I have tried to do this," the man writes, "but my busy practice limits this." Dr. Spock does not chide the man to spend the necessary time with the child, but sends the doctor — along with scores of anxious mothers — to the child guidance clinic to determine the child's adjustment.

Although Dr. Spock's mail frequently begins by praising him, the letters often end by revealing a substratum of problems experienced by the middle-class, a declension from the ideals depicted in his book. The letters begin briskly, referring to a problem, requesting reference material, and end revealing, unwittingly and indirectly, lives as troubled as those of women who wrote to the Children's Bureau. The difference betwen the two bodies of mail is that the Spockian generation, trying so intently to lead lives of balance and good cheer, experience difficulty acknowledging aberrations — a husbandless home, a struggle making ends meet, and emotional trouble in pursuing model mothercraft. The woman who wanted reference material on an epileptic son with an explosive personality tells Dr. Spock, "I try to give him a great deal of affection, although I am a working mother — his father left us five years ago. Sometimes it is so difficult to maintain my control that my hands shake." And she ends her letter revealing how unconfident and reliant on experts the Spockian mother has become. "Does he need the help," she writes, "or do I?" A second mother describes her husband who drinks to excess and slams out of the house when her 2½-year-old and 13-month-old children cry or make noise. She requests Dr. Spock's professional opinion about a separation and reveals how well she has learned the lessons of *Baby and Child Care*. "I may have to work full or part-time," she writes. "Do you feel that it would be better for my children to stay with my husband and his poor influence and my upset condition, and the tension, and have me home full time."

The deviations from the projected norm that often mark letters fulsome with praise for *Baby and Child Care* are related most often as personal failings. "But we continue to find parenthood to C_____ an almost unbearable drain. What can we do? What should we do?" one mother asks. And another confesses, "We like to read and listen to music. Maybe we have neglected some aspects of A _____'s development in our own selfishness."

This is an extraordinary collection of letters for they tell us among other things, how women have internalized the values *Baby and Child Care* teaches and yet reveal in many cases how difficult it is to live according to this wisdom. When aberrations do occur they are viewed as problems to be tackled by experts and consultants from outside, for the world of *Baby and Child Care* is essentially one of optimism and balance. Curiously, the equanimity that marks the manual has Freudian roots. Accepting Freudian insights on the stages of childhood, the book counsels defusing each of the potentially dangerous phases with maternal behavior like "take it easy and follow his lead" in weaning and toilet training, or "you can distract him with a toy if you want, but don't feel that you've *got* to," on handling the genitals. The manual uniformly stresses the congenial. For the balky two-year-old, the mother is taught, "When it's time for bed, or going outdoors, or coming in, steer him while conversing about pleasant things. Get things done without raising issues." Though *Baby and Child Care* acknowledges Freud, it is not the Freud who wrote *Civilization and its Discontents.* Painting so comforting a world has robbed permissive literature of its true ability to reassure. *Baby and Child Care*'s Freudian world is not only scrubbed of seething ids, constraining and punishing superegos, and fixations in oral, anal, and genital stages in the nursery, it is heavily decathected from the mother's point of view. Insisting on the ultimate ease and benevolence of the world, this regimen leaves behind advisees who are foundering in the breakers of true Freudian waters, the clash of their psychic needs with those of their offspring. Also left out of this scan are the people whose economic struggles preclude the comforts essential to Spock's child-rearing scheme.

The nature of the advice tends to exempt certain mothers. To use permissive techniques requires households with enough bedrooms and belongings for all members. *Baby and Child Care* addresses the problem of whether siblings should share a room, cautioning "out of the parents' room by six months if possible," without considering homes where children must share beds. The advice presumes a catalogue of belongings and a set of relationships: telephones, refrigerators, a pest and rodent free house in adequate repair, accessible physicians, a nuclear family composed of mother, father, and baby, with an occasional recognition of one other sibling. The larder is filled with food, the "feeding problem" being the recalcitrant child, not an inadequate food supply. The modality of child rearing itself involves endless conversations and verbal exchanges. To argue, as sociologists and psychologists recently have, as to whether or not child-rearing practices of the working classes are more or less permissive than those of the middle class pays insufficient heed to the practical dimensions implicit in child-care advice.

The advice in *Infant Care* earlier in the century was also middle-class in orientation. Yet working-class women interpreted this literature to fit their lives. The Children's Bureau encouraged this translation through the celebration of "Baby Weeks," personal visits of bureau personnel, and detailed correspondence with troubled women, as well as with women who wanted to begin informal neighborhood "conferences" on child care. Spockian middle-class rearing rules appear less appealing to the working class and have no provision for the spread of child-rearing lore by an oral mode, or informal network. "Dr. Spock?" one contemporary mother commented, "He's for rich kids. How can he help my children? He doesn't know my child."

Although the ideals set forth in *Infant Care* of 1914 emphasize single family dwellings, sunny nurseries, ample food for mother and child, and adequate maternal rest, there is a recognition of the problematic side of the rearing process for some people: the existence of poverty, rural isolation, and the difficulties of the mother wanting to do her best but proscribed from it by physical or psychological barriers. These dimensions, both emotional and political in a broad sense, are missing from *Baby and Child Care*. Just as *Baby and Child Care* relegates disturbed women to the counseling center, the manual sends poor women to the social worker, for the normal home for Spock has room for neither the personal dilemmas women may face as caregivers nor the social problems of poverty.

References to folk custom or ethnic child-rearing practices, acknowledged in the earlier literature, are absent from *Baby and Child Care*. In trying to guide women to the new scientific child-rearing standards, *Infant Care* alludes to the older ones, thereby including women guided by their lights. Mrs. West speaks of the tradition of "biting the baby's finger nail," believing it "will prevent him from becoming a thief," or feeling "ill luck will follow if the baby looks in the glass." Trying to lead women to the new nurture, *Infant Care* refers to the traditional practices of offering babies table tidbits, wine, cider, beer, or tea and the use of soothing syrups. Although the references are largely negative, mentioning them addresses those women who resorted to them. On traditional practices *Baby and Child Care* is silent, pointing indirectly to a different audience of readers.

Despite the narrowed base of permissive literature, reviewers were impressed by the easy language of Dr. Spock's manual and scarcely noticed its omissions. Dr. C. Anderson Aldrich, prominent pediatrician of the period, wrote, "One is immediately struck with his friendliness toward the people who are to read the book, and there is not a vestige of the carping criticism so often seen in such works." And mothers, too, are taken with the down to earth, non-technical language. "I feel as if you were talking just to me," one mother wrote. "You make me feel as if you thought I was a sensible person." For these mothers the homeostatic pattern of easy balance between mother and child is temperamentally congenial. These letters frequently include descriptions of curtains made, husband's job histories, cataloguing of how food is prepared for the baby, or when he or she has a bath. The language of the kaffee-klatch reveals how likely it is that many mothers have accepted the Spockian view of balanced, breezy child rearing. But it also reveals more.

Many correspondents take pains to write about their contentment in raising children according to the tutelage of *Baby and Child Care*, but even the most complimentary letters display genuine difficulties that the writers cannot bring themselves to acknowledge. These letters, often running to several pages and heavily insistent on cheerfulness, relate the most dire experiences without any effect. One mother describes her move from New York to Montana. In New York she and her husband had lived with her parents. Arriving in Montana at midnight, her 2½-year-old "promptly pulled a corner cupboard over onto himself." His leg was broken. While in the hospital he contracted measles. "Finally he was over the broken leg and measles and this lasted all of three weeks when he fell on the floor furnace and sustained 2nd degree burns on both of his hands." During the three-year residence in Montana, this boy "got his arms caught in the washing machine wringer and cut his head open on a battery. . . ." But what the mother makes of all this is nothing short of astounding. "I kept gaining more confidence and learned to cope with these little problems without becoming quite as upset (at least until it was all over with)." Perhaps the massive denial that is resident in Spock's advice did serve this woman, at least in the short run, for she writes about another of her children, a four-year-old, who "recently got hit by a car but fortunately came out of it alright." To women like this correspondent, problems on bedwetting, the need for finding friends for a two-year-old to "form . . . habits of cooperation," and making nursery school a happy experience are lumped in the same category as mangled arms and burnt hands. This woman learned a lesson implicit in Spock — how to whistle a happy tune on the darkest night, even when it's inappropriate.

A few women are exceptions and do write to Spock critically about the most serious difficulties. One recently widowed woman takes Spock to task for the way he deals with the issue of the death of a parent, concentrating excessively on guilt feelings of the child and too little on reality. She tells Spock what the death of a father means. "A little boy not wanting to sleep in his own room alone like he always had before. Watching him try very hard to be a man, trying to solve a mechanical problem. Or a little girl wishing she could go to Heaven to see Daddy. . . . You have to stop crying, the tears do not just flow on forever, but in over a year now I have experienced what one *does* get over and what one does *not*. These and others are the *real* problems of death in the immediate family which you scarcely mentioned, Dr. Spock."

Other women, potentially critical of the book, probably do not write because they don't read it as a philosophical tome; they may view it as a reference work, thumb through the index for "rash" and "fever" and ignore toilet training and weaning.

The largest body of criticism of *Baby and Child Care* comes not from parent users, disillusioned with its precepts, but from people distrustful of Spock's politics. Dr. Spock has been a controversial political figure, a one-time spokesman for SANE, a defendant in a conspiracy trial for voicing opposition to the war in Viet Nam, and a third party vice-presidential candidate in two elections. Dr. Norman Vincent Peale's view of a direct line from self-scheduled babies to indulged, protesting youth sets the tone for negative comments about the book. One furious mother writes, "I have just torn your book apart with my bare hands." Another scrawls "traitor" across the cover and sends the manual to Dr. Spock. A third ambivalent woman waivers and opts for Spock. "Give up Spock," she exclaimed, "why I'd rather give up my husband." The *National Review* publishes a poem entitled "The Spockery of Dr. Quack."

> I do not love thee, Dr. Spock
> The thing is this: I've got a block
> Against the sort of seedy hat tricks
> You're sneaking into pediatrics.
> Let a mother ask you why
> Her kid is nervous — *you* reply
> She's stuffed the moppet's head with rot
> About a Communistic plot
> And if she only had a brain
> She'd run right out and go in SANE.
> Well, Mom, let me say beware
> Of all this bogus baby care,
> And don't let Benjy muddle you
> You know more than you think you do.

On a milder note, but still critical of Dr. Spock's political views, the following story was related: "Dr. Spock was giving an anti-war lecture at Western Reserve. There was a poster announcing that Dr. Spock would speak on the war. Some student had written under it 'Next week Gen. Maxwell Taylor will speak on the toilet training of children.'"

It is ironic that Dr. Spock, a political activist in his own life, can be linked with purveying a conservative child-rearing creed. If critics had looked at the ideas conveyed in *Baby and Child Care* more closely, they might have concluded they were antithetical to social and political involvement, rather than conducive to activism. The mother of Dr. Spock's manual is an apolitical person without any social involvements outside of her own home. She exists largely to rear her young and has time off only to pursue a few private activities — "a movie," "the beauty parlor," "a new hat or dress," or a "visit [to] a good friend." The manual's emphasis on getting along, avoiding confrontation, and pursuing a balanced life could, one might imagine, more easily lead to conformity than to political protest.

The variety of stories told about Dr. Spock's activism — some highly critical, some bemused — do point, however, to the schism between the private and social facets of child-centeredness. The split was much less apparent in the Progressive period. Political advocacy on the part of child-care experts like Dr. Josephine Baker, head of the Bureau of Child Hygiene in New York, for example, or of groups like the P.T.A. was not uncommon, nor considered unseemly behavior.

By the 1960s the private and public spheres of child nurture were separate issues, in part encouraged by the success of Spock's own advice. For the very purveyor of this wisdom to take public, political stands on nuclear testing and war outraged his audience. So well had many middle-class Americans absorbed the lesson of the isolated maternal figure along with her offspring mediating their environment to provide optimal experiences, developing cognitive traits, and multiplying sensory input, that the very thought of their patron saint edging them out of the home in a grander cause set them astir. The triumph of the Spockian dictum of a privatized child-rearing world, shorn of political concerns, may, in part, explain the vehemence with which Dr. Spock has been attacked for his own peace activities.

Dr. Spock has stood resolute before critics of his politics, but has yielded to certain faultfinding in *Baby and Child Care.* He has toned down the permissiveness of the first edition in the 1957 and 1968 revisions. A quantitative study of Spock's advice in the area of toilet training, discipline, and children's behavior in articles he wrote for *Redbook* and *Ladies' Home Journal* measures a notable decline from the 1940s to the 1960s in the emphasis on nurturance and a new stress on more structured child-care practices. He indicates why he has changed his mind in the 1968 revision of *Baby and Child Care:* "A lot has been added and changed, especially about discipline, spoiling, and the parents' part. . . . nowadays there seems to be more chance of a conscientious parent's getting into trouble with permissiveness than with strictness. So I have tried to give a more balanced view." Yet the changes are more apparent than real, for the ease and balance of the art of child rearing continues to be underscored, and the privacy surrounding the dyadic relationship of the mother and child is unchallenged.

By 1976, a new revision of *Baby and Child Care* was available. A core assumption of Spock's *oeuvre* appears changed and the mother-child twosome is stretched into a triad to include the father. Affected by feminist critiques of his work and crediting his associations across the country with young people in the anti-war movement in helping him to see the light, Spock assigns a new role to the father in the child-rearing process. In 1976 Spock recanted: "I always assumed that the parent taking the greater share of the care of young children (and of the home) would be the mother, whether or not she wanted an outside career. . . . Now I recognize that the father's responsibility is as great as the mother's." Infants called "he" in earlier versions now become "supposing the baby is a girl"; caregivers become mother, father, child-care center, or sitter (one can "assume for the discussion that it's a woman, though there is no reason why it should not be a man"). In 1945, Dr. Spock had extended the necessity for the continual presence of the maternal figure well beyond the physical requirements of nursing, cautioning that two-year-olds show increased dependence, and "this should be taken into consideration if the mother is thinking for example of taking a job, going on a trip, or having an elective operation." It was not sufficient for the mother to be present most of the time in early Spock, but mandatory that she be present all the time. For home is the school of infancy in this literature, the curriculum is articulated in a child-rearing text, and the teacher-trainer of choice is the mother. By 1976, Dr. Spock saw the plausibility of replacing the maternal figure with a father, baby sitter, or child-care institution. Yet old beliefs, particularly deeply held ones, do not easily change.

The 1976 text continues its emphasis on the primacy of the sequestered home the book has always stressed. "While we're waiting and working for a more humane society I hope there will always be men and women," Dr. Spock muses, "who feel that the care of children and home is at least as important and soul satisfying as any other activity, and that neither men nor women will feel the need to apologize for deciding to make that their main career." The elevation of the father to an active participant in the household has created the new configuration of the triad, but it is a tableau which on the whole is still a solitary and isolated one. The formulation of the triad continues to stress the private features implicit in the cult of childhood to the exclusion of attention to child rearing's place in the larger social fabric.

Baby and Child Care emphasizes the symbiosis that rests at the heart of permissive advice. Curiously, the interdependence of mother and child has a commercial as well as a moral element. The language in which child rearing is discussed is often that of modern marketing. Children are a product to be turned out by the home. The mother, not only literally the original producer, is more importantly its refiner and packager. The lure is held out before her that with attentiveness, emotional vigilance, and her uninterrupted presence she can provide an environment from which a superior individual will emerge. Spock's correspondents fathom the product orientation and product maintenance implicit in the manual. The first fan letter written to Dr. Spock from a new father stated, "In largely the same manner that I have previously sat down and studied manuals on the operation of the contact camera or the proper upbringing of Irish setters . . . I entered the realm of pediatrics with the good Doctor Spock as guide and mentor." Thirteen years later a mother sent Dr. Spock a revealing parody, equating a child with a product. She remarked, "Today on purchasing even the simplest modern contrivance, a parts check list, and assembling and oiling instruction sheet is included that prominently proclaims, 'STOP — READ THIS FIRST,' for even the simplest minded owner's edification.... A glossary of terms, language, schedules, with appendix and footnotes should be required reading for parents while infant is still hospital incarcerated."

Product maintenance advice in the manual has useful consumer features, particularly in medical diagnosis. Through Dr. Spock's words one mother recognized signs of pyloric stenotosis before her physician and a second woman noticed intussusception in her baby. Yet *Baby and Child Care* is more than a medical dictionary, or a first aid manual, or even a Heath kit. It embodies a world view, just as the earlier literature did. This world of rearing the young, in contrast to that of 1914, is free of dissonance or conflict, or the recognition of poverty or cultural difference. Such a world has invented a motherhood that excludes the experience of many mothers.

Selected Readings

Antler, Joyce, and Stephen Antler. "From Child Rescue to Family Protection: The Evolution of the Child Protective Movement in the United States." *Children and Youth Services Review* 1 (1979): 177-204.

Apple, Rima D. " 'To Be Used Only Under the Direction of a Physician': Commercial Infant Feeding and Medical Practice, 1870-1940." *Bulletin of the History of Medicine* 54 (Fall 1980): 402-17.

Ashby, Leroy. " 'Straight from Youthful Hearts': *Lone Scout* and the Discovery of the Child, 1915-1924." *Journal of Popular Culture* 9 (Fall 1975): 775-93.

Bane, Mary Jo. *Here to Stay: American Families in the Twentieth Century.* New York: Basic Books, 1976.

Beck, Rochelle. "The White House Conference on Children: An Historical Perspective." *Harvard Educational Review* 43 (Nov. 1973): 653-68.

Berrol, Selma. *Immigrants at School: New York City, 1898-1914.* New York: Arno Press, 1978.

Bremner, Robert H. "Families, Children, and the State." In *Reshaping America: Society and Institutions, 1945-1960."* Ed. Robert Bremner. Columbus: Ohio State University Press, 1982.

———. "Other Peoples Children." *Journal of Social History* 16 (Spring 1983): 83-104.

Bronfenbrenner, Urie. "Reality and Research in the Ecology of Human Development." *Proceedings of the American Philosophical Society* 119 (Dec. 5, 1975): 439-69.

———. *Two Worlds of Childhood: U.S. and U.S.S.R.* New York: Russel Sage Foundation, 1970.

Brophy, A. Blake. *Foundlings on the Frontier: Racial and Religious Conflict in Arizona Territory, 1904-1905.* Tucson: University of Arizona Press, 1972.

Brown, D. Clayton. "Health of Farm Children in the South, 1900-1950." *Agricultural History* 53 (Jan. 1979): 170-87.

Bullough, Vern L. "Bottle Feeding: An Amplification." *Bulletin of the History of Medicine* 55 (1981): 257-59.

Cavallo, Dominick. *Muscles and Morals: Organized Playgrounds and Urban Reform, 1880-1920.* Philadelphia: University of Pennsylvania Press, 1981.

Clement, Priscilla. "With Wise and Benevolent Purpose: Poor Children and the State School at Owatonna, 1885-1915." *Minnesota History* 49 (Spring 1984): 2-13.

Cohen, Ronald. "Schooling and Age Grading in American Society Since 1900: The Fragmenting of Experience." *Prospects: The Annual of American*

Cultural Studies vol. 7. Ed. Jack Salzman. New York: Burt Franklin, 1982, pp. 347-64.

————, and Raymond Mohl. *The Paradox of Progressive Education: The Gary Plan and Urban Schooling.* Port Washington, N.Y.: Kennikat Press, 1979.

Cohen, Sol. "The Mental Hygiene Movement, The Development of Personality and the School." *History of Education Quarterly* 23 (Summer 1983): 123-49.

Coleman, James S., et al. *Youth, Transition to Adulthood: Report of the Panel on Youth of the President's Science Advisory Committee.* Chicago: University of Chicago Press, 1974.

Coles, Robert. *Children of Crisis.* 5 vols. Boston: Little Brown, 1964-78.

Davis, Glenn. *Childhood and History in America.* New York: Psychohistory Press, 1976.

Elder, Glen H., Jr. *Children of the Great Depression.* Chicago: University of Chicago Press, 1974.

Fass, Paula. *The Damned and the Beautiful: American Youth in the 1920's.* New York: Oxford University Press, 1977.

Freidberger, Mark. "The Decision to Institutionalize: Families with Exceptional Children in 1900." *Journal of Family History* 6 (Winter 1981): 396-409.

Glassberg, David. "Restoring a 'Forgotten Childhood': American Play and the Progressive Era's Elizabethan Past." *American Quarterly* 32 (Fall 1980): 351-68.

Grubb, W. Norton, and Marvin Lazerson. *Broken Promises: The State, Children, and Families in America.* New York: Basic Books, 1982.

Horn, Margo. "The Moral Message of Child Guidance, 1925-1945." *Journal of Social History* 18 (Fall 1984): 25-36.

Hostetler, John A., and Gertrude Enders Huntington. *Children in Amish Society: Socialization and Community Education.* New York: Holt, Rinehart and Winston, 1971.

Jones, Landon Y. *Great Expectations: America and the Baby Boom Generation.* New York: Ballantine Books, 1980.

Karier, Clarence, Paul Violas, and Joel Spring. *Roots of Crisis: American Education in the Twentieth Century.* Chicago: Rand McNally, 1973.

Katz, Michael. "Missing the Point: National Service and the Needs of Youth." *Social Policy* 10 (1980): 36-40.

Keniston, Kenneth. *All Our Children: The American Family under Pressure.* New York: Harcourt Brace, 1977.

Knapp, Mary, and Herbert Knapp. "Tradition and Change in American Playground Language." *Journal of American Folklore* 86 (Apr.-June 1973): 131-41.

Lasch, Christopher. *The Culture of Narcissism: American Life in an Age of Diminishing Expectations.* New York: W. W. Norton, 1979.

————. *Haven in a Heartless World: The Family Besieged.* New York: Basic Books, 1979.

Leavitt, Judith Walter. " 'Science' Enters the Birthing Room. Obstetrics in

America since the Eighteenth Century." *Journal of American History* 70 (Sept. 1983): 281-304.

Levenstein, Harvey. " 'Best for Babies' or 'Preventable Infanticide'? The Controversy Over Artificial Feeding of Infants in America, 1880-1920." *Journal of American History* 70 (June 1983): 75-94.

Macleod, David. *Building Character in the American Boy: The Boy Scouts, YMCA, and Their Forerunners, 1870-1920.* Madison: University of Wisconsin Press, 1983.

Mattesick, Paul W. "Childlessness and Its Correlates in Historical Perspective: A Research Note." *Journal of Family History* 4 (Fall 1979): 299-307.

Mergen, Bernard. *Play and Playthings: A Reference Guide.* Westport, Conn.: Greenwood Press, 1981.

Mindel, Charles, and Robert Habenstein, eds. *Ethnic Families in America: Patterns and Variations.* 2nd ed. New York: Elsevier, 1981.

Murphy, Cullen. "Kids Today." *Wilson Quarterly* 6 (1982): 61-82.

Olneck, Michael, and Marvin Lazerson. "The School Achievement of Immigrant Children, 1900-1930." *History of Education Quarterly* 14 (Winter 1974): 453-82.

Ravitch, Diane. *The Troubled Crusade: American Education, 1945-1980.* New York: Basic Books, 1983.

Rhodes, Sonza L. "Trends in Child Development Research Important to Day Care Policy." *Social Service Review* 53 (June 1979): 285-94.

Rothchild, John. *The Children of the Counterculture.* Garden City, N.Y.: Doubleday, 1976.

Ryerson, Ellen. *The Best Laid Plans: America's Juvenile Court Experiment.* New York: Hill and Wang, 1978.

Schlossman, Steven. "Before Home Start: Notes Toward a History of Parent Education in America, 1897-1929." *Harvard Educational Review* 61 (Aug. 1976): 436-67.

————, and Stephanie Wallach. "The Crime of Precocious Sexuality: Female Juvenile Delinquency in the Progressive Era." *Harvard Educational Review* 48 (Feb. 1978): 65-94.

Stambler, Moses. "The Effect of Compulsory Education and Child Labor Laws on High School Attendance in New York City, 1898-1917." *History of Education Quarterly* 8 (Summer 1968): 189-214.

Steere, Geoffrey H. "Freudianism and Child-Rearing in the Twenties." *American Quarterly* 20 (Winter 1968): 759-67.

Sulman, Michael. "The Humanization of the American Child: Benjamin Spock as Popularizer of Psychoanalytic Thought." *Journal of the History of the Behavioral Sciences* 9 (1973): 258-65.

Sutton-Smith, Brian, and B. G. Rosenberg. "Sixty Years of Historical Change in the Game Preferences of American Children." *Journal of American Folklore* 74 (1961): 17-46.

Thomas, Mason P., Jr. "Child Abuse and Neglect. Part I. Historical Overview, Legal Matrix, and Social Perspectives." *North Carolina Law Review* 50 (Feb. 1972): 293-349.

Tiffin, Susan. *In Whose Best Interest: Child Welfare Reform in the Progressive Era.* New York: Greenwood Press, 1982.

Trattner, Walter. *Crusade for Children: A History of the National Child Labor Committee and Child Labor Reform in America.* Chicago: Quadrangle Books, 1970.

Tyack, David, Robert Rowe, and Elizabeth Hansot. *Public Schools in Hard Times: The Great Depression and Recent Years.* Cambridge, Mass.: Harvard University Press, 1984.

Violas, Paul C. *The Training of the Urban Working Class: A History of Twentieth-Century American Education.* Chicago: Rand McNally, 1978.

Zuckerman, Michael. "Dr. Spock: The Confidence Man." In *The Family in History.* Ed. Charles Rosenberg. Philadelphia: University of Pennsylvania Press, 1974, pp. 179-207.

Contributors

N. RAY HINER, Professor of History and Education at the University of Kansas, received his M.A. and Ph.D. in History from George Peabody College. He has been the recipient of a National Endowment for the Humanities Fellowship and has completed post-doctoral work at the Menninger Foundation where he was a Fellow in the Program for Interdisciplinary Studies. Professor Hiner's research and teaching interests are concentrated in U.S. colonial history, the history of education, and the history of childhood and youth. He has published widely in professional journals and is a co-editor (with Joseph Hawes) of *American Childhood* (1985). He is currently writing a book on the impact of children on the life and thought of Cotton Mather.

JOSEPH M. HAWES is a faculty member and Chairman of the History Department at Memphis State University. He served in the same capacity at Kansas State University from 1973 to 1984. His works include *Children in Urban Society* (1971); *Law and Order in American History* (edited) (1979); and *American Childhood* (edited with N. Ray Hiner), 1985. He is currently working on a history of child psychology in America. He teaches courses on the History of the American Family and the History of American Childhood.

ROSS W. BEALES, JR., is a member of the history faculty and Director of the Interdisciplinary Studies Program at the College of the Holy Cross, Worcester, Massachusetts. In addition to the history of childhood and youth, his research interests include community and religious history as well as historical editing. He is currently working on a study of the family and community life of Ebenezer Parkman, an eighteenth-century New England minister.

D'ANN CAMPBELL is a member of the history faculty and Dean of Women's Affairs at Indiana University. Her research and teaching interests include the history of women, utopian societies, World War II, and quantitative methods in history. Her articles have appeared in *Arizona and the West, New England Quarterly, Pacific Historical Review,* and *History Teacher.*

JOHN G. CLARK is a social and economic historian at the University of Kansas. Among his several publications are *The Grain Trade in the Old Northwest* (1966); *New Orleans, 1718-1812: An Economic History* (1970); *Three Generations in 20th Century America: Family, Community, and Nation* (1976, 1982); and *La Rochelle and the Atlantic Economic During the Eighteenth Century* (1981).

PRISCILLA FERGUSON CLEMENT teaches U.S. social history and women's history at the University of Pennsylvania, Delaware County Campus. Her research has concentrated on children and poverty in nineteenth-century America, welfare and poverty in America, and juvenile delinquency. She has published articles in the *Pennsylvania Magazine of History and Biography; Newsletter of the Philadelphia City Archives;* and the *Social Service Review.*

BARBARA FINKELSTEIN is a member of the Department of Educational Policy, Planning, and Administration and Director of the Center for the Study of Educational Policy and Human Values at the University of Maryland. She is the author of numerous articles on the history of education, family, and childhood. She is the editor of *Regulated Children/Liberated Children: Education in Psychohistorical Perspective* (1979).

PAUL A. GILJE is a member of the Department of History at the University of Oklahoma. He is interested in the history of early American society and popular culture. He has published essays in the *Journal of Social History, Maryland Historian,* and the *Journal of American History.*

WILLIAM G. McLOUGHLIN, JR., is a member of the history faculty and Chairman of the American Civilization Program at Brown University. His research has focused on American social, intellectual, and religious history. He is the author of *Isaac Backus and the American Pietistic Tradition* (1967); *The Meaning of Henry Ward Beecher* (1971); *New England Dissent: 1633-1830* (1972); and *Revivals, Awakenings, and Reform* (1979).

DANIEL T. RODGERS teaches American intellectual and cultural history at Princeton University. He is the author of *The Work Ethic in Industrial America 1850-1920* (1978) and has published essays in the *Journal of Interdisciplinary History, Journal of Social History,* and *Reviews in American History.*

REBECCA J. SCOTT is a member of the history faculty at the University of Michigan where she teaches Latin American history. Her research interests include the comparative study of emancipations and post-emancipation societies of Cuba, Brazil, and Louisiana.

PETER G. SLATER teaches American history at Mercy College in New York. He has published essays in the *American Quarterly, Twentieth Century Literature,* and *The Psychohistory Review.* He is the author of *Children in the New England Mind: In Death and Life* (1977).

DANIEL BLAKE SMITH is a member of the Department of History at the University of Kentucky. His research has emphasized family and social history, and he has published articles in the *Journal of Interdisciplinary History, The Psychohistory Review,* and *The William and Mary Quarterly.* He has recently published *Inside the Great House: Planter Family Life in Eighteenth-Century Chesapeake Society* (1980).

MARGARET CONNELL SZASZ is a visiting scholar in the Department of History at the University of New Mexico, where she teaches American History and American Indian History. She has published several studies in Native American History, including *Education and the American Indian* (1974, 1977). Currently she is working on a book on Indian education in colonial America.

PETER UHLENBERG is a demographer and sociologist who teaches at the University of North Carolina. In his research he has concentrated in part on the size and composition of successive cohorts entering old age, their socioeconomic and political environment, and the implications of historical change for the way these factors interact to affect life experiences.

NANCY POTTISHMAN WEISS has recently returned from Southeast Asia where she served as Senior Fulbright Professor of American Studies at the University of Indonesia. Based on this experience, she is preparing articles which provide a comparative analysis of Asian and American child rearing. Her previous research has appeared in *American Quarterly, Journal of Social Issues,* and *Center Magazine.* She is currently working on a trashy novel.

ROBERT V. WELLS is a demographer and social historian who teaches at Union College in Schenectady, New York. His articles have appeared in the *Journal of Interdisciplinary History, William and Mary Quarterly,* and the *Journal of Social History.* He is also the author of *The Population of the British Colonies in America Before 1776* (1975) and *Revolutions in Americans' Lives: A Demographic Perspective on the History of Americans, Their Society* (1982).

DAVID K. WIGGINS, a sports historian, is a member of the Department of Health, Physical Education, Recreation and Dance at Kansas State University, Manhattan, Kansas. His primary research interest is in the history of black athletes in nineteenth-century America. He has published articles in the *Journal of Sport History,* the *Canadian Journal of the History of Sport,* and the *Research Quarterly for Exercise and Sport.* He is currently working on a biographical study of Peter Jackson, a black boxer in the late nineteenth century.

MELVIN D. WILLIAMS is a faculty member in anthropology and the Director of the African Studies and Research Center at Purdue University. He has published articles in several professional journals and is the author of *Community in a Black Pentecostal Church* (1974). His most recent book, *On the Street Where I Lived* (1981), is an ethnographic account of a black neighborhood in Pittsburgh.